*Until the Singing Stops*

# Don Gold

# UNTIL THE SINGING STOPS

## A Celebration of Life and Old Age in America

HOLT, RINEHART AND WINSTON

*New York*

Library of Congress Cataloging in Publication Data

Gold, Don.
    Until the singing stops.

      1.  Aged—United States.  I.  Title.
HQ1064.U5G53     301.43'5'0973     79–2351
ISBN 0–03–041501–2

Designer: Jacqueline Schuman
Printed in the United States of America

All photographs are by the author.

*For Phoebe*

Old persons have nothing to lose by telling the truth.
—*Malcolm Cowley*

*Until the Singing Stops*

# A Personal Note

My grandmother, my father's mother, was named Phoebe. She was a strong woman, in both physique and will, and she was an influential factor on my life. A woman of many passions, she could devour a meal that would have filled three men, not because she was gluttonous, but because she was inspired by good, hearty food. She had large hands; when I was a child, I thought that they were the most enormous hands I would ever see. Yet she was not clumsy or a bully. She had a personality amply spiced with wit that charmed almost all who ever met her. She took life seriously, but never at the expense of the joy she felt in being alive. Whatever problems arose, she dealt with them.

She died in her nineties a few years ago, and those of us who loved her attended the funeral. It was not a large crowd. She was not famous. She had not been a force in the outside world. Yet, within her family she was dominant, the matriarch who held her family together despite the crises that threatened its solidarity. She managed that for decades, and when she weakened, she did not topple; she simply quieted down, became less assertive, seemed to wait for death.

If, as Henry James noted, aging is "a reluctant march into the enemy country," she resisted the enemy as long as she could. She capitulated eventually, but it was not a willing surrender even at the end. I do not know if she ever granted death its invincible power; she did not speak of that to me. She must have come to accept it, as she had accepted, and transcended, so many other challenges to her well-being.

I remember once sitting beside her and telling her that I was about to do something I feared but that I had to do. "Don't be afraid," she said. "You're doing what is right for you and you're not hurting anybody. Don't ever be afraid."

I cannot measure her influence on my life. I simply know that it existed. And when she died, the continuity of my own life was interrupted. Something had stopped and something else was beginning. But I could not, and did not want to, forget her. I found myself thinking about her as each year fled by. And finally I realized that she had not been properly honored in her lifetime. More important, I realized that there must be others like her. I wanted to meet some of them.

I knew all along, and now I know it more than ever, that we treat the elderly badly in this country. We avoid them and their problems; we are reluctant to join them. Our wish, our delusion, to remain young keeps us away from them. As a result, they languish in loneliness, in rooms filled with souvenirs of the past, in impersonal nursing homes. We cannot bear their reminder of our mortality. I knew all that. However, the image of my grandmother tantalized me. If she could survive, if she could sustain the will to survive, others must as well. I wanted to find them, to discover how they had lived their lives, what they cared about, how they viewed old age.

I am not a sociologist and will not try to impersonate one. I can appreciate statistics, but I cannot be moved by them. I wanted to talk to older people with the same eagerness that I bring to talking to my closest friends. I wanted to act as a conduit between them and people who read books. What could they tell me about growing up, about living one's life, about growing old? I wanted to find out. I remembered some lines by Walt Whitman:

> Youth, large, lusty, loving—Youth,
>      full of grace, force, fascination,
> Do you know that Old Age may come
>      after you, with equal grace, force,
>      fascination?

I drafted a letter and sent it to friends, acquaintances, business associates—dozens of people I felt I could trust. In it, I said simply that I wanted to interview people 65 or over, people who had led affirmative lives. They did not have to be well known; they did not have to be conspicuous achievers. They did have to manifest a sense of spirit, a positive attitude toward life.

The response was almost overwhelming; the nominations arrived quickly and in abundance. Out of them all, I chose approximately forty candidates from various parts of the country, and I set out, tape recorder in hand, to chat with them about their lives.

The interviews were not rigidly structured, but in each one I attempted to cover most of the same general subjects. I wanted to unearth these people's feelings about America in the twentieth century, from their childhood to the present. I wanted to know about their relationship with their parents, with their own children. I sought their views on the physical life and its benefits, on morality, on the family. I wanted to talk about sex, love, marriage, religion, health, travel, the arts, politics, work, and retirement. I wanted to explore their passions, their hatreds. And finally, I wanted to listen to their talk about grief and death.

I made appointments and travel arrangements, and I headed out into their world. Many months later I returned home, my suitcase filled with tape cassettes and my mind filled with images I will not easily forget.

Out of all that material, more than fifteen hundred pages of transcripts, I have attempted to create a representative array of self-portraits. I could not include everyone I interviewed, which saddened me, but I could, I realized, include those who affected me most. They comprise a diversified group: men and women who have, for the most part, lived quite different lives. They are rich and poor, believers and nonbelievers, gentle and tough; few of them were ever at a loss for an opinion. Not one, of any age, showed the slightest hint of senility, that phenomenon we are just beginning to understand (what we have often called senility may in fact not be that irreversible decline that has stigmatized the aged for so long). Without exception, they made me feel at home, relaxed in their presence, assured that they would be cooperative. They were patient with my questions and prodding, seemingly limitless in their wish to aid me. For my part, I have edited their words with care, eliminating my own presence and, I hope, letting them emerge undistorted and with clarity. Everything that went on between us was spontaneous, and I have tried to preserve that in the editing. I did not rewrite anything; I simply pruned and ordered passages to make a manageable book possible.

When I began, I did not have a title for the book. I found it during an interview, just at that point when the interview was coming to an end. Milton Rettenberg was talking about his father and how his father died; it occurred to me as he spoke that the lives of all the people I interviewed had the quality of joyous song. They lived fruitfully until the singing stopped, just as Rettenberg's father had sung as death approached.

Before the book was completed, I read a short essay by May Sarton, in which she noted:

The myth of old age as chiefly disability, as a sad ending of everything most desired by man, has been created by the young. But even in my time there have been superb examplars of the old as fertile and joyful givers—Casals, Stravinsky, Stokowski, Rubinstein, Georgia O'Keeffe, Wallace Stevens, the Will Durants, Cousteau; the list could be endless. Each of us has known at least one old person who continued to be life-enhancing to the end, who made one look on old age as something marvelous, to be attained as all good things are, because of a passionate commitment to life.

If the whole of life is a journey toward old age, then I believe it is also a journey toward love. And love may be as intense in old age as it was in youth, only it is different, set in a wider arc, and the more precious because the time we have to enjoy it is bound to be brief. . . . Old age is not an illness, it is a timeless ascent. As power diminishes, we grow toward more light.

In my own search I found her words to be true.

The people I interviewed are not Pollyannas, smiling blankly in the face of reality. They are not escapists eluding pain. They are, in every case, people who have been deeply involved in the experience of living. They have resisted disenchantment and conquered cynicism.

What I have attempted to bring together here are slices of the reality of age. They don't contradict the despair that is rampant among the aged. That is real, too. But if there are clues in the words of those I interviewed, they should be useful, as useful perhaps to those who are not yet old as to those who are.

In any case, there are insights to be gained from good conversation. I left this experience, as a journalist, with some of my views altered, some of my perceptions heightened. More about that at the very end of this book. Now it is my turn to introduce you to some of my new-found friends.

# May Martin

$G$uthrie, Oklahoma, is an immaculately preserved small town studded with nineteenth-century buildings and carefully kept homes. It is a short drive north of Oklahoma City, but it has none of the bustle of that large city. Guthrie is serene. May Martin first moved to Guthrie— to a farm a few miles north of it—when she was 12. Her father and mother, both teachers, came to Oklahoma from Nevada, Missouri, transporting their family (six children) in a covered wagon. The year was 1895.

May Martin remembers growing up in Guthrie, going to its schools, marrying her husband, George Martin (whom she has always called Sugar). For a while, from 1908 until 1920, they lived in Amarillo, Texas, but Guthrie drew them back, and they settled there. George, who worked for a lumber company, became Guthrie's U.S. postmaster. He died in 1959, at age 79. May remained in the tidy house she and her husband had first moved into in 1926.

She is still there, a figure instantly recognizable in downtown Guthrie to those who knew her as a teacher in Guthrie schools for twenty years. At the same time, she was active in politics, local and national. A staunch Democrat who began working for her party when women first got the vote, she stopped only a few years ago, when she felt she had done all she could and wanted to let others take over.

Today in her mid-nineties, she shows few signs of debilitation. She is lean, active, alert, and articulate; she is eager to meet people and to talk to them. Until the spring of 1978 she drove her own car. The last one was a 1955 Chevy, which she sold, for a handsome price she won't reveal, to a local boy with a perceptive eye for a near-antique car. She didn't need any help negotiating the deal. In fact, she needs very little help on any front.

She plays bridge regularly, attends meetings of various Guthrie organizations, works in her church, keeps house, cooks, welcomes visitors. Her memory is good. So is her health. She wears glasses, but the only time she has ever really needed a doctor was when she had a minor accident a few years ago. She goes out, somewhere, every day, even without the car. Although she never had any children, she has many relatives *and friends with whom she keeps in contact. She is a superb cook and an able gardener. Most of all, as she puts it, she is "a real westerner and an old-fashioned woman."*

We lived on this farm north of Guthrie, and we'd never lived in the country before. We came toward the end of August, and the day we went to school we'd heard about Indians and cowboys and we thought we'd all be kidnapped and killed. Coming home from school, we saw the cowboys. It was prairie country, but it was fenced in. And they were herding cattle. I didn't know what to do. They had some kind of a tent fixed up. And these cowboys were running the cattle in there. And then they'd come out all wet. We didn't know what was going on. And one of the cowboys was Will Rogers, and the other was Tom Mix, both young boys. Yes, Will Rogers. So they scared us kids. We thought they were wild, you know. We just ran like somebody was after us. And they had lariats, you know, and just scared us to death.

Anyway, this ranch had bought a carload of cattle from Texas. And they brought them in and unloaded them that day, and they sent them in for a dip so they wouldn't bring the Texas ticks into Oklahoma. And they'd run them in those baths as fast as they could run them. They just hurried them in there and hollered. And oh, we thought they were Indians, you know. We just ran home and told Mama and she didn't know what was going on because kids don't know what they're telling. But anyway, when my dad came home, he knew what it was. But we thought they were trying to get us.

You see, Oklahoma had only been open six years. But Oklahoma had built a schoolhouse every three miles. Kids come mile and a half one way, and a mile and a half that way, back and forth. And they was all educating their children. So we all really paid a lot of attention, and we all had a good time. And once a month—you can see how progressive the people were—the men and women had a meeting at the schoolhouse. They either had supper or a pancake frying, and had the kids say pieces. We all had to learn to say a piece, sing songs. And that was their get-together, their community life. The men and women took over. We kids sat and ate. But then I saw what a wonderful thing it was in that day and age that they had that much ambition.

Working hard all day and then once a month just taking time out, men and women, all the kids come in big wagons. We put chairs in the back of the wagon. And all went to it. And everybody went to church on Sunday. They built a church a mile and a half away. Had stores at Mohawk. Just like you have anyplace else. You could sell butter. I know we bought coffee for ten cents a pound for Mama. And we saved those little strips because you got something for it, a prize. We lived just like everybody else. But only now do I see that they were very progressive.

My mother canned fruit, dried fruit, and knitted our stockings and our gloves, made her boys clothes. On the sewing machine. Oh, yes, sewing machine. See, my mother was a smart girl when she got married. High school teacher. In that day and age that was something to be that well educated. I'll tell you, we had everything that was going in those days, for that day and age. Took a daily *Saint Louis Post-Dispatch*. I couldn't read it. I didn't know what it was. But that's how my father kept up with all the world news, local news, state news. He cared about ideas. And Mama kept up with the latest fashions on sewing. She was smart. She must have been, to raise her kids like she did.

Now, before I got married, I told my husband I couldn't wash. Mama said we couldn't. She washed on the washboard. Then finally we got an old big washing machine with a wheel turning around and the boys had to turn that wheel. Turn it by hand. And we had a wringer and we kids loved that wringer. Fought to see who was going to get to wring. And Mama would let us hang it out. So I told my husband when I was going to get married, I can't wash because Mama said I couldn't, didn't wash them clean. So he said, "Let me tell you something. When we get married, you won't ever have to wash. We're not going to have a washboard in the house." Never had one all these years. Send it out. It isn't too satisfactory, but I'm not doing it myself. Never have. But wasn't that something for a man to say that? Unusual, sure was.

I thought this town was perfect when we moved here. We thought it was perfect. We lived on the main street. My brother went past a man in a yard with an old kettle, pot boiling something. What do you think—it was a man making Wrigley's chewing gum. Wrigley's chewing gum. Making it right here in Guthrie in the early days. They've always done things, people here in Guthrie. I say my folks were progressive, but everybody else was, too. They all kept up with things.

We're all just about the same, even now. I'm the same. Of course, they all say I haven't changed a bit. If I didn't like it, I wouldn't live here, because I could live anywhere in the United States I want to. But I like it. I wouldn't live anyplace else.

I can go downtown. Every man, woman, and kid says, "Hello, May!" They've all gone to school with me at some time or other. Now, this morning I had a lady come from Wichita, Kansas—she and her daughter. She went to school with me, too. So I knew all the folks.

I had a beautiful home life. If anybody was sick in the neighborhood, my mother went and bathed the woman the next morning, cleaned up the kitchen, fixed something for the kids' dinner, and then come home and done her own work. She was kind. Her father was a teacher, principal of high schools, city superintendent, also. He wouldn't help us with our studies at night. "You'd pay attention to what the teacher said, you wouldn't need any help." Mama never said a word. After Grandfather went to bed, she got us around the table and helped us get our lessons. And she helped my father. She was a high school teacher. She knew all about algebra and all that. She helped him get his algebra lessons to teach the kids at school the next day. She was something.

He was very stern. He said, "Did you hear your mother call you?" We'd say we didn't hear her the first time. That was all that needed to be said. He said, he thought if he'd ever spanked me, I'd a died. I was so scared. I'd seen him blister the boys. But oh, I would've died. He said he believed I'd a died. I was always frail. And here I'm the strongest woman in the family. And do the most of any of them.

I learned one thing, never to say anything about any of the neighbors. Don't come in and say that Mrs. so-and-so is doing something wrong, because she's head of that house. And whatever she says is all right. We never dared come in and say anything against so-and-so. No. I knew I was supposed to be honest. And never owe anybody anything. And to go to church. And behave myself. And to be careful about the boys.

I'm more like my mother. The biggest compliment I've ever had, that my sister in Oklahoma City said, was that I'm more like Mama than anyone in the family. Because I am a kindhearted person. I say "damn it" once in a while, but that's all right. I do that—I go ahead and do it. But I am kind to people. And I do nice things for people.

I helped more people during the Depression because I was in a position where I could get on the WPA or get in the sewing room or get jobs, or send them a bag of groceries unbeknownst to who got them, sent them to them. I done those things because I believe in it.

When we was little kids, I went to school. Let me see, one of the things I learned there was about six sticks, in McGuffey's reader, which I think he's one of the best for young people, of any books I've ever seen. Because there was a new moral to every story. And you see in this bundle of sticks, as long as you keep them together, you could build with them, but one at a time, you could do nothing. And that always made me kind of stay with the gang, as the saying goes. Not get off by myself. And we brothers and sisters always stuck together.

I used to play a lot of tennis. Sugar did, too. We played tennis. Had a tennis court. But I never felt bad. You know, I don't let myself feel bad. I decide if I'm able to get up in the morning, everything's okay. I don't go around moaning. Everything all right. The day is lovely, and I've had a nice time. And I just hope that I always act a lady. That's one of my ambitions. Of course, I was just raised that way. I'll say this: I am quite well respected here in town. I'm an example to the kids and the grown folks. And the young married folks in our church say, "I'm going to be just like Mrs. Martin. She does everything, plays bridge, goes to the football game, comes to church on Sunday." And I have entertained my church circle for more than fifty years. They've been in this house for fifty-two years. But I finally decided it's time for some of the other women in the church. I told them last time they was here, I said to our preacher, "I don't mind having you. I like to have you. But I think maybe I'm keeping somebody else from having them."

He said, "No, you're not. They don't want to." I said, "Well, I want to, but I think it'll do them good to have it." It does you good to do things. I believe in doing things.

My mother and father talked about that. They talked to all we kids that way. Because in school they had to teach the children. My mother taught school until I was in the fourth grade. We lived in a little town; the street was right in front of our house. And the back of our house was acreage where we had a cow and some pigs, and the schoolhouse was just about a block away. So Mama would go to school. We had a housekeeper tend to the babies at home. Mama would come home at recess and nurse the baby, go on back. So anyway, I heard her tell how some kid done something wrong, how bad it was. So we just were kind of raised that way.

That kind of family is not here anymore. That's the trouble. They got away from us some way. I don't know why. Well, I'll tell you. I know lovely people in this town whose children have gone haywire. You know, most people drink nowadays. I don't. But I think that's the root of all evil. That and too much money. They don't have the kids work. Now we got up and helped Mama get breakfast every morning before we went to school. Because she got up and went to school, too. And then we come home, and we'd help get supper in the evening. Pop would read that paper. Mama would see that the kitchen was in order. Then Papa would go to bed, and then Mama would help us get our lessons. So we was just taught, we was just raised that way. I couldn't do anything else because I don't believe in that. I believe old-fashioned. I tell my girls here in town: I'm one of these old-fashioned. You can take all the highballs you want. But you know, I'm old-fashioned, I don't drink. And they don't get mad at me.

The sexual revolution—oh, I think that's pitiful. Pitiful. It's the ruination of the married life. Well, you know, getting married is a mystery. There's a lot of mystery to it. And if they have all of that over with before they get married, why do they get married then? I think that's causing a lot of trouble. Of course, I don't believe in women having too many children. They're not able to finance them and educate them. I think that's all right. I'm for that. Just limit their family.

The little girls ask me about love. Well, I was so in love with my husband I didn't know any different. I had other boyfriends, but nothing like him. It was just shivers. He was so perfectly lovely. Treated me like I was a queen. I have been spoiled. He never come in that door ahead of me. Never. Even if he had a sack of groceries. I said, "Run on, Sugar." And he never said "damn it" before me without saying "excuse me." Now I say it before the preacher, anybody; I don't care whether they like it or not. I don't give one. But then, no, I was just so in love with my husband. After I met him and got to know him, the others didn't entertain me.

I think the reasons Sugar and I got along, we never had time to fall out. We was always making a living and having a good time. We never had time to fall out. Not that I didn't ever get mad at him or him mad at me, but he always said he forgave me. And I forgave him.

Well, I just wanted to be with him. I was happy. And after we was married, we had such a nice time. I'd say, "Sugar, we haven't got sense enough to know that we're old folks and married. We're still having a good time." And we'd sit at the table and he'd say, "I don't want you at one end. I want you to sit by me so we can hold hands while we're eating dinner or supper." And then he said, "I don't want you in the kitchen washing dishes after. That's the only time I'm home. I want you to be dressed up and sit in the front room with me." So I guess that's love.

When I was a girl, all the teachers went to normal school in the summer time for a month. And he sat clear across the room with what I called the old men. All the boys who had mustaches I called old men. I was just a young kid, you see, and he'd kind of smile at me. I never looked at him. And I remember he'd try to—as we walked down the steps—get hold of me and make me walk with him. And I'd jerk away from him and walk with some old woman, and we'd laugh all the way down, making him walk with old Mrs. Smith.

Well, we used to have opera troupes come through from New York City and put on a show at the opera house. He wrote me a letter—he was teaching school out in the country. And, you know, we didn't have telephones in those days. And he wanted to know would I go to the opera house to see *The Wizard of Oz*. I'll never forget going to that opera. So of course I wrote back and said that I would. And he was boarding with a man out in the country who taught and was the principal of the school at Crescent. Big shot. And Sugar never told him he'd written me a letter too. So I got a letter from this principal saying, "You won't need to answer this letter, but I'll be at your house at four o'clock on Thanksgiving day and spend the evening and take you to see *The Wizard of Oz*."

Two of them. Sugar was boarding with him. And I had already written Sugar—Sugar was my pick. So I didn't know what to do. Mama always had a nice Thanksgiving dinner for us. That's a part of our tradition. That's the way she believed, in having a nice Sunday dinner and a nice birthday dinner and those things. So here comes Sugar, first. And, oh, I was so tickled to see him. And he hadn't been there more than fifteen minutes than here come this other old boy. And I know I had heart trouble. And Sugar didn't know what was going on, and I couldn't explain it. And my little brothers and sisters was feisting around there. And Sugar had given them a nickel to get them out of the house and get some candy. But I never got a chance to tell him this, about the other one. So I went in and I told Mama. Mama says, "Cross the street to those old maids, go over and see if one of them would go to the show." He had tickets. They had cost four or five dollars. So I went over and asked one of the old girls if she'd be tickled to death to go with him. So Mama had us all come in and have supper. I just choked on every bite I ate. I was just scared to death. I was afraid Sugar would get mad and leave. And he was the one I wanted.

So after supper, before we went to the show, I said to the principal, "I ran across the street and asked one of the girls if she'd go to the show with you tonight and she said she'd be tickled to death." And he said, "I don't know who she is." I said, "I'll take you over and introduce you to her." And boy, I saw that pleased Sugar. I didn't call him Sugar then. I said, "I'm going with Mr. Martin." I didn't want Sugar to get up and go home. And so I took this old boy over and introduced him to this girl and she was thrilled to death. They went to the show. And we ended up good friends. And he said to Sugar later that he always liked me. And Sugar would say, "Yeah, I did, too."

Our courtship was perfect. Sugar liked me and I liked Sugar. We went to everything that came along in town. We'd go to the circus. Here in Guthrie. And they always had some good show about once a month at the opera house. Sugar always took me to see the show. We'd go to the ball games. And once a month Sugar would hire a horse and buggy, and we'd go take a buggy ride, all over the county. Hottest Sunday, parasol over our heads. Go along and have a good time.

Religion has been important to me. I believed in it. I was just raised that way—to go to Sunday school and church, and I don't know any different. I thought that was part of life. Well, I'll tell you something. I have been blessed a thousand times. I've had several accidents. Been in a terrible accident once. Home seven months. Got out of it good as new. As I say, I've had lots of ups and downs, but it's always worked out. And my minister's always come to call on me. My church life has been beautiful. But you know, I'm the kind that would tell him to go someplace if it didn't suit me. I wouldn't humor them. But Sugar was so kind and gentle. I'd say to Sugar, "You get down there and pray for them, and let me out of it because I'm hotheaded." I don't take any fooling. And when I worked for the Democratic party, nobody refused to do one thing that I ever asked them. In the whole state. So that's going somewhere. Because I had a program in my mind that I wanted certain things carried out.

But religion has helped me. I think it has. I think it has sustained me in lots of ways. I have never been uneasy about dying. If I die tomorrow, it wouldn't worry me at all. If I die next week, it wouldn't worry me. Because I lived a life, I don't need any last minutes.

I don't believe in people being sick. I'm not a Christian Scientist, but I think it's all up here, most of it. And old age the same. It's all upstairs. I don't let myself be afraid. I don't go out at night. I don't answer my door after I lock up at night. And I always hook my screen when I come in my house. I've had people knock at my door at eleven-thirty at night. I didn't enjoy it. But then I don't go around saying I'm afraid. I lock up my house. And I say if it's God's will, I'm all right. I don't worry.

I've been in every state in the United States. I've been to Alaska. I've been to Panama City. I've been to South America. I've been to Jamaica. I've been to the White House several times. To Europe. And would've gone again if Sugar had been able. We was planning on going back.

When I was in Oklahoma politics, why we was in certain districts. And we all went to every state, to a state meeting. Well, that took me all through the southwestern states. Then when Sugar was postmaster, they all had state conventions in their states. We went to every state then. And then Sugar and I have always traveled. We used to always go to Colorado every summer. And I've been to Yellowstone, Grand Canyon, the Great Lakes, Saint Lawrence, the Frontenac Hotel. And I've just been everywhere. And then I was head of the war-bond drive for Oklahoma, and I had to go everyplace. We had regional meetings, and I'd go to that.

I saw lots of things that I never forget.

Well, now, have you been to Sitka, Alaska? Well, that was one thing up there. I saw a great big house, I thought it was some hotel or something. And a lot of people on the porch, and they had a fence and they had climbing roses all over the fence. I'm a lover of flowers, I love flowers. I went over there to just see what was going on. So when I come over to the fence to go see, all those old men just come a running out there like their grandma had come. And so I said, "Well what is this?" "It's a old folks home for men." I said, "Oh, so pretty," because it was beautiful. "Well, we don't like it." I said, "Why don't you like it?" "Not any women up here." I said, "Oh, you don't want any old women. They're so ugly and mean. What do you want with one?" I said, "Well, you're just hard to please." I tickled that old man to death when I told him that. I thought that was kind of funny. But everyplace I've been there's been something funny.

*Oklahoma*—that play. Wasn't that beautiful? I loved it. You know, something about it. I don't know whether it's because I'm an Oklahoman or not. When I was in New York City one day, my brother introduced me to one of his friends. "Now, May, he's a real easterner," he said of this young man. I said, "Well, I'm certainly glad you are because I'm just a real westerner and an old-fashioned woman." So he and I sat in the backseat while we took a drive, and he says, "I don't think you're very old-fashioned myself." I said, "Well, I can enjoy life, but I'm one of these well-behaved gals."

One of the books that made the biggest impression on me years ago when I was young was *Shepherd of the Hills*. It's about a young man who raised violets and sold them. And he met some young girl who was selling violets, too. And she liked a certain kind. So he kind of became infatuated when she said he was charming. Every day he'd pick a certain kind of violets and take them to the door. And the long and short of the story is they finally got married. But that impressed me more than anything. That's the first book review I ever gave. *Shepherd of the Hills*. I gave it in school and I gave it at clubs, churches, women's meetings. They want somebody to tell them something, pep them up.

I love politics. I got into it when women could vote. I didn't know what to do when they went to vote. I said, "Sugar, I don't know how to vote." "Oh, I want you to go vote," he said. I thought it was for men and men only. It wasn't nice for women. I was raised that way. And so anyway, I said, "I don't know how." He said, "I'll take you up there and introduce you to them." And I was to help count the ballots that night. That's the funny thing. And I didn't know anything about that. So I went in and they asked me, "Are you a Democrat?" I said yes. And that took care of all of it. So that's the way I vote, straight Democrat. I don't look. Because I know there's something on there that I wouldn't like. I know something about them. But there's just as much I know about the other side. I just vote straight Democratic, no questions asked. I tell them that's my party. I am voting my party. And the hardest thing I ever done was to have to vote for McGovern. I cried. I cried all summer. Oh, it made me so mad.

I began to work for the Democrats when Roosevelt was coming along. About that time. And Sugar said, "Well, now the women can vote, and somebody ought to take hold of that and do something for the women." They'd all been taught, like I was, that it was dirty, it wasn't fit to do. So they had a county meeting, and Sugar says, "I want you to come and I want you to get some of your women friends and you women take part in it." The men were running it, you know.

So I went and, by hoagie, a man got up and nominated me for the county vice-chairman. Well, I said, "I don't know what to do." "We'll tell you." Well, you know, they didn't have to tell me too long. They didn't tell me very many times. Sugar said, "I'll help you. We'll all help you." And they all helped me.

In the fall they needed to get it going. There was a man here in town, he was running for district judge. And he had a good-looking wife, and she drove a car. Of course, I drove one, too. But she just wasn't afraid of anything. So he said, "Bess will go with you and you go around this county." I went to school in Mohawk. I knew everybody in Mohawk. I had a sister got married and landed in Orlando and run the newspaper. She taught school there. Well, I knew from there. I had a sister that got married who lived down here at Coyle and her husband runs a store. I knew those people. Sugar lived out southwest of town. He knew all those people. And I had lived in Crescent. I knew those people. I went to those towns. People I knew. And I went to the banks. Always went to the banks, because you know all the banks run the towns. You know that, don't you? Well, to make a long story short, we got around, and I knew enough people in Guthrie, ask them if they want to come. And we got back to town and we had 170 people lined up to come to the Democrats' meeting at the hotel. I never realized I'd have to pay for it. But I went in and signed it up, and this guy says, "You know, May, if they don't come, you'll have to pay the hundred and seventy dollars." Oh, I didn't know that. Well, I had to tell that to Sugar, but I didn't know how to tell him. I'd been a teacher of school enough so that I didn't have to take any of our money. I'd just take my own money. So that night before we went to bed—we always had an understanding. We wasn't to go to bed mad at each other or hold anything away from each other. Then we didn't have time to fall out. So I said, "Sugar, I've got something to tell you." And I told him. He said, "Don't worry about that. I will take care of that. It won't cost you a penny. Just go down there and have a good time."

So I went down to the hotel, there's that judge of the state supreme court, and the national committeeman. And they said, "We come out to help you out. First thing that's ever happened in the state for the women. And we want to back you." Well, that was something. And so we went in, and not only did we have 100, we had 220 people. And it thrilled the women to death, and the men got up and bragged on them and told them to get in there and back me up. That they had a leader and this and that. Then we went down to Oklahoma City to the district meeting, and they put me in as vice-chairman of my district. Well, I didn't know any of this, this was all Greek to me. I never asked for anything, because I didn't need it. But I was just doing it because I believe in the Democratic party myself. I'm a believer. And so then I got along so fine with those Oklahoma City women—they couldn't all get along among themselves. They liked me. And then we had a state meeting, they put me on as the state vice-chairman. Just because I could get along with people. I believe in getting along with people.

And then, anytime there's this going-on in Washington, President Roosevelt invited me to everything that went on. Everything. Oh, I was crazy about Jim Farley and President Roosevelt. Oh, Jim Farley. He was something. He met you once, and he knew your name and where you were from. He'd start out saying, "Mrs. Martin, come here I want to shake hands with you." He always knew me. I went to President Roosevelt's banquet the night he was inaugurated President. I went to the inauguration. First time. Sugar and I sat on the third row near the front, in front of the marine band. And said hello to everybody. Oh, the President, I loved him. When he'd come to Oklahoma, they always had us come down to meet him.

One night some man said bad things about Roosevelt on the radio. And I heard that program. Oh, I was so mad. I really was. After church the next morning, I went down to the depot and sent President Roosevelt a telegram. And in it I told him that I heard that talk last night,

Saturday night. And it upset me so. I was determined to work harder than ever and line up the women stronger than ever for him. And that was on Sunday I sent him the telegram. Well, on Monday I got a telegram from Washington to come to some Democrat meeting. I guess they was going to line us up then. So I went, and when I got there, they had an invitation for me to come to the White House to President and Mrs. Roosevelt's reception. They was entertaining the cabinet and the Supreme Court and so on. So I went to the White House. And when they announced me, "Mrs. George Martin," President Roosevelt flashed his smile. I said, "Mr. President, I was afraid you didn't get my telegram." He said, "Listen, Mrs. Martin, I've already answered it." And he put his arm around me, and I said, "I was mad as I could be, but don't worry, we're not going to let you down." And Mrs. Roosevelt was standing there and she said, "Oh, I know just what you two were talking about." And I said, "Well, I'm talking about making love to the President." I felt that I could say that, an old woman like me. Oh, I've had a good time.

And listen, politics is not dirty. It's just you. You. You can be just as nice. I've never met a man that wasn't a gentleman. Never.

They've always treated me with the utmost of respect. They introduced me as a real sport and a good Democrat. But they know I don't drink, and I don't fool around with the men. It's all business with me. And they helped me out on every occasion. They never left me high and dry.

I think the women's rights people have gone too far. Well, talk about this liberating women. A women's place is in her home. I kept my home intact. I belonged to all of my clubs. When I taught school, I used to say there are certain things in my life that I want to do.

Now I've quit. I just vote a straight ticket. But I help my friends out. I campaign with my garbage man and my laundry man. And my girl friends I play bridge with.

At the rate some people work I think they should be retired. See, my husband was appointed postmaster and he served fifteen years. Well, he was ready to retire. He said he enjoyed retiring because it was the first time in his life since he was 17 years old he hadn't punched the clock.

I don't think you can do a good job if you don't love what you're doing. Now I like to keep house. I don't do too good a job, but I don't live in dirt. Anybody can come in my house as soon as the door's open. But I'm not a fanatic. Once a week I have a maid a half a day. That takes care of things, sanitary. I think that if you don't like your work, you shouldn't be in it. I don't think there's enough money to pay you. I enjoy being a housewife. I enjoy it. I like to cook, like to have the girls over to play bridge. I don't mind going in the kitchen and washing dishes. Don't bother me at all. I like it.

When I was in London, we was taking a tour. And we came down through town, and I was on a busload of people. And I thought, Oh, do you see what I see? Just got up and clapped my hands. And they all said, "What is it?" I said, "American flags. Prettiest things I've seen since I've gone to Europe." That's the way I feel about it. And when I came back to New York Harbor and I saw the Statue of Liberty, I said the same thing. This country has always been good to me. It's been good to the people. It's been good to people. Better than other countries.

I was at a hotel in London and the men was all drinking. And they got to telling some story about the United States and England and France and Italy. And the story ended up that the United States got the best of the deal. There I sat. I said, "Well you know why, don't you?" Oh, they thought they'd say something that didn't make me mad, because they all liked me. And I said, "You know why, don't you?" They says, "Why?" I said, "Because we're financing all of you. We're keeping you all on wheels." It's the truth. I'd say, "Some of the American money built that building." I can tell it because they're all alike. Well, that's some of the aid program. American money. I won't be outdone.

You can be what you want to be. You can be a ditch digger, a drunkard, a United States senator. You're making your own life. I believe in it.

I still have my same old-fashioned ideas. I believe in common decency first. If you're that way, you are respected. I think that's why I'm respected around town. They all know that May's a good old gal, but she's on the straight and narrow path. I know that times change, though, and I've got a lot of confidence in the next generation. Well, listen, they have lived when a man walked on the moon. And they have so many advantages now that I didn't have. And school, and cars, and motorcycles, everything in the house. They have a wonderful opportunity, young people, if they take advantage.

I can't talk about Sugar's death. It's too touchy. As for me, I don't worry about it. If I'm going to die, it wouldn't worry me at all. I feel that way about it. I may not have sense enough to know the difference. I am not uneasy. And I'm not scared that I'm not going to go to the right place. I don't think about it.

# Theodore Levy

*T*heodore Levy lives in a rambling old apartment on Manhattan's Upper West Side, which he shares with his wife of more than fifty years, Henrietta. For readers of the many magazines devoted to magicians, however, he is better known as Theo Doré, for sixty-five years one of the most gifted magicians in America. He has had more than three hundred tricks and articles published in those journals. He has lectured about magic, taught it, appeared on radio and television, done a command performance at the U.N. for delegates to the General Assembly and their children. He is the author of Magnetrix, a book about tricks done with the aid of magnets, and a second book of his tricks is due to be published in the near future. Over the years he has entertained at the homes of J. P. Morgan, Marshall Field, Cornelius Vanderbilt, Moss Hart, and George S. Kaufman, among others.

Levy's has been a busy life. An ardent magician, he could not support himself, his wife, and his daughter through magic alone. But he is also a gifted painter, and he used some of that talent to work as a display artist for a number of New York City department stores, including Macy's, Gimbels, and Alexander's. When he retired from that work a number of years ago, he spent more time performing as a magician and doing his own paintings. Those paintings line the walls of his apartment, along with awards he's won for feats of magic.

A small, sturdy man with gray hair and trim mustache, he is alert and astute. He was the last of thirteen children. His father, a clothing designer in London, came to America when he was 21; his wife and three of their children joined him a year later. In the United States the father became a tailor to support his family. Theodore was born (in New York, in October 1892) when his mother was in her forties; he remembers hearing that she thought about not having him and is grateful that she did. He gained a fascination for magic from his father, and as soon as he got through high school, he set out to make a living in ways that intrigued him, artfully, and that included magic whenever possible.

Today he remains lively and active, performing for children and *people in nursing homes. Although he refers to himself as "an elderly gentleman," he admits that he performed at a party the day before he entered the hospital for surgery in early 1978.*

*He owns a playing card with the inscription:* WHAT DORÉ DOES CAN'T BE DONE—ORSON WELLES. *It is not likely that he will ever make that card disappear.*

I was 8 years old in 1900. One of the things I remember in New York then are streetcars with horses. I remember that very well. I remember during the winter the drivers were encrusted with ice and snow. There was no protection. I remember a very terrible strike of the people who were running the trolleys. And I remember someone in my house—his name was a real novel name, Wooley Hill. And Wooley Hill never did anything in his life, you know. And he always "ran" everything. So Wooley came down and tried to run the strike. And I remember very vividly the helmeted police grabbing him and beating him and sending him home.

And then I remember a youngster, fellow who lived in my house whose name was Hayes. Hayes was a boy my age. And I remember very vividly him running down and shouting all over the street, "My cousin won the marathon!" And he was thrilled.

I remember going to Central Park. I remember watching the big sailboats on the lake, which still exists.

I'll tell you a story. I was a youngster—how old I was I don't know. Maybe 10, maybe 9. And next door was a candy store, a penny-candy store in those days. Nobody had much more than a penny. And he had a sailboat in the window, an aluminum hull with two sails. And when I came back from the park, where I saw these enormous six-foot, eight-foot sailboats, and I saw the sailboat in the window—I went in and I said, "How much is that sailboat?" And he said, "Twenty-five cents." Well, a quarter was a fortune. So gradually, I got together twenty-five cents. I think he saved it for me. And on Saturday I got the sailboat, and my sister and I went up to Central Park to sail my sailboat with the other sailboats. There were hundreds of them in the lake. So we went up there, and I put my sailboat in the water, and I gave it a push. And I gave it enough of a push to push it ten feet into the water and it sailed about two minutes and the wind blew it over and it sank. And it's still there.

My father had a tailor shop. And he used to do a lot of work for the police department. Now, I was artistically inclined. My father's wool samples were glued on beautiful white cards. I used to pull the wool off and I had a nice white card to draw, like Charles Dana Gibson, who was alive then, in his heyday. And "Tad" was a cartoonist with the *New York Journal*. And he'd do marvelous cartoons, mostly fighting. James J. Jeffries, world heavyweight champion. And I would do these pictures, and my father put them in the window. I would copy Tad's signature as well as his cartoon. One day a big burly Irish police captain came in, you know, and he had his suit made. And he said to my father, "You know Tad?" He said, "I know him very well. He must be a friend of yours to give you one of his pictures." So my father says, "No, that's not one of his pictures. My little boy made that."

While these police officers were hanging around waiting to have something done, they asked if I could play checkers. Well, at that time I think I was about 12. So my father went out and got us a checker set. I got to playing checkers with these police officers. They used to play checkers in the police stations in those days. There was no TV, no radio. They had to do something. They all played checkers.

So I became quite expert. For a while they used to beat me. Then I went down to Madison Avenue and I got a book *How to Play Checkers* for ten cents. I had a fine memory, and I memorized all the moves. The checkerboard was numbered, and then you learned that if somebody moves from 12 to 13, you move from 14 to 16. So I studied that, and it came very easy to me. And I started to beat all the policemen. And in the neighborhood was Saint Bartholomew's Boys Club, and that was part of Saint Bartholomew's Church. That was Forty-second Street. Now it's on Park Avenue. So I joined the club. And I was in the club about six months, and I went into the library, and there was a sign in the library that said checker tournament. And it said this cup will be awarded to the winner of Saint Bartholomew's checker tournament, 1906. And the cup was right there alongside of it. So I entered.

After about three weeks I had all wins. No losses. So I went over to the man who ran it and he said to me, "You played everybody, but you didn't play Greene." I couldn't find Greene. I went to his home. He moved away. So they decided that as long as I didn't play

Greene, and the runner-up had played him and lost, that I had to play the runner-up for the cup. He was 21, and I was 12. So came the big night. They had the table set in the library and had chairs all around and they announced it. And there was sixty people there. I won the first two games, and then he won the next two. I got careless. Then I won that big fifth game, which I won with a nice three-star move.

Then came the presentation, two nights later. They brought me into the governor's room, the conference room, and there were these five directors of the Saint Bartholomew's club. Mr. Reed, of Reed & Barton, was presenting the cup, and there were all these fine gentlemen there. All big successful men—naturally, if they were directors. And he had the cup, and this is Saint Bartholomew's, and this is the little Jewish boy. And Mr. Reed said that he was very happy to present this cup to Theodore Levy. Here.

And I was to keep this cup for one year, and that next year it would be contested for again, and the one who won it twice out of three times could keep permanent possession. And with that he gave me the cup. And they all wildly applauded. And after they all got through, I said, "Gentlemen"—at 11 or 12 years of age—I said, "Gentlemen, I appreciate getting the cup, but I'd like to call your attention to the fact that this tournament does not say anything about running three times for the cup or twice. The sign said on the announcement of the exhibition that this cup was to be awarded to the winner of the checker tournament. It didn't say anything about running three times or twice."

So Mr. Reed said, "Is that so?" He said, "Just a minute, I'll go out and get the sign." So I said, "You don't have to go out and get the sign. I've got it here." And I took it out of my pocket. Mr. Reed said, "Well, the young man is right." The cup is still here, in my apartment, today.

A few years ago I picked up *The New Yorker*, and there was a full-page twenty-thousand dollar ad of Reed & Barton. So I wrote them a letter, and I told them the story of winning the cup and that I still had it. And that Mr. Reed himself had presented it to me. And it was more than seventy years ago. I said that when I got the cup, it was like silver, but now it's very dull. And I said I was wondering how this could be cleaned. A couple of weeks later I got a letter of apology from a gentleman who was not Reed or Barton, told me that the company had changed hands, and that he was very happy to hear from me, that every once in a while he hears from other people who have Reed &

Barton souvenirs or whatever. And that if I would send them $1.50, they would be very happy to send me their silver-cleaning fluid. How do you like that for real concern? A multimillion-dollar concern and somebody gets a letter that he got a cup seventy years ago, presented by Mr. Reed, the owner of the company, and they write and tell him—send them $1.50. It's a lesson, it's a lesson for all people, that you can throw sentiment out of the window.

I had the same experience with Henry Morgan. Henry Morgan is the president of the Morgan Trust Company, and he's a grandchild of J. Pierpont Morgan. A few years ago, they opened this little bank on Wall Street, and he, Henry Morgan, was the new president. So I wrote him a letter and I said to him, Congratulations on your appointment as president. And I said, I wonder if you remember a Christmas party that your grandfather gave in Glen Cove, Long Island? I was the magician and you were 6 years of age. And you helped me. And I did something to you—I pulled some little silks out of your shirt and you didn't like it too much, and you nearly started to cry. I said, I wonder if you remember that party? I said, Finally you started to laugh and you enjoyed it, and we all had a good time. And we all had Christmas dinner. I said, I'd like you to know that I'm now 80 years of age. So he sent me a very curt letter thanking me. You know, it didn't mean anything to him.

I think that all people have a tendency to cling to the past. I think that we all look back and we think about the good old times, which is trite. People in 1900, the turn of the century, eight years after I was born, they probably looked back and talked about their good old times. Right? And if you read about the pioneers, you feel how they had the good times because they weren't dependent on the A&P to supply anything. They had the cow. And they didn't rely on anybody to give them a ham. They had a pig, right? So maybe to them those were the good old times. I think that we have a tendency to look back and cling to the past. I don't cling to the past. But I can look back at some of the pleasant things that have happened to me.

My father was an amateur magician. In England he made suits for magicians—for professional magicians. He didn't do magic per se. But he saw magic and he was interested. And in this way I somehow gravitated to it. My father made me trick pockets, and that was, let me see, seventy years ago. And today I see the magicians using these pockets, and some of them think it's brand new.

My father and mother were completely different types. My father was a natural quiet man. He wrote poetry. He was a fine Talmudic scholar. He spoke a beautiful English because he was an Englishman, and I remember him telling me that when he first came to this country, people used to point to a window, say, and ask him, "What do you call that?" And he would say "That's a *window*," because they said, "windah." In those days he had enough qualifications to call himself a rabbi because in those days there were no seminaries where you graduated. And some of his friends who had a lesser Hebrew education than he put a sign in the window: REVEREND. And they would officiate at marriages. But they gradually became known as reverends without half the qualifications my father had. My father should never have stuck to what he did, but he did.

And these so-called reverends would come to my father and tell him that they had to go to a funeral or they were going to officiate at some affair, and my father would write out their speeches. Forty, fifty, sixty years later, his sons did the same thing. I did the same thing. I used to write out speeches for school principals, believe it or not.

Mother had a terrible temper. She was fiery. Mother was good-looking. Both of my parents were short. This is something that I always wanted to correct in my lifetime. I never could correct it. There were a lot of other things I could.

I don't think my mother was particularly literary, but my father was. My father once burned a pair of pants pressing them, because he was so interested in telling me a story of the Bible. My father gave me the desire to go to the library, to read, to be literary, and he liked people with a fairly good degree of education.

A fellow got up one time and lectured, and he said morals was the result of geography. He said that a traveler years back went to Arabia, and he was wandering through the sand dunes or whatever, and he came to a stream. And on the other side were a dozen Arabian women. And they were washing in the stream. And they all had their faces uncovered. And when he came out and they looked across and saw a stranger, they couldn't put their veils on because they had discarded the veils. So they all picked up their skirts and brought them over their heads, exposing themselves. So he said morality is a question of geography. And I believe that. I mean, all education, all intelligence, all wisdom is a question of geography. You can take Einstein. If you sent him into the middle of an African forest, he would starve to death, right? So the so-called ignorant savage can survive, right? And his family. And they know how to eat and pick grasses that grow, that are beneficial and nourishing. And the greatest scientist in the world wouldn't know what to do. He'd die.

What is right for you may be wrong for me. I'll tell you a story. This professor gets on this boat, and he has to cross this body of water. And a fisherman is rowing the boat. The professor says to the fisherman, "Did you ever study philosophy?" The fisherman says, "No." He says, "I never heard of it." They're rowing, rowing, rowing. The professor says, "Did you ever study astronomy?" "No. What's that?" He said, "Then you've lost three-quarters of your life." While they were talking, a storm came over, and the boat sprung a leak, and the boat started tipping over. The fisherman said to the professor, "Did you ever study swimming?" He said, "No." "Then you lost your whole life." And he dived into the water.

Well, what is good and what is bad? Let me try to separate some of my rushing thoughts.

In the first place, when you think of families in my day, they were competely different then. Our family sat down at the table to eat. The night before I got married I came home late, and my mother said to me, "Do you know what time it is?" The night before I got married.

No one disobeyed our parents. It was unthinkable. Disobey your parents? We would sit down and if we said something bad, my father didn't hit us—my mother did it occasionally—he would look at us, just look at us, and we kept quiet. My family would no more think of criticizing our parents than they would think of jumping off a cliff. We were obedient children in our day. I know Italian families in my neighborhood were the same way, and German families. The children stayed home—that was their home. It was unthinkable that a child, a young daughter or a young man, would say I'm leaving home, I'm taking an apartment. Whoever heard of that? What are you, a bum? I remember my mother telling me quietly that so-and-so smoked cigarettes. It sounds funny today, right? And don't go near her. Don't have anything to do with her. My mother warned me and I listened to her. I thought that was something terrible.

Some children were brought up in a very religious atmosphere, compelled to go to the synagogue or to church, in the morning or the afternoon or in the night, or part of their Sundays, and got to hate religion. This is a common experience because it was forced on them, you see?

We were brought up without television, without radio. We were more self-entertainers. Pianos were in a great many homes. The child took violin lessons or took piano lessons, or took elocution lessons. We entertained ourselves. Parents didn't buy expensive toys for their children. I was brought up with the toys of my cousins who happened to be wealthier. So they gave me their magic lantern without the chimney, and I ran all over New York trying to get a chimney for it. Or my father would take a string and tie a knot and take a button with a hole, and run the string through the hole in the button and show me how the button could cut something or make a noise, or whine. Or show me how to make things out of paper. So that today I'm a craftsman. I can do all kinds of things. I can amuse for an hour with a handkerchief. That's all I would have to have. We became more self-reliant. And I think that we all learned how to speak better because we had conversation. Today they only listen. And they watch TV. I mean, you see a child watching TV for hours. Not only a young child, but older children. And you can call it good or you can call it bad. Stays in front of the TV and he doesn't have to worry about amusing himself. We amused ourselves.

When people ask me, "What did you know about sex?" I always think of the story of the poor boy who said he was so poor that he was 21 years old before he found out that a chicken had any other part except a neck. I didn't know what sex was. Now whether my parents were at fault or not, I don't know, but neither one of them ever told me anything about sex. My father spoke German when he wanted to say something to my mother and not have the children understand. I went to Hebrew school. Saturday mornings. And I was confirmed there. I was 13 when I was confirmed. And one of the teachers was Mr. Content. He got ahold of us one day, Mr. Content, and he brought us into a classroom and he sat us down, and he talked to us about sex. For about a half an hour. When we left him, I said to one of the boys, "What was he talking about?" Evidently he was talking about social diseases. So I said to one of the boys, "What was he talking about?" He said, "He was talking dirty." That goes back seventy, eighty years. That was our conception of sex.

I think that if a person likes art and you open up galleries to them and classes, and education, they become art conscious and they want to paint or they want to draw. And I think it's the same thing with music. So the same thing in my opinion is happening now to sex. You are opening up avenues of education to the extent that they all want to try it. I didn't know anything about it, so I wasn't interested. I didn't want to try it. I was 17 when I surreptitiously made a date with the girl who lived upstairs—a very lovely girl. And her mother didn't want her to go out with boys. And my mother didn't want me to go out with girls. So we went to an amusement park in the Bronx. And three blocks from the house we separated so our parents wouldn't know. See? And I held her hand, and I think I kissed her on the cheek in one of the dark tunnels. And I thought about her for three weeks.

Once I delivered for my father some clothing or something, and a woman said to me, "Well, come in, come in." And she took me into the bedroom. And pushed the bed up and down and said, "Isn't that nice and soft?" I was 16. And I had a conception of that woman when I left. And that conception was, She's a dirty slob. Because she had her waist open, besides showing a little of her breasts. And I got out concerned that my sisters wouldn't dress like that. Certainly my mother wouldn't. And this was my mentality. Not today, of course. Today they would grab her and throw her onto the bed. You can't go back. What are you going to do?

I had a sister who said that her husband was wonderful in bed. She said he was wonderful when it came to sex. Never kissed her from one end of the year to another. Never wrote her an endearing note. Never gave her flowers on an anniversary. Never knew when she had a birthday. Never held her hand. Never put his arms around her. But he was wonderful in bed. You want to call that love? I don't know.

I would define love as a deep interest, a high regard for the other person. I do feel that regardless of how inward a person is, that there must be some outward manifestations. This I think is important.

My wife was in the hospital with me. And she was in a completely different building and different floor. Very difficult to get to her. They used to take me down in a wheelchair, you know. Then it was her birthday. She celebrated her 78th birthday. I teach magic, and I asked a young protégé to bring in some watercolors. And he brought in watercolors and a pad and a couple of brushes. So I painted pictures for the nurses and one or two doctors. So when my wife's birthday came, I painted her flowers. And I wrote happy birthday on it, like it was a card, with flowers. And I gave one of the porters a little tip and I asked him to bring it down to her on her birthday. To a person like my wife, she appreciates that more than if I would say, Darling, I'm going to give you a fur coat.

I met my wife at the YMHA. That is, the first time I actually dated her. But my wife met me when she was 8 years of age, maybe 10. My wife belonged to an organization that was connected with a synagogue. The rabbi got me to entertain for his class, his school. And my wife was in the audience. She remembers it very vividly. Of course, I wouldn't know a little girl in the audience. I'm eight years older than she is. And then she joined, when she was 18 or so, the ladies auxiliary of the YMHA at Ninety-second Street. Somebody had to go to the ladies auxiliary and talk to them about coming to a dance we were planning. We were having some kind of a holiday dance, very important. Little bit out of the ordinary, dress occasion or something. Two or three of the boys were asked to go over there, and they all got faint about it—talking to the women. Shows you how times have changed, right? And then he asked me if I would do it. So I walked over there, and they were holding the meeting. They were waiting for somebody to come over because they were told that somebody was going to tell them about the dance. And my wife was there. I got up and I addressed the girls, with my usual oratorical forensic ability. So at the dance, of course, they were there. I asked Henrietta for a dance. That was our getting together.

The courtship lasted a couple of years more than it should. It went about three years or so. It was a beautiful courtship. Henrietta's mother was the only one that liked me. Her father wanted me thrown out of the house. He was terribly confused because he couldn't figure out how anybody with the name of Levy couldn't speak Yiddish. And I was the artistic type. I was different. But her mother saw that Henrietta was a different girl when I came there. I used to play the piano a little bit. Henrietta sang. And her mother saw this—that there was a light there, you know.

I was still supporting my mother. I was 32 before I got married. I was such a good guy, which you don't find today, do you? Well, we finally got engaged and we got married. We had an engagement party that few people have today. We hired a hall, we had a band. And we had a good time. I had tickets for the theater that night. And we left the party and had dinner out. It was beautiful.

We had the wedding in a small hall in Harlem. And we stayed overnight at the Majestic Hotel, and we had a trip to Niagara Falls and Canada.

We have managed to make it work for fifty-three years. Give and take. There's a thousand jokes about this. A fellow says, "How are you married so long?" He says, "Well, we compromise. When we first got married, my wife wanted red drapes, and I wanted green drapes." He said, "So we compromised and got red ones." See? The fellow said to an old man being interviewed, "You're so healthy. You're so vigorous. How do you account for that after more than fifty years of marriage?" He says, "Well, I'll tell you, young fellow. When we first got married, we made an agreement. If we had an argument and my wife was wrong, she had to go into the kitchen, do the dishes, stay there. If we had an argument and I was wrong, I had to leave the house, walk around the block. I've been walking for fifty years."

We have one daughter who makes up for twelve. Well, in the first place, she's 50 years of age today. She lives in Santa Fe, New Mexico, on her second marriage. Beautiful girl. Highly talented. She had a mother who did things—like making her play the piano at the age of 4. And then she studied and became a very, very fine pianist. She did concertizing. She received a scholarship from the United States government, one from Spain.

At the height of her career, she became ill, and she was hospitalized for two years, and it broke up her life. She received all kinds of offers while she was in bed. So she got divorced and she went off to Aspen. Aspen, the music colony. And there she met a young fellow who was studying composition. And he was walking around with music that he composed. And nobody took any interest in it except Ruth. And Ruth criticized it and they played. Well, they got together, eventually got married. She took over his three kids. So somehow or other Ruth financed a house and they became quite successful. And his compositions are played all over the world. The government sent them to Poland, to Europe. He wrote a ballet. She collaborated with him. She became, contrary to her father, a very successful businesswoman. President of a little music company. And he is quite successful. He's a very fine gentleman. He has a doctorate today, he's a musicologist and a composer and a writer. Lectures in dozens of colleges all over the country. A very fine educated man. Lovely fellow. And they have now a beautiful little place in Santa Fe. We go out there nearly every year.

What is being religious? Well, I think that my first analogy is as a child. My father and I were standing outside of our house, and a man passed by with his prayer shawl and a book under his arm, and he walked past us and said hello to my father. When he was out of sight, my father said to me, "He thinks he's religious. He's going to temple now to pray."

So we have people who wouldn't do you a kind thing, but they think they're religious because they go to synagogue every day. They'll stand outside this door here and won't open it because it's Saturday and they're not allowed to open a door, so they wait for you to open a door, see? But they wouldn't do a good turn for you, and this is what in my opinion being religious means.

As far as I'm concerned, I go to the synagogue maybe once a year on the holidays, and I buy two tickets because they charge. Did you ever hear that story of the fellow who tried to get in the synagogue? On a holiday, a high holiday. The fellow at the door said, "You can't go in." He said, "I got to go in. I just came from California and I want to see my brother." So the fellow at the door says, "Well, go ahead, you can go in. But don't let me catch you praying."

So I go into synagogue and Henrietta joins me. And I sit down and I hear the rabbi deliver a sermon, which I don't hear too well. And I hear the choir. And I stay there a few hours till it's over. And I do this because I want to feel that innately I'm a Jew. And I want to feel that I still have my religious Jewish instincts. And I keep this up. And I'll do it as long as I can. But as far as being religious is concerned, I think I've gone out of my way to be kind to people, to do things for people, within my ability. And I think this is being religious. I believe in a God. Whether he believes in me, I don't know.

To older people, unless they're financially stable, I think health is the most important part of their lives. And in my day, where there were no pension plans, I worked more than fifty years of my life. Today you can work twenty and retire on a pension. I worked fifty years.

My parents didn't have Social Security. Neither did my wife's parents. We all made a little living in our lives, you know. We weren't bums. Some people today object to the fact that something's taken out of their salary to pay Social Security. They don't know how fortunate they are.

Yes, the cost of being sick. Another thing that's condemned that's a blessing is Medicare. People in our state survive on Medicare. We're contributing to it. We're paying money out of our little incomes, every single year, toward Medicare. We're not getting it for nothing. Every single month they're deducting it from our Social Security, right to this day. Over the years. It may not cover all the expenses. I got a hospital bill myself, close to eight thousand dollars for twenty-two days. Medicare covered 80 percent.

I don't think that any sensible person looks forward to going to a hospital. I think a person who looks forward to going to a hospital is out of his head. The hospital is a torture chamber. It's going back to medieval days. You get through it because you have no alternative. Personally, I couldn't wait till I got out fast enough. I painted in the place after I was well enough to get out of bed. And I kept myself busy that way. Most of the patients are satisfied to watch TV. My mind doesn't work like that.

A great experience, travel. You meet different people. It's a different life. You're waited on. You're catered to. For a few weeks you live like a millionaire. It's like the fellow said when he saw the funeral with the beautiful flowers and a beautiful coach, and he turned around to his son and he said, "That's living, boy."

I was standing outside my house one day, I was just about voting age, and a little fellow came over to me and he said, "Would you like to be a poll clerk?" I said, "What is that?" He said, "Well, you come down. You get fifteen dollars a day at the election. Are you Republican or Democrat?" I said, "I don't know what I am." He said, "Well, you got to be a Republican because this is a Democratic district and we can't find any Republicans." So I became a Republican poll clerk. In those days there was no women's suffrage. Only the men used to line up. Women did not have the vote. And the men used to line up, and when you asked them to write their names, they couldn't write them. They were illiterate. So they had to put a cross there. You wrote their name, they put a cross. And this was my experience as a poll clerk. And I always look back to that and think to myself, these were the men who said, "Women, they want the vote?"

I remember one time walking down Fifth Avenue and there was a table there with a lot of women suffragettes. And I was walking with three or four boys, young men. And the women stopped me and asked if I would sign a petition. And one of them said, "Do you believe that women should have the vote?" I said, "Yes, ma'am." She said, "I bet you don't know what district you're living in, do you? Can you tell me the name of your congressman, senator?" We couldn't. And she said, "You boys are stopping us from having the vote. Look at how ignorant you are of what's going on."

Women should have all the rights men have. Absolutely. Why not? I mean, what are they? Different human beings? My wife has been for women's suffrage as far back as I can remember.

I don't remember that I was writing political letters per se, but I have written letters all my life, and still haven't stopped, and won't stop if I can write. And they've gotten me some very, very funny experiences. The last letter I wrote was written a few days ago. And it was written to the Mrs. Adler Matzoh Ball Company because we got a can of matzoh ball soup without matzoh balls. Right from my friend Louie Rosen, the butcher, on the corner here. So matzoh ball soup sells for eighty-five cents. Well, Louie's a good friend of mine. He's a kosher butcher, without whiskers, you know, a college boy. Does a good magic act for an amateur. So he sold me the matzoh ball soup for sixty-five cents, like he does everything else he gives me. Henrietta says, "Where's the matzoh balls?" I said, "I don't know." I cut the top off and it sunk right to the bottom. So I sat down and I wrote them a letter.

Henrietta saved plaid stamps. I don't know how long she saved them up. And then she looked in the book and she said, "I've got four books and a half, what can we get? What do we need?" We need a card table. All right? So we get the books, and we went down to Eighty-first Street and Third Avenue and we gave the books and we took the card table out, in a case. I took it to the door. I called nineteen cabs and they wouldn't take it. Finally we got a cab, cost me two dollars and a half. We got it home. And after we had it home, I opened it up. It had a guarantee for thirty days. Guarantee. And after six months we

sat down—we used to play Scrabble every night with the table there—
we noticed that the table was wobbly. And then it got a little more
wobbly, and finally one leg fell off.

So I wrote a letter to the company. I told them that my wife had
been saving the plaid stamps for three years, and finally managed to
get four and a half books. And we decided we're going to get a card
table. And I know that the guarantee was thirty days. But shortly after
the guarantee ran out, the table started to get wobbly. The legs. And I
wrote to Mister President—always write to the president of the company, never write to anybody else, only the president of the company,
nobody else—and I said, I am 80 years of age, and my legs don't
wobble. I said, After a while one leg fell off, and sir, I still have both of
my legs. One of them hasn't fallen off yet. I said, Your table is built
with steel piping all around. I said, You can rest assured that with this
steel piping you could build a house on top of it. I said, I'm surprised
that this happened. My wife and I would like to play Scrabble. So I
said, We felt a little inconvenience—I took my family Bible, I put it
on my knees to support the one corner of the table. But my wife,
I said, objected to it. She said it was sacrilegious to do that. There we
are, sir, I said, with all of our *Encyclopaedia Britannica*s on the floor,
reaching all the way up—just enough to support one side.

Well, I don't remember every word I wrote, but the phone rang a
couple of days afterwards. This was out in Detroit someplace, and
somebody's voice says, "This is Miss Kelley, Mr. Scranton's secretary."
President of the plaid stamps. "And as soon as he gets through
laughing," she told us on the phone, "he's going to send you a card
table." And sure enough, here it is. See?

Another letter. We had a gas stove here, and it didn't work. We still
have it, but now it works. The landlady is responsible for the stove,
not the Con Edison Company. They have no responsibility whatsoever, only with the gas connection. You also can run into a very serious
thing with the Con Edison Company, which I learned lately. If you
have a leak and call them up, they'll shut off the gas, and they won't
fix it. The landlady's got to fix it. So if you ever have a leak, don't call
up the Con Edison Company. I found that out lately. But this is before that.

This wasn't a leak. It was just the gas wasn't right. So I wrote a
letter to the president, Mr. Luce. I always tell them my age. See?
It's a game. Some of these letters are heartrending. They cry. And I

told him how much we suffered with this thing. And I told him that the landlady would not replace the stove. A couple of days later I got a call. "This is Mr. Luce's assistant, public relations," blah blah blah. "He turned the letter over to me, and, Mr. Levy, we're very sorry. It's not the policy of the company to do anything." He said, "It's up to your landlady. We only connect the gas." And he said he was very sorry and he hung up on me. No he didn't hang up. He started to hang up, to excuse himself. I said, "Just a minute." I threatened the hell out of him. I said, "I wrote you a nice letter, but you've got the wrong guy if you think that I'm stopping here." I said, "I'm going to see that this gets plenty of publicity. I have connections with *The New York Times* and the *Post*, the *Daily News*." And I said, "It's up to you to take care of this. The gas is not running."

Well, I don't know what the hell I said. I don't really remember. It's ten years ago now. He said he was very sorry. He hung up. I don't know what I said to him, but ten minutes later the phone rang again. "Mr. Levy?" "Yes." "Mr. Levy, after business hours tonight we are sending over our foreman to look at your stove." Well, about eight o'clock that night the bell rang. Three guys outside. One was the foreman of the district, dressed in a regular business suit. And the other two guys were repairmen.

"Mr. Levy?" "Yes." Took them in and showed them the stove. There was not enough light in there. Well, they were here from eight to half-past ten. The foreman looked at it, told them what to do, and went out. I had them. You know, those holes in the burner—they bored them out. And they broke the bits, they broke two bits, and they came back the next night and they spent hours again. The foreman came back to see if I was satisfied the third night. Not only that, I had him fix the refrigerator, too. Because they had turned off the refrigerator—I had a gas refrigerator, the only one in the world—so they fixed the refrigerator because I said it was their fault, they turned off the gas. Well, I gave them a couple of dollars.

Another case. Right after World War II. I have a typewriter, see? My lodge gave it to me when I retired as secretary after twenty-six and a half years. My fraternal lodge. I had this typewriter. It was an eighty-five-dollar typewriter. The lodge bought it and I had it at home. It was a new typewriter. And after a couple of months it skipped—started skipping.

Well, I called the company up and I told them about it, and they said, well, it's a portable. They don't send people out to fix a portable. So I took it down to Park Avenue, because I was younger then. But they monkeyed around with it there and I took it home again and the same goddamned thing, you know?

So then I wrote a letter to the company. One day my bell rang, and a fine gentleman came in with a little bag. "Typewriter here? Royal typewriter?" Yes. So he came in and I showed him the typewriter. He said, "They made a mistake. It says office machine here. We don't fix portables in the home."

He started walking out. So I said to him, "Just a minute. Would you do me one little favor. I had it down in your service station. The machine doesn't work. Look at this skip. What's wrong with this?" He gets out of there, doesn't fix it.

I picked up the paper a few days later and I read—I don't remember this guy's name—about the president. Irish name—John MacMahon—whatever. I know the first name was John, I know that. I read that John MacMahon, president of the Royal Typewriter Company, announces that their engineers have now perfected the electric Royal typewriter, blah blah blah. All right. I write like a college chum. Dear John. Dear John, was thrilling to read of your promotion of the new Royal typewriter electric that your engineers have worked out, perfected under your direction. If I could meet you at the club, to tell you personally about my problem, I wouldn't have to write this letter. I tell this story. Would you do me a personal favor for old times' sake? You know, the undertone of it—a very gentle undertone, without saying anything, you know? If you do this, I'll give you the old college yell. You know, something like that. These guys all go to college, right. They don't take any high school boys to be president of the Royal typewriter company. Could I go wrong on this? Oh, by the way, I never sign my name Levy. No, never Levy. Because as soon as they get these letters, the first thing they'll say is some Jew bastard wants something. So I never sign my name Levy. It's always Theodore Doré. So I tell him that for the old college try will you kindly, before your engineers work on the electric typewriter, have them perfect my typewriter? And I said, there's one weak part in there. I tell him it's skipping.

Well, two things happened practically the same time. Henrietta has an appointment with a doctor. I'm working. I'm not home. She has an appointment with a doctor, two o'clock. About quarter after one, the phone rang. And then an agitated voice gets on the wire. Who's this guy? He's vice-president in charge of service.

And he says, "Mrs. Doré?" Yes. "We got your husband's letter." My wife knows as much about these letters as a Chinaman. I never tell her. She didn't know what they were talking about. He says, "I'm sending a man over to pick up the typewriter." My wife said, "I have to go to the doctor." "Mrs. Doré," he said, "it's very important for us to pick up that typewriter." He said, "I'm taking a cab over. I won't have to park or bother." He said, "Please let me pick up that typewriter. I got to get it over here." His boss must have given him hell.

Well, Jesus, Henrietta waited. This guy sent over somebody to pick up my typewriter. And he said, Mr. MacMahon is writing Mr. Doré a letter. Well, a couple of days later I get a letter. Now, I don't know to this day, and I don't think anybody could tell me, whether Mr. MacMahon had a good sense of humor, whether he saw through my letter and answered me in like vein, or whether he fell for it. You could never tell, and I don't know. But he writes to me, "Mr. Theo Doré. Dear Theo, it was certainly good to hear from you again. And I do hope to meet you at the club in the very near future." And goes on like an old college chum. And by this time Mr. so-and-so, you know, has undoubtedly taken care of your typewriter. You can rest assured . . . And goddamn right, they took care of that typewriter. They took care of that typewriter without any trouble.

I enjoy everything I do. I do it with enjoyment, for the simple reason that I don't do anything I don't enjoy. That's all. I do everything. Home here today, I vacuum and I even do the laundry. If it's necessary, I do ironing for my wife. And I don't mind doing that. I don't think anything is demeaning. I think that marriage is a partnership. We should help one another.

In this book I'm reading right now the author spends a couple of chapters talking about people who have jobs they don't like. But why don't they quit? People don't have the courage to quit. And do what they want to do. They should. If they have the courage. A lot of people have done so. Have quit their jobs and gone out and made good, doing what they want to do. But this requires courage. People are looking for security. They don't want to take a chance. And probably their wives don't want to go along. I think this is more of an influence than anything else. Their wives don't want to go along with them.

I think I adopted new ideas as an entertainer, as a magician. I've adopted new ideas with new materials in art work, or new ideas of going and seeing others' art work and things like that. I think I have. I think that I can safely say that for an old man I'm not stagnant. I think most old people don't want to advance, don't want to learn anything new. I'm willing to learn something new.

Mrs. Roosevelt said that one of the unfortunate conditions of being old is losing your friends and your relatives. They pass away. And it's a natural thing. My wife is the only living relative of her family. Her entire family is gone, she's the only one left. And I have lost so many of my old friends and relatives—and there's no replacement. You can't replace them because the new generation, new friends, new relatives, whatever, that you meet, they don't have the same background that you have—they can't go back all those years. Well, I just have to take it as it is. You just have to face it, that's all.

I don't think we have any control over life or destiny. It just happens. I have a situation right now that I'm trying to control. But I'm not dealing with it. Both of us were in the hospital. What if it happened again? What are we going to do? Or suppose we are incapacitated? I'm not dealing with the problem now and I should be. I don't think that I'm very bright not to consider it more seriously. And I feel a little conscience stricken that I'm not dealing with it. I don't think that I can deal with it religiously. I learned this in one little story. The rabbi sat next to the priest at the boxing match. And the fighters came in, and one of them got down on his knees and prayed before the fight, and the rabbi said to the priest, "Do you think that will help him?" And the priest said, "Yes, if he can fight."

# Carey McWilliams

*Carey* McWilliams *lives in an immaculate modern apartment in an old building near Columbia University on Manhattan's Upper West Side. It is several worlds removed from where he was born, on a cattle ranch just outside of Steamboat Springs, Colorado, on December 13, 1905.*

*McWilliams was raised on that ranch and spent one "truly dreadful" year at the University of Denver before leaving to attend the University of Southern California. He found a new sort of life on the West Coast. In 1927 he completed law school and joined a "Dickensian" law firm in Los Angeles. The law fascinated him, but so did writing. He did both. He wrote a biography of Ambrose Bierce. He contributed to a number of magazines. He got involved in California politics. From 1938 to 1942 he was the head of the state division of immigration and housing, dealing with the welfare of alien immigrants, including Dust Bowl migrants.*

*His book on the plight of farm workers, published in 1939, led him to correspond with John Steinbeck, whose* The Grapes of Wrath *had been its fictional counterpart. For several more years McWilliams combined writing and the practice of law. He wrote for the* Baltimore Sun *(and got to know H. L. Mencken) and the* New York *afternoon paper* PM, *and in 1945 he became the West Coast editor for* The Nation, *the liberal political magazine.*

*In 1951 he came east to edit an issue of* The Nation *devoted to civil liberties; he never left New York. In 1955 he became editor of* The Nation *and remained in that post until 1975, when he retired.*

*Today, McWilliams lives with his second wife (he has one son by each of his two wives) in a comfortable apartment filled with books, including the eleven he wrote, mostly during the 1940s. The titles reflect his interest in labor, minorities, civil rights. He is a busy man, writing a new book (a political memoir), writing articles for* The Nation *and for newspapers, doing book reviews, and lecturing. His views blend the populism of the open West and the sophistication of the urban East. He pays attention to America; as an experienced observer, he can either criticize it or praise it, knowledgeably.*

It was marvelous to be a kid in Colorado. And when I listen to people that I meet and I read all these books and articles about parents and children and so forth, I really have very great difficulty in identifying with this business because, from my point of view, I had ideal parents. They were both very hardworking people. They were devoted to the two of us, my brother and myself. We knew it. It was the kind of household in which you didn't talk about unkindness. But we had assigned work, work we had to do. It was on this big cattle ranch, and we spent most of our time with cowhands, you know? And we didn't mind the assigned work, the chores and the work and the things that we did, because it was outdoors, with horses, riding and going around. And we greatly enjoyed being with the cowhands in the bunkhouse. I've often wondered if either of our parents understood the kind of talk that we heard in the bunkhouse, what they would've thought about it. But my father was a teetotaler, wouldn't tolerate guns. No guns. They could have them you know, but they had to be under lock and key. No drinking on the ranch. If they went to town and got drunk, that was their business. That kind of thing.

It was absolutely beautiful country, indescribably beautiful. And it developed very fast once the railroad went in there. You know, the West developed by a series of retreats or movements. Silver mining moved eastward from California. Cattle started in Texas and went up to Kansas, Oklahoma, Wyoming, Montana. Never got into northwestern Colorado because the range was there. Had to wait until this crazy modern railroad was built right over the crest of the Continental Divide. It was supposed to go to Salt Lake City but got as far as Steamboat Springs and stopped. But the minute that railroad was built, the last big hurrah of the open-range cattle industry was staged in northwestern Colorado. There were more cattle shipped from Steamboat Springs after say, 1911, than from any other point in the United States. And it didn't last very long. It lasted from then until about 1921. And then the open-range cattle industry was dead. But these were big outfits, big ranches with lots of cowhands and so forth, roundups.

The town itself was very funny. My father one time owned the townsite. It began to grow. There were springs, mineral springs. And as kids, we would be in snowshoes and sleds and so forth. But skiing, we didn't know from nothing. One year a very romantic character with some blue corduroy skiing costumes came into the community from Norway. He thought this was great, marvelous skiing country. And as kids we tagged along in his wake, and we helped him to sell these skis. So we all began to get into some skiing. Today it's a big ski resort with condominiums and all the rest of it. And the big jump is on the mountain that my father owned. He used to curse it. He couldn't find anything to do with it. It was too steep. And there it is today, with all this great skiing.

With the springs and the skiing, people began to come in. And it grew to fourteen hundred, maybe two thousand people. But in the early period, the proper housewives of the town insisted that it had to run on the up and up. So the saloons and the houses of prostitution and all that were moved across the river into a special community, which inevitably was called Brickland. So the town itself had a façade of piety. You wouldn't think it was really a western town in these respects, you see. But you go across the river, it was quite a different story.

So it was a really wonderful way to grow up because the attitude of our parents was essentially that we could pretty much run wild, because you know, we might get frostbitten or we might break a leg, but otherwise what could happen? It was a very safe place, and they knew this. And so we were subject to minimal restrictions.

I think it's changed a lot. The range cattle industry was the real basis of it, and that's all gone. It's a recreational community, changed almost beyond recognition. I would feel probably quite ill at ease there, even though I still have many old friends there. I think it's changed a great deal.

It was once the kind of community, for example, where there was a Negro couple and their children who ran the springs. It was an outdoor pool and an indoor pool and a lot of private pools. But they ran it. It was a Negro woman who took in washing. They were the only blacks. And as a kid I didn't even think of it as being particularly odd or different. Nobody even bothered to explain. And another thing very interesting about this community. By general consensus you didn't inquire too much into anyone's antecedents. Well, it was just the nature of the West. You didn't want to inquire too much. I think it's a very positive attitude, because many of the families whose kids I associated with in the school, I didn't know where these families came from or what the background of the family was. There was one Mexican-American family there. No Orientals. There had been Indians, youths.

But the Indian presence had completely vanished. And there was a very, very democratic kind of attitude. My father was the kingpin in the community. Everybody more or less deferred to him.

And there was a wonderful outdoor life. Incredibly beautiful country. As a youngster I thought that this country must have been there for all time and eternity, that it would be there for all time and eternity. It gave me an enormous feeling of stability. And yet some of those mountains where I used to ride the herd, ride the range, ride the range all day, are being ripped up. Developed. Around Hayden and Craig, Colorado, they're doing all kinds of mining and strip mining and what-not. So they'll have changed even the contour of that beautiful country before they're through with it.

Since my childhood, first of all, I would say that I think the whole society has become tremendously dependent upon money. And this creates a great dependency. I think it's gone a great distance toward undermining individualism in this society. I attribute a lot of this to the persistence of the Cold War over the last thirty years. The artificial prosperity that it generated, you know—we thought this was going to go on forever in the fifties. Gross national product and all the rest of this. And there would never be a day of reckoning. Nobody thought of this at all. In the meantime we've distorted the economy beyond recognition. You couldn't even call it a capitalistic society anymore. What it is nobody exactly knows. But in the process of this, this enormous growth, in the process, has come the reliance upon money, a tremendous corruption. Particularly at higher levels of the corporate world—tremendous corruption. Lack of individualism. Unwillingness to accept individual responsibility. Rip-offs, crimes. The guy who's money-dependent doesn't want to create a ruckus in the corporate structure, goes along with what he's asked to do, toes the line pretty much. You've heard quite a little bit about whistle blowers, but I've noticed that whistle blowers don't get very far. They're treated as traitors. Out they go. I'm very disappointed. I think that we always had this tendency to identify the American Dream as such with this specific economy. That was a great mistake because the American Dream in my judgment is something much more—something quite different. I think it is an attitude of mind, an attitude towards people, an attitude towards other people. For example, not only in this community that I speak of—that was a marvelous place to grow up in—but I have a tremendously, madly mixed heritage. And I associate this with the idea of America. I have misgivings about ethnicity as it's being emphasized in this country at the present time.

My family on my father's side were Scotch-Irish, Presbyterians, Baptists—that kind of thing. Very rigid. On my mother's side they were Catholic, French-Canadian, German Catholic. You couldn't imagine a more bizarre mix. They were not intellectuals in any sense. I didn't get any of that side of my life from either side of the family.

But I'm very proud of this heritage. I wouldn't have it any other way. And I'm a little distressed by the emphasis on ethnicity and all that, because it's done in a context which seems to imply that this is a defensive coalition against certain other groups. It's Italian-Americans against Jewish Americans, and it's this and this. I don't like that. In Colorado then, they appreciated the differences. There were no questions asked. There was nothing that you could call discrimination in that sense.

My father was, from the point of view of the cowhands, a humorous square. He always wore a coat and a vest, and collar, tie. He wore a buck hat that would befit a Mormon bishop. And you know, cowhands are very style conscious. They want to see what kind of reins you have on your bridle, and the width of your stirrups, and the kind of oil that you have on your spurs, what kind of saddle you have. They couldn't understand my father. He was like a city gentleman out there. But they had great respect for him because he was one of the finest judges of livestock—cattle and horses—imaginable. They had great respect for him. They just laughed uproariously behind his back. Because he was very taciturn. He was always preoccupied. He didn't show affection. He was universally regarded as a very decent man. I sensed that. For example, in this particular part of Colorado, there were ranches of 160 to 180 acres. I'm referring to then, not now. They had a certain number of cattle and cows, and they would have a certain number of calves. My father would buy the calves and buy the hay. Now all of this very large kind of operation was done just on a word-of-mouth basis. Never any contract. Nobody ever questioned his word about anything.

My mother was very warm, very, very sweet, a lovely person. I don't think you could find anyone who knew her who didn't have great respect and affection for her. She pretty much ran the family. But she, too, was very busy. She couldn't spend very much time with us. They didn't have domestics. Although my father was unquestionably the wealthiest man in the community, he lived a very Spartan kind of life.

And she was very affectionate, very concerned with us, very interested in us, but also very busy.

I have friendly recollections of the ranch. I have friendly recollections of the people who were around the ranch. Very much so. I have very few unpleasant recollections of the community, as a matter of fact.

Both of my parents were absolutely very strict. You paid your bills, you did what was expected of you. If you had an obligation, you met it. If you promised somebody that you'd do something, you'd do it. That sort of thing. They instilled this in us. Didn't have to make a point of it. It was so obvious that this was what we were supposed to do, that we went along with it. I still have my mother's sense of conscience. She was very regardful of other people. She was very sensitive to other people. And their problems. And I've got quite a bit of that from her. My father was very paradoxical. He was very close to us in a sense, and very remote from us in a sense. He was not the kind of guy who you could sit down and chat with.

My brother and I were together most of the time. But the family, as such, didn't do a lot together, except when we went to Denver at stock show time and when the state legislature would meet. My father was a state senator. We were much more together then than we were on the ranch.

When my father left the farm to go to Kansas City to work in a clothing store, his intimate friend was his cousin, Homer, who was virtually the same age. And they became very, very close friends. And the cousin was the person who lent my father the money that he went out to Colorado and started this crazy store—the New York Emporium, he called it—with. Now, this cousin died at age 98 in Kansas City. He never married. He left his entire estate to the hospitals of Jackson County, Missouri, that served Protestant, native-born, white Americans. It was a fourteen-million-dollar estate. The trustee had some doubts about the constitutionality of it, and it was taken up to the United States Supreme Court. And with Bill Douglas dissenting, they upheld the will. Now, this was the background of my father's family. They were southern. I think they were biased about disorder, against Catholics, Jews, Negroes, the foreign-born. In 1943, after one of my books on prejudice was published, I was in Kansas City to speak to the Missouri State Conference of Social Workers. And just as I was about to be introduced, I could see this tall stately figure with his cane coming in. Sits down in the first two or three rows, puts his hands on his cane, and looks at me very intently. And I thought to myself, Well, Cousin Homer, you're not going to like this. But I said what I had to say. And the next day I went around to see him and we had a very pleasant chat. We talked about the ranch and my parents. He used to come out and visit us almost every summer. Never a word about what I had said.

Now, I don't know exactly where the family got these biases. They were sort of built into that situation. My father, in moving west, shed them. He really didn't have them. This was a very bizarre background for me to come from, because it has nothing to do with any of my interests.

I think all of my books, I could safely say, are attempts to relieve my ignorance on a subject, of getting intensely interested in a subject and writing about the subject during the time that I was intensely interested in it. And I got interested in farm labor not so much out of a compassion for farm laborers as such; I got interested in it because it was so inherently interesting. The drama of it, thousands of people, big strikes, all this sort of thing. And this has been the story of my books.

For example, my book *North of Mexico*, which has had a tremendous sale and has been very, very influential, is still regarded as the key book about the Spanish-speaking in the United States. I was not the person to write that book. I don't even speak Spanish. I don't have intimate ties. But the reason I wrote that book is I got immensely curious about this situation. And the more I studied it, the more I checked it out, the more I talked with people about it, the more interested I became.

The same thing in a way with blacks. I have had no experience with blacks as such. I began to have an interest in them. And then when I really began to understand, I was appalled at some of the discrimination that was going on and was not even questioned. People took them for granted. So I got deeply involved. And the four years that I spent in the state job were very important because I moved all up and down the state running into all kinds of situations. Dealing with welfare recipients, how they were getting along, what their problems were, and so forth, including Indians. So I got an eyeful. And I acquired a lot of information that I used in the book.

I have a theory that one of the problems in American life is that we move from one extreme to another. And we do it so fast. We go to permissiveness and we'll swing into something else when it doesn't work out the way we think it should work out. And with respect to a lot of this consciousness raising and sexual promiscuity and whatnot that goes on at the present time, I have my own very serious reservations about it. The idea that a child can be raised by only one parent, for example. Or that people can live together as husband and wife for brief periods of time or longer periods of time but seem to have no obligations with respect to each other is foreign to my kind of nature. I don't cotton to it. I don't make a point of agitating about it. But, are women better off because of the pill than they were before? I wonder.

Mobility has a lot to do with the decay of family life. The small town is evaporating, disappearing. It's not a situation where your uncle is around the next corner, or your grandparents. My family is scattered. We have a son who is in San Francisco. We have a son who is in New Jersey. My brother is in Los Angeles. Keeping the family together is a very tough problem, a very difficult problem.

I've found two or three things that interested me about the so-called aging process. One of them that's been very revealing to me is that from 1951 until the time I resigned I lived such a rat-race existence, night and day, weekend, vacation time, whatnot—no staff, you know? Incredible rat race. Then when I retired, I suddenly began to see human relations and personal relations in terms that I hadn't been aware of. Been too busy, really, to perceive. Well, I found out a lot of interesting things. Nuances about relations between people. I had more time to listen to them. More time to perceive. More time to spend with my wife. More time to become aware of some of her problems, problems of being a wife with intellectual interests of her own. And I was aware of them—I mean, I could not have been unaware of them. But at the same time, I didn't really perceive them, didn't have a real feel. I got a much better feel for personal relations just simply because I've had some time to observe and to meditate a bit about it, think about it. And I couldn't when I was down there. I was getting up at seven in the morning.

I think a lot of social or economic and cultural changes have taken place in the country that have undercut marriage to a great extent. Kind of lives we lead, the speed with which they're led. The volatility of modern life, the tremendous contacts of people coming together, impinging on one another and so forth. There's no time. This is the key aspect of it. There's very little time for anything. I've been married for many years. We're a perfect marriage, as far as both of us are concerned. Despite all our tensions and the quarrels and the rest of it, we have a mutual respect, and we get along very well. She has imagination. She understands me very well. And I think I understand her. We came from very dissimilar backgrounds. We have acquired many interests in common which we didn't have at the time of our marriage. And it's worked as a marriage. I was talking about this experience of really understanding people better since I've retired, having more perception, in-depth perception, of some of their problems. This includes even our son, Jerry, who's now in his middle thirties. Well, I knew that he had problems growing up in this kind of family, to the kind of parents who were busy. I was aware of this but not nearly so aware as I should have been, simply because I was too preoccupied, I was too caught up in this rat race.

My sons are very much alike in some respects, quite different in other respects. But they're both very, very bright guys. And I'm amazed —I'm really amazed. The one at Rutgers is, I think, quite brilliant. The other one is equally brilliant, but in quite a different way, in his music and so forth. But they're clearheaded, bright. We've had a marvelous relation with them. And Iris feels toward the son at Rutgers as though he were her son. And he feels that way about her. There's a very, very good relation. Very good relation.

They both gave me pleasure when they were growing up. But here again, the one that's at Rutgers—my first wife and I were separated when he was at a fairly young age, which was very painful all the way around. It was a friendly separation and I went to see him all the time. But I didn't spend as much time with him as I did with the other boy. And I didn't spend as much time with the other son as I should have because of the business.

I never have been religious, but my father would write out a check to every church in the community, including the little Catholic church. Same amount. And his attitude was, well, if the boys, meaning my brother and myself, if they're enrolled in the Sunday school of their choice, it won't do them any harm, and it might be a good idea. But he was not insistent about it. We did go. Of course, it was kind of a social thing to do. I really have no religious feelings that I'm aware of.

I retired at the end of 1975 and I hadn't been sick for a day. I didn't even have a cold, and in January of 1978 I go to my doctor, who we've had for twenty years, for the annual physical checkup, and he says, "You have to go down to the NYU Medical Center immediately." He said, "This looks like it might be a dangerous tumor." So I go down there, and the doctor says, "You have to be put in the hospital immediately, as fast as I can get you in." So I get in there, and I have three operations before I get out. I hadn't any awareness at all, and I had enjoyed perfect health. Well, I was shocked at the suddenness of it and the fact that it was so unexpected, and the fact that I had no symptoms of being ill. I was tremendously shocked. Another thing—an impression I've had about growing old is what somebody—I don't know who it was—once said, that old age is one of the most surprising things that can happen to a person. And I'm sure that this is true because we're all perfectly aware of the fact that we grow older. We all know older people. We see them, we associate them with grandparents, parents, and so forth. And yet they are not us. We don't identify—we can't identify with that state. It is imaginatively impossible to really identify with that state. And that's why it's such a surprising thing, such a surprising thing to suddenly more or less realize that there are some things that you can't do which you did so easily. That you have less energy than you had, have to watch time more carefully than you did. That you begin to count. I'm 72. Well, gee whiz, suddenly I'm 72 years old. What's that mean? 73, 74, 75. What is the expectancy here? Suddenly very foreshortened. Even, you know, with all the geriatric marvels of our time. Still it's a foreshortened period, greatly.

I've been very busy since I got out of the hospital.

I'm pretty much immune to fear. At times I've been vastly worried that I wouldn't be able to support my family or I wouldn't be able to do the things that they'd need, and we were running out of resources, never having had much in the way of resources. And I've worried a great deal about things of that kind, and I suppose you could say I was afraid, I was afraid of the consequences of not being able to do this. But I don't think that's quite fear.

I think it was a mistake when I, for reasons that had nothing to do with my own feelings, decided to go to law school. I was working full time at the *Los Angeles Times* and going to school, and I had a marvelous schedule. They let me work out my own schedule so that I could carry a full-time job and at the same time go to a liberal arts school. It occurred to me one day that it was kind of silly for me to get my Ford roadster up in Hollywood, drive all the way down to USC, attend my classes, drive down to the *Los Angeles Times*, work in the afternoon and the evening, and then drive back home. The law school was right across the street from the *Times*. So I said, Well, why don't I enroll in law school? So for no better reason I enrolled in law school. I don't really regret the time that I spent practicing law. But it was something that I didn't really want to do. What I really wanted to do was be a writer. So there was a period there of ten years, twelve years, spent on this kind of detour. I think this was largely responsible for the failure of the first marriage. I regret that, the failure of that first marriage, because of its impact on our son. He had kind of a rough time of it.

We went to Turkey one year, and that was a tremendously moving experience in many ways. I was deeply stirred by it. And it made more of an impression on me than the ordinary tourist sites that you see, the galleries that you visit, the things that you see in Rome and Madrid and London and Paris and so forth. I was very much interested in Eastern Europe. And Prague made a tremendous impression on me. We were in Prague just before the going got rough. Dubček was still there. Those people interested me. And the life there interested me, and the city I thought was fascinating.

And also Ireland. This is very funny. The first day we were in Belfast—we were there on two occasions—I thought it would be fun to check the city directory, the telephone directory. You know, there are columns and columns and pages and pages of McWilliams. Incredible. Forget about checking it out.

I was greatly influenced as a youngster at the university—a freshman at the University of Denver—by discovering *Smart Set*. And I became a great Mencken enthusiast. I would get the first copy that was on the newsstand, read all the books that Mencken reviewed, and became a real Mencken fan. And I think this was a great influence because he said certain things at exactly the time they needed saying in American life. That there was a lot of guff in this country. You shouldn't take it too seriously. And listen to these ministers. Just listen to what these ministers are actually saying. He was concerned with the American scene. And he was not impressed with names. He was not an editor allied to big authors. He would take a piece from a lumberjack or from a convict. Very much interested in the American language. And it was a tremendously influential kind of thing because it made you open your eyes to what was going on around you. For example, I got very interested in cults in Southern California. Largely as a result of his kind of interest. He did a lot of pieces about cults, some of them appeared in the *American Mercury*, some in other magazines.

I began to look around. For example, when I first went to Los Angeles to live, it was just as the big move was on the way. I thought this was one of the most hideous cities imaginable. It didn't have anything like the compactness and the kind of elegance that small cities like Denver had. Then after about eight months, I became fascinated with it. I had begun to feel that I had a ringside seat at the circus. I couldn't wait to get out the next weekend and explore what the hell was going on.

Mencken really opened my eyes to a lot of this. I had a very good relationship with him, got to know him. And tried to emulate him as an editor and never succeeded, in the sense that he was so prompt in acknowledging requests or queries. Say yes or no about a manuscript, wouldn't hold it, would give you good leads, and so forth. Excellent, excellent editor. I think Mencken was great, was a real influence, no doubt about it.

And then I noticed when I was reading Mencken that Mencken was always talking about Bierce. Well, not always, but he frequently talked about Bierce, and he was sort of intrigued by Bierce. That was clear. And then it occurred to me, Well, here I am living in California. Bierce lived in California for years. Why shouldn't I find out what I can find out about Bierce? But before that I was wandering around in the stacks of the Los Angeles Public Library one day, shortly after I went to Los Angeles. And I suddenly came on the collected works, which was a very imposing collection, twelve volumes—and I thought, Well, that's that fellow Mencken is always talking about. And I began to read a little—picked out *The Devil's Dictionary* and I was hooked very promptly. So I started making inquiries. Mencken encouraged me to do this, because he wanted to know more. And this became a fascinating adventure, because I got to know all kinds of immensely interesting people.

Bierce was a great influence—a great influence in a very odd way, because he is thought of as a cynic, a skeptic, and all the rest of it. Fact is, Bierce was a man of very, very intense, deep feeling. And he never really recovered from the tremendous trauma of the Civil War. Never did. And his disappointment in the kind of society that came out of the Civil War. Terrible disappointment to him. He had come from an abolitionist family, intensely abolitionist. He was the first person in his county to enlist in the Indiana regiment. He had a tremendous war record. And to come out of this and then see what was happening to this society. He was badly wounded in the war and he just never recovered from it. It gave him a deep feeling that nothing really matters. But he didn't mean it in that sense. Everything matters; therefore you had to say that nothing mattered. I was very much moved by his letters, and I began to see what kind of experiences he was having, and that he had had in his later years, and how disappointed he must have been. And then he decided to go to Mexico. He first went down to see all the old battlefields. And some of the letters he wrote from that trip were absolutely beautiful, very beautiful letters. And then he disappeared in Mexico and that was that. No trace. A very deliberate disappearance. Very deliberate. He couldn't imagine himself growing any older. He was quite alone and he sort of felt that he'd had it. But he wouldn't commit suicide. He was unquestionably shot or robbed, or he was in the thick of the fighting.

Maybe I'm a special case. I watched Richard Nixon's career from 1946. And I thought, even then, that I had him pretty thoroughly cased, and I did. So I never was surprised at anything. I must say that Richard Nixon was the most important political figure in the United States in the period from, say, 1946 to the time he left the White House. This was really the years of the Cold War. I have to cut back here. Years ago I read a book by Karl Jaspers, the German philosopher, that made quite an impression on me. He was telling about the change that was taking place, that men and women were becoming more and more identified with their function, that personality was disappearing. And Nixon was a classic example of this. He was so obsessed with his career as a politician. There wasn't anything else. He wouldn't know a political value if one came up and bit him. Winning was the thing. And in this respect, with respect to his career as everything, he was a great deal like a great many Americans. I think they had his number long before

Watergate, but they didn't want to acknowledge it to themselves because they had sort of identified with him. They were capable of the same kind of self-deception, or deception, that he was capable of. And the same kind of phoniness. So he was not too far removed from them. I wasn't surprised by Watergate at all.

On the other hand, the civil rights movement certainly has improved this country. From my point of view, civil rights didn't start with Martin Luther King. It really began in World War II, that's when the true nature of it started. And it would've gone along at quite a different course had it not been for the onset of the Cold War. The Cold War put it in a deep freeze until the Montgomery bus boycott. Then it came out in the open. And in the South—it first started in the South, the heart of the old Confederacy. Very interesting. I think the civil rights movement had a tremendous impact, and I think it achieved its objectives. Because no one who was ever interested in racial issues would've thought that just recognition of civil rights would do the trick. But it was absolutely the first step. Until we'd taken this step, we couldn't go the rest of the way. And you look all over the country today—the victory has been achieved. They vote, they move, they associate, there are no arbitrary discriminations, and so forth. To that extent, it's unquestionably had an enormous impact. Nevertheless, there is a tremendously difficult road that lies ahead. But at least you've got this much. And mind you, it took a hundred years after the adoption of the Civil War amendment.

Women's rights, I think they're making headway and gain, and I think it's a plus. I think it's changing aspects of American life. I think it's good that women are getting into certain kinds of roles and functions. And where they've been arbitrarily discriminated against, I think it's all for the good.

What I do have some reservations about is consciousness raising in itself, on a particular issue. Because I think this tends to make it very difficult, it makes it too easy for politicians, and it makes it too difficult to build the kind of solid political coalitions that you need. It's all right to have black power and to have Italian-American power, and to lift the awareness of women, but the consciousness raising begins to take on an aura as though this were the only cause in the world. So then, you see, the women judge politicians not on overall practical basis—what is this guy like in terms of his entire voting record, behavior, and so forth—but how does he stand on the ERA? And I think that's unfortunate.

People work for money and they're unhappy at their work. It's gone much too far. It's gone much too far. And I can almost give you a date —it was 1956 when the census figures showed that service employment had for the first time exceeded industrial employment. Now, at about that time I did any number of pieces and editorials trying to focus attention on the fact that something very interesting was happening in this country. The business journals—*Business Week, Wall Street Journal,* all of these—were euphoric because the Protestant ethic had gone down the drain. The credit card had come in. Marvelous. And I thought to myself, These people are out of their minds. They're supposed to be spokesmen for capitalism. The Protestant ethic, the work ethic, is pretty fundamental to this. Now, you throw that out the window, you encourage people to buy things that they can't pay for and don't need and that are probably ecologically and otherwise harmful—what the hell are you doing? If you just worship something called gross national product, which would include switchblade knives and you name it, what are you doing? And what is happening? What happens when you throw out this concept of work, this having to actually pay someone to have some responsibility for your own life and the lives of other people. And for the quality of work. And what happens, I think, is a disaster. The other day there was a story, one of those wonderful left-hand stories in the *Wall Street Journal,* about a guy who had a big conglomerate and who's now in trouble with the IRS and the Securities and Exchange Commission. You should see the purchases that this guy charged to that company. This is commonplace.

From the time I resigned, I started to do a book about this. I started saving clippings, stories, about corporate corruption. And that file is going to push me out of my study. There are two or three stories in the *Wall Street Journal* each day. I think this is very bad. How must any kind of John Doe citizen feel? Even if he's not too bright, he's vaguely aware of what the hell is going on. And the temptation is to join them. I think that capitalism has come up against the consequences of its own successes, and it doesn't know how to cope with them at all.

Yet, I am an American. Well, there's a certain kind of quality about American life, there's a certain sort of personal freedom of motion and movement and so forth. I think it's somewhat exaggerated because of the dependencies that we're creating and insecurities that we're creating. But it's still there, and there is still this American Dream thing, the embers of it are still there. It's still there. I know all kinds of people who are very idealistic.

I was a Franklin Roosevelt fan, of course. His personal attitude, his freedom, his free and easy way, the way the people walked into his office and he greeted them. His whole general attitude was one of openness and his feeling for people. And these wonderful stories about Roosevelt's Warm Springs and Roosevelt in various contexts. I think he was personally a very great human being. He had personal qualities, apart from his political genius, that I think came from his having had polio. I think that if you look at his career, up until then he was rather insensitive. He was very ambitious, very insensitive. But then when this struck him and he was out of the swing of things for quite a time, he was trying to develop his muscles in Warm Springs, saw these young people, and got a feeling about their life—all that made a great difference with him. And the informality of the man, I think he was a much greater man than any of his successors—a greater human being.

A lot of things annoy me very much indeed. The stories of brutality that I read in the paper. I can understand, I know sociologically, how they happen. But it doesn't change my attitude when I read that a 14- or 15-year-old kid has taken a blunt instrument of some kind and struck a 60-year-old woman over the head. These stories happen all the time. The senseless brutality. Part of it, I think, is there is no morale in this society. Yes. There is no morale. What have we done lately as a nation that we can all agree is an extraordinary achievement? For example, you read all these stories about how these programs, these ambitious programs in which we throw all these millions of dollars, how they fail. Somebody rips it off here, somebody rips it off there, and so forth. And then you take out this biography of Harry Hopkins. Here is Hopkins, who set up the WPA program, did an enormously useful amount of constructive work, schools and sidewalks, libraries and so forth. A minimum of rip-off in it. Here was Hopkins on a salary of $12,500 a year, and because they couldn't force him out of his job—they knew he was too close to Roosevelt—some of his critics who were constantly putting him down cut that by $2,500. The poor bastard died broke, in debt. Now that was great morale there, wasn't it? He was interested in seeing that something was done. And I'm sure this permeated all the way down through the WPA. Accomplished tremendous amounts. That was the spirit of the New Deal. Now that's what I mean by morale. In the book about Hopkins, he tells about people in business dress who were out with a shovel because they'd lost everything they had, they needed work, working on these projects. And they would be interviewed first. These people weren't resentful. They thought it was marvelous. This was something wonderful—this was a great thing that they were doing. That kind of attitude is very good. That makes a project work. Now where do you find that in American life today?

One of the ideas that certainly has descended upon me in the last ten years is the fact that the models of different types of economies are all screwed up. Here we are less capitalistic than we've ever been in our past. We still call this capitalism. It doesn't have hardly any relation to it. I don't know how to name it. I wouldn't know. And at the same time, see, socially it's tending to become a socialist country. So what is coming out of this? What's happening? We've got to think that none of the models are any good. And we desperately need to try and find out what's happening. Because I don't see how you can cope with problems unless you have some kind of concept in your mind about what's happening in the society. Why do these problems arise? What direction a society should move in and so forth. And we don't have any models. We're improvising.

I suppose one has to assume, to believe, that the young idealists will rescue us. And to want to believe that. And I'm sure it's true. I'm sure there are lots of bright minds around. I think what's happened more than anything else—thirty years of Cold War, and the Cold War is not over—during the period from 1945 to the time that we withdrew from Vietnam, tremendous changes took place in this country. Institutions were sort of undercut. This business about New York City and its fiscal crisis. And the story the other day about the underground facilities of all the older cities, water mains and sewers and all, being in terrible shape. Now, the real history of this thing is that during World War II there was no chance to maintain these facilities. Everything had to wait until the end of the war. At the end of the war there were shortages, and it had to be postponed again. Then there was the Korean War. Again, couldn't be done. No sooner was the Korean War out of the way than the Vietnam War began to heat up.

So what we're seeing in some of these cities is simply the fact that they haven't had a chance, or they haven't wanted to do anything, for almost twenty-five or thirty years. So they're in terrible shape in terms of their basic structure—our cities. For example, there's been an awful deterioration of transportation in New York. This was one of the finest mass-transit systems in the world. And look at it today. And I'll tell you something else—as a people we're historically spoiled, and we're reluctant as a people to face the fact that there are finite resources. You can talk about energy, you know, but Sartre said only catastrophe will change people. You can talk about energy shortages and all the rest of it until you're blue in the face, and they will not stop driving those cars. Until there's no gas at the station.

My sons have a sense of conscience about all this. They do, indeed. And that's one of the reasons why I have some hope. I know their friends, and I know a lot of young people. We developed a contributor at *The Nation* who I was very proud of. He used to teach at Northwestern, and now he's at La Jolla, and his name is Stavrianos. Well, this book of his—the title of which I just love—is *The Promise of the Coming Dark Ages*. You know, there is a kind of dark age coming. I think there is, as a matter of fact. Well, along with this there are a lot of promising things that are happening, developments, as it were, in the dark ages, so-called. I think it's a pretty good concept.

Last Sunday my wife and I went to a small meeting of friends of a friend who had died. I was very disappointed in this gathering. Some people there seemed to think that it was no occasion for any real memorial, where people could really say what they thought about him and his achievements and what he was as a person. They wanted it to be strictly informal. So they had these people down there, and one of them got up and said, with his glass, "Cheers." And this was it. It seemed to me to be in bad taste. It disappointed me. That a person who had played an important role, as he had, and meant as much to many of the people as he did to me, as a friend for many years, I would've hoped that there could've been someone to say something that would have had some meaning to it. I don't think it was adequate. I've had quite a number of very close friends die recently, and I've been disturbed by that attitude. We have kind of an obligation to say something about our friends. This notion that it is somehow lugubrious—I don't understand this attitude, I think it's deplorable.

My friends have meant a great deal to me in my life. And if I have a religion, it's a religion of friendship, in a sense. I believe in loyalty, being loyal to friends, and people that I've learned to respect in my life that I've seen face all kinds of difficulties. I've seen them under stress and so forth, and I have a great affection for them.

I don't have any fear of death. I don't spend any time thinking about it. I think about my own life in terms of the things I want to get done. I wonder if I'll have the time. I wonder about the security of my wife. Will I be able to complete all these projects, all the things I want very much to do?

# Frances Teresa

*F*rances Teresa is an exuberant, chubby, active woman in her early seventies. She lives with her husband, Michael, in a one-story, brown-and-yellow stucco house on a well-kept residential street in Santa Barbara, California. The house is less than a mile from the Pacific Ocean and a few miles from the mountains she can see through her windows.

Mrs. Teresa is fond of pointing out that Teresa was her middle name before she married Michael Teresa, so she is Frances Teresa Teresa. One of ten children, she was born in Boston on July 28, 1907. Her father was a fisherman who became a grocer. When she was 6, the family moved to Little Italy in Manhattan and stayed there until she was 10; then they all moved to New Jersey. After finishing high school she attended an art school and studied interior decorating.

In 1935 she married Michael, and they continued to live in New Jersey; they had two sons and adopted a third son. Mrs. Teresa worked consistently at various office jobs. In 1962 they moved to California; they tried Los Angeles (too polluted) and San Francisco (too chilly) before they settled in Santa Barbara, in 1963. Her husband retired at the age of 59, after twenty-eight strenuous years with the Ford Motor Company. Mrs. Teresa worked at the Santa Barbara General Hospital until she had a heart attack at the age of 63. At that point, she decided to call a halt to formal work and devote her time to herself, her husband, her interests, and her home.

Today she does volunteer work, exercises and swims at least five hours a week at her local YMCA, works in her yard, maintains her house, cares for her husband, drives the family car, and keeps in touch with her children and grandchildren.

Although she no longer goes to a daily job, she keeps busy. Her conversation reflects an awareness of the world around her, tempered by a strong devotion to traditional values.


In Little Italy in Manhattan I was never permitted to go out at night. I lived on the ground floor. And you know, there were always men lurking in corners to frighten little kids. One night I was coming from the store and there's a man hiding under the steps. And I ran back to the store. I said, "I'm afraid to go home. Somebody's under the step." When I got there, he was gone. I screamed and yelled, so I guess he ran away. But you know, I was frightened as a child living in such a place.

My friends were afraid of my father—they called him Captain. He had a fisherman's boat. About thirty-five feet, with a galley. And when he got to New York, they called him Captain Sal—Salvatore. He used to sing a lot and was invited to weddings and dances and what-have-you. And I'd go along with him. I learned to dance with my father. We used to have a lot of fun with very little money. Well, let's say, you just made some homemade macaroni, and Mrs. Pudello down the street just made some tomato sauce. Well, the two would combine, and the families—these were all families, kids and all—would make the spaghetti and they would fix it all up and have lots of fun. Honest to God, by the time you were through, the men were chasing each other down the hill with a handful of spaghetti. We kids used to love it. On the last day of Lent, we'd go singing with our father door to door to the neighbors. And that meant inviting us in—until midnight. And we would sing and dance with them. American songs. We all spoke English. We were all born here—the children. And we'd mix the two. My father sang Italian songs, opera pieces, which I still remember. Had a very good voice. That's why we were invited out so much.

When we were kids, there was more of a family group. You know, my mother would take us to the Williamsburg Bridge, seven kids following her. She'd take us to the movies. Seven kids, Mom at the end, the mother chick. How I loved it. We'd go down to the Jewish part of town, oh God, we loved that. Mom would buy material, and my mother made me the most beautiful maroon coat with monkey fur you ever saw. So the teacher wanted to know where Mom got the material. She said in a pushcart. You know, she'd go down and get a piece of material and make a dress. Get a piece of material and make me a coat. I was one of the best-dressed kids in school because Mom liked to sew. And I never remember my mother going to bed before two or three o'clock in the morning. If she wasn't ironing and washing, she was sewing for us.

I think we've become a lazy nation. I really do. I'm still ambitious, and I shock everybody because I'm so ambitious. What are you racing around for? Because I can't help it. I never could stay still and do nothing. I look at television and I'm making slippers for some kid. I don't even know the kid yet. He comes in the house and gets a pair of slippers. And things like that—I just do it to keep busy. I've always been like this. I think I wear some people out. They're tickled to death to get rid of me because I'm always saying, "What have you got to sew? You got something to do?"

My mother was a darling. She was a mother who just lived for her children. My father was not around very much. My father was a very fun-loving person, loved fun. But he made money. He was a fisherman. I think he sold beer on the side, you know, against the blue laws. This was many years ago—I'm 70, so you can imagine how many years ago that was. A good sixty-five years ago. But that was it. He was always doing something. He was always making money. He wasn't a highly educated man. Then after a while, he used to import his olive oil and cheeses and sell them on a retail basis. My father and mother said they were both born in Italy—but wait a minute. When I got to Italy in '72, I discovered that my father wasn't even born in Italy. I discovered my father was a Frenchman. But he was brought up by Italian people and never spoke French in his life. And I'm taking up French now because my father was a Frenchman who never spoke French.

I was Papa's right arm. I was very good in the business. I was a little salesperson at 8 years old. My mother was having babies, you know, upstairs. And I would order and the man would say to me, "Gee, you're the littlest salesperson I have." I'd say, "Well, my mother's upstairs sick with something." I'd never tell him she's having a baby. That's the way I started. Then she used to have these poor people that needed help. Guess who was sent to those people? Little old Frances, because I spoke two languages. I speak Italian fluently, you know, and English. And of course, with the judge—I would interpret from the widow to the judge to get her help. Mama said, "Take Francey with you." They'd pull me out of school to take care of the widow. I've done that all my life. I'm still doing it.

I remember this. Getting carried out of a building and a fire going on, in Boston. And I said to my father, "Pop, did we ever live in Boston near a fire?" He says, "Do you remember that?" He said, "You couldn't have been more than four years old." He says, "Yeah, I carried you out because the fireman said that the house might burn next. But it didn't," he said. But we all had to get out. And I remember that.

My mother was so generous to people. I've seen her take food off our table and say, "Go down to Mrs. Benedetto. They have no food. Take this pot of food to them." I did that as a child. No asking for it. My mother didn't have to be asked. My mother gave very generously. I always wished I could be like her. They tell me I am, but I don't know. I think I still lack her goodness.

My father had a sense of humor. I have a brother you ought to meet, you could see where it comes from. He's very similar to me in the humorous view of life we both have. I love life and I love people. And I think it shows. I really love them. I really love people. You ought to see us in the Y. You'd think we were going to Oshkosh forever. Everybody wishing us luck on our trip. You know, this is the sort of thing we build up wherever we go. I have such a decent husband. He's such a sweet person. He allows me to do anything.

Exercise is very important. I'm a tennis player. And I swam all my life. It's when I stopped walking that I got fat—I'm getting rid of the fat, but very slowly. It's a year and a half, and I've still got, I'd say, another year and a half to go to harden up a bit. But the weight I'm losing. I've lost over twenty pounds so far. I just padded it all on. I stopped when I had arthritis of my feet, of all places. I had to stop walking. And I ran from doctor to doctor, and I got so disgusted. This foot paining me like a toothache. And one says, "You gotta cut it," and the other one says, "I wouldn't touch it. You got diabetes." Back to my doctor I went. He says, "Tell that clown you don't have diabetes." It was $238 worth of tests to tell the doctor I didn't have diabetes. Well, anyway, I dumped him fast. And I went to the Y to start walking again, be human, you know, alive again. And this is where it started. And I walk on my toes. I swim. So I'm doing it.

My parents believed in being fair. Be fair with people. Would you want that person to do that to you? That's the way we brought up our children. Let's face it. You want to get treated in this world the way you treat others, I told my children. I say you go around sneering and hurting people's feelings, that's the way they're going to treat you. Maybe they won't, but somebody else will. And this is the golden rule we were taught at home. My parents were very strict with us. We couldn't go out, you know, because the city was bad, and the world was kind of bad in their eyes. And they were strict—Dad was brought up as a Sicilian anyway, although he's a Frenchman. He wanted his girls to stay as nice as could be until they married, and this sort of thing. This is the way we all went along. And we're hoping our children follow suit, you know. But I thought at times they were a little too strict with us kids, you know, the older ones. The younger ones got a better break than we older ones did. I remember wanting to go to a dance one night, and I had put on a little powder—that's all, no rouge, no lipstick. Oh! I never made the party and the powder had to go off. That's how strict he was. Now that was ridiculous. But Dad was very possessive. You know, he couldn't die until I got there.

My father was a diabetic. Didn't know he had it. And some kid threw a stone and hit his big toe. Well, that big toe became black, and they started chopping him. First the toe, then the ankle, and so forth. And guess who signed the papers? I did. He was full of gangrene. So he was dying. After all this shock the man was dying and had gone totally blind. And the doctor says, "Look, this man should be dead three days ago. What's holding him up?" And they said, "Well, there's one daughter that's the apple of his eye, and she's up at the lake." So they said send for me. So they did. They got one of the neighbors about two hundred feet away from our cabin to tell me that I was wanted on the phone. I ran over. I couldn't imagine what happened. They said Pop's dying, and they said they think you should come in. Something is holding him back. So we closed the cabin. We went there, and I had to hit my father's face—he was in a coma—to let him know I was there. He says, "Francey. Francey." And he died that night, very peacefully. Now, isn't that awful? You know, there he was, this is how possessive my father was all his life about me. Which is cruel, because, gee whiz, you know, you wanted to have friends. I had a brother who was just as bad. A guy stopped dancing with me and was talking to me, and he said, "Is that guy making a date with you?" This is the kind of family.

I think we're too easy with divorces. We shouldn't give these divorces out just because you twisted your eyebrow this way. Let's face it. We all have troubles. We all go broke. I've lived on a quarter for a whole week with little kids that I had to bring up. I managed. I think the parents today are all so busy doing their little thing, drinking, going to parties. I never did that. I worked. I worked when I was married and my children were growing up. But I come in the house, strip off my office clothes, and start cooking and baking. I made sure those kids did their homework.

One time my son Bob got into trouble in school, and he was sitting out in the hallway. And I met a neighbor and she says, "Gee, Fran, I see Bobby in the hallway." I said, "Hallway?" I said, "Hey you, Bob. Mrs. So-and-so saw you. What were you doing in the hallway?" He says, "Oh, I got smart and they threw me out." I said, "Come on." Next day I took off early, went down to see his teacher. She says, "Well, all you mothers have to work." And she said, "You expect us teachers to do your job and our job." I said, "Wait a minute. You're not doing my job. My kids can't even go out of my house when they come home from school without telling me where they're going. I have a phone right at my elbow—three boys, you know, I have to be careful." I says, "If I have any doubt that they're going to a kid's house, I call that kid's house to find out if they're there." I was very strict with the boys.

When I was a young girl, I couldn't come out of my bedroom without my bathrobe on. My father thought that was very bad, we start walking around in our slips. Now, I don't know whether that's good or bad. But outside of one divorce, which was no fault of my son's, in the family, everybody is very happily married. I have eight grandchildren. We're bringing them up the same way—we're strict with them that they don't go living with this guy and doing that with that one. We don't believe in it. I'm sorry, we don't. We think we've got to keep some decency in this world.

This kid across the street's been living with a Jewish girl for three years. All right. She got him to go back to school. Guess what? He's going to marry his little Jewish girl friend in the Jewish faith. I don't care what he marries, what faith he marries, but at least they get married. We're very happy about it. To me marriage is important. I think it holds a family together.

I could have dumped my husband twenty years ago. There wasn't anything that could hold me to this man. But I stayed with Mike. I see that Mike eats properly. I see that Mike stays alive. I moved away three thousand miles so he could be in warm climate. He wanted to go to San Francisco. He didn't want to go to Florida, where it would've been closer to our family. I went with Mike. I mean, that's devotion. That's love. We're married forty-three years. I mean, I don't know how you can prove love. It isn't just that garbagy word *love*—they're really killing it. Is that love? That passionate baloney, bed scenes and all that. That's not my idea of love. That's an individual thing. You do it, keep it private. Love is sharing, loving, doing for each other. Just because Mike got sick and couldn't do all the things a man in his fifties should anymore, I should've left him? I got busy. I went to school. I took up languages. Everybody laughs at me, they think I'm a nut. But this is why. I have to take my mind away from other things, you know. I'm being deprived of things most married people have, but the man is sick. What can you do? He's my husband.

I think you gotta have a sense of humor. You've got to. You've got to forgive, too. One time he was very friendly with this friend of ours, and she was working in his plant. And he'd taken her back and forth to work. Oh, talking things out is another one I'm trying to stress. So I says, "Gee, Mike, I hate to tell you this, but you're being talked about so much." I said, "Somebody said to me, 'What's the matter? He thinks more of her than you?' " I said, "Don't you think you ought to be a little more discreet? People really draw the wrong meaning." And he listened to me—he did. After that, every time they went anyplace, outside of work—they went to work together and I was home with the kids—I would always be with them. You know, he had to use discretion. But I just would talk this thing out. I'd pull him in the bedroom. The kids knew when that bedroom door was closed, father and mother were having a serious talk. I say talk it out.

I met my husband at a speakeasy, Keeley's. Keeley's is underground in Newark, where the railroad goes over. That's where it was then. And right next to us was a table of a bridal group. You know, they had come from a wedding. Well, he's looking at me, and he said, would I dance with him? Well, when I got on the floor I said, There's no dancer he is. He never learned to dance, by the way. Anyway, I danced with him and he took my telephone number and he wanted to see me again. Took me home, too, by the way. That Wednesday he called up. In the drugstore, by the way—we didn't have a phone in the house then. But luckily he found me home. I was married to him in thirteen weeks. Neither one of us was the marrying type when we met. Never say those words. Even in jest.

My kids meant everything to me because I never had any more. And I don't know why. I had this hunch that if I didn't have them together that I'd never have any. I was right. I had two twenty-three months apart and never had any more. I had a serious operation and that was the end of my motherhood. I wanted about six children because I believe in large families. So we adopted one. I had so much fun in my family, with my brothers and sisters. We were always so popular, bring your brothers along, you know. Nice marriageable-age brothers. Oh, were we popular.

We had a marvelous relationship with our children. We used to take them camping. We're great swimmers. We all like the water, and we used to throw the kids in at 9 months old and they'd swim to us. And we built a cabin for them. Oh, you'd die laughing—this cabin. Nobody had money in 1945—right after the war. I fell in love with this lake this friend took us to. And we stayed with her one week. So I says, "Gee, Aunt Bee"—that was the owner of the property—"if you ever have a piece of land, will you sell it to me?" So we went around, we picked a piece of land, and she says $200, $225—something like that. Imagine! You know how many years it took me to get that $200. We were living in the cabin and still hadn't paid for the land. That's how much money we had. Every time I had $10, I'd give it to her, to pay $200. We had an old garage. We tore it up piece by piece. You couldn't buy nails in those days. I sat down with a bunch of rusty nails, and I hammered them even while they were pulling them. And that's our first one-room cabin. But there was a lake there. And those kids were with me every summer at this little shack made out of an old garage. And we had it for seventeen years.

My kids are very good, extremely good for boys. Now don't forget, I'm talking about boys. I have one at the moment that I'm not seeing too much of, and I think he's influenced by his wife. Either he's busy starting up his business, the computer business or something. But he promised in his last letter that they'd come up and see me. It's some misunderstanding there that we have to straighten out. But the love is there.

I go to church every Sunday. I'm extremely religious. I'm the only one in the family that goes to church. I think it's because I'm a Sunday school teacher and because I always feel that one hour of prayer a week isn't going to hurt me. And I've always swayed my husband. I didn't sway him on that. I married him, you know as a non-Catholic, and after we'd been married twenty years, he said, "Could I take the sacraments?" And he is now a Catholic, and he's a better Catholic than I am. Goes to communion every Sunday with me and all.

I said I think that we can spare one hour a week to go to church.

And I feel there is a God. I just like it. It's good for my soul. It's just beautiful to me to sit there in church, and for one hour think of God and sing his praises. We sing a lot in church. And I've done a lot of work for the seminary—Saint Anthony's Seminary in Santa Barbara. We do a lot of work there. Mike is a pottery teacher, and I do the selling. I'm a seller. I can raise from six hundred to eight hundred dollars a year. I try to. Whatever I raise, they get. I go out and get donations and all.

I think I'm a little careless at times. Go around barefooted at 70, you know. It's very undignified and very unhealthy. But I'll run out in the garage barefooted, and my husband yells at me. But I don't know. It hasn't done me any harm. I walk to the pool barefooted. Mike says, "When are you going to grow up and be a dignified lady?" I just can't help it.

I know I have to take care of myself. I've always been on my own. I have buried all my family. The boys all disappeared and left it all up to dear old Fran. And it's been that way ever since I was a child. Every time there's been trouble, I get calls yet from my brothers and sisters that something's gone wrong.

I was almost kidnapped when I was a kid. I know what it means to be afraid. In New York. I'm an avid reader. And the first thing when I could crawl was to go to the library. And I was going to the library with my brother. You must think I'm making this up. Everything I'm telling you is the truth, because I think I've had a very exciting life. And we're walking along and this man wanted to know where Great Jones Street is. It was off the Bowery, by the way. And we had to go in that direction. So we said we were going. And all the while this man is talking to me and my brother, he's saying, "When I get there, I'll have the boss give you a doll," to me, little kid. And my brother Joe, who just died recently, was with me. So we get to this building. I says, "I'll stand right here near the door." And he says to my brother, "You wait for her over there." And all of a sudden he's calling me upstairs. "Come up, little girl. Come up." And I says, "No, no." And suddenly I was afraid. This man is up to no good. And he comes down and picks me up to carry me up. And I screamed and I scratched his face and I pulled his hair, and my brother hears and he comes in. And he sees my brother and he drops me and he runs away. I don't know what the man was up to, but that was the worst. And from then on my mother wouldn't let me go to the library unless I had a grown-up with me, because of that experience. That was the only time I was truly afraid. But look how close to being kidnapped I was.

I went to Italy to see where my parents came from. I found a cousin there. He wanted to know who the little girl was that wrote to his mother all those years. And I said, "I'm the little girl." And he says, "How did you learn to write Italian?" I says, "I never went to school. I never learned to write Italian." I says, "I used to write phonetically. As my mother spoke it I would write it." He says, "Well, it's funny, we understood it." But I have taken Italian since, to improve my grammar a bit. I still write to him, and we keep in touch. Very handsome. I want you to know he has a title. Sir or knight in Italy. When they talk to my cousin, they take their caps off.

I went to California very indignant. I wasn't going to join any political party. I was an independent voter, which goes very bad over there. We weren't allowed to vote in the primaries. So I am now back to the Democratic party.

I was a judge on the election board and I kept the mayor from voting. No, I didn't stop him from voting, but I stopped a person on the street that he brought in that had moved away over nine months. And I bucked the mayor, and I was backed by the election board. They all went hysterical when I did that one. Can you imagine bucking the mayor? I did it.

We never did like Nixon, of course. Watergate proved our point that he was all we think he is. In fact, just reading about him, you know he hadn't been any nicer throughout his whole lifetime. I think you're a bad egg from the beginning. It shows even as a child. I really mean that. I says to Mike, "I bet they used to call him Stinky in school."

Feminism? Me? I like being a woman. Because I like the protection of a man. I like being married. Yes, I worked, but that didn't mean a thing. We shared everything together. Money's never meant that much to me. I get two checks every month. I sign those checks and my husband puts them in the bank. I think he's better at money than I am, and I don't care. And this is the way it's been all my life. Money has never meant a thing to me. I just sign it, and it's a commodity to be used. That women's lib is for the birds. I have always had good jobs. Now, mind you, I was a woman paymaster. I got paid as well as any man in that plant. I was even making more money than my husband in those two or three years that I had all that responsibility.

The women's-libbers, they want to be equal with men, but then they want the courtesy of being treated like a lady. Now, why demand that when you want to climb poles and hold signs and stuff like that? I don't mean that they shouldn't do these jobs. They should. But act like a lady. Let the man open the door for you. I'm sorry, I like that. And I always will. I demand it from my sons. I have three boys. We all got together, they came home, I forget where they had been, but that was the one night the three boys were home with their mother and father. We went out to dinner. And one young lady came to the table and was talking, and not one of my sons got up. I didn't say nothing. When she left, I said, "I'm ashamed of all of you." They said, "Why?" I said, "That girl came to the table, and not one of you had the manners to get up and let her feel that she was a lady." And they said, "Oh, Ma, we know her. She's in school with us." I said, "I'm sorry, but I'm still at this table." You know. From that day to this, I have never seen a person walk in the room that my sons aren't the first ones up. It left an impression, and I wanted it to stay with them.

I'm for civil rights. Blacks are human beings. They're American citizens. They should have the same privileges that we're getting. I don't know how they could possibly say that their schools are so bad, though. If we hire these people as teachers, don't they have to meet a certain qualification to be accredited? Well, then why do they say that their schools are so poor and the white schools are so good? I'm stumped on that one, because I think if we hire a teacher, she must have the qualifications to teach. Whether she's teaching in a black school, a white school, an Italian school, an Indian school, any kind of a school. Don't forget. There was no worse minority than the Italians in the East Side of New York. Now, why are we out of all that? Our children all went to college. Because we sent our kids to school. Do you think it was very easy for me to make the money I made and go around with the same old pair of shoes while I was paying nine hundred dollars a semester for my child to go to college? That was very important to me. Every one of my children had better jobs than their father will ever have. They're living in better homes than we ever had. And they always say, "Don't ever worry, Ma. If things get that bad, three of us, we'll be there to help you." And I believe the boys would help me. Right now we haven't needed them. But I'm just telling you—don't you feel proud that your child is doing better than you? When my son took me to his office, I asked, "Where's the boss's office? Where's your office?" There. And it was the same office, you know. My son, as boss of all these people in this building. Well, that made us feel good.

When I went to Italy, my cousin said, "You can come and live over here if you want to." He owns a whole block—I think my grandfather owned it and now he owns it. And he had a lot of people living in those two streets. And he says, "With your pension you could live like a queen here." And I believe the man means it. But when I see the men all in the plaza smoking their cigars, and all the women sitting behind windows, that's not my kind of life. I like going out with my husband and being with my husband. Going in restaurants with him. The freedom is what I enjoy. The freedom of this country, and I says, No thank you. I says, There's no place like America. There isn't. I told him that right to his face. With all his money.

What do we want out of life? We're getting everything—I mean, what would a lot of money mean to me? I've got a new car, a '78. I've got a beautiful house. You have to see it to appreciate it. I've got three lovely children. I've got eight grandchildren. I may get another daughter-in-law. There's one in the making. So I've got all I want out of life, as long as my kids come and see me now and then. Hug me and tell me they love me and all. That's all I want. I'm happy.

John Kennedy. I waited six hours to see him one time. He was six hours late. In Newark, in one of the big halls there. And there I sat, and when I saw him, that was it. I fell in love with him. They say many little things about him I don't like to hear, but to me he's still . . . Oh, when he walked into the room, he just brightened the whole room up. There was a few thousand of us. That man walked in there, he just brightened that whole room up. We all were waiting six hours for this man to get there. There we sat, we waited. But there he was. He had something that I haven't seen in any other President. Radiance. I tell you, he walked in and everybody was happy. You know, everybody clapped and howled just to see that lovely face. He had a nice face. So rosy and so nice, and that big smile. They could say anything they want about him, but that was the impression I had about him. I just loved him.

I'm against forcing people to retire. I wish my health would have been better. I'd still be working. I still do volunteer work, though. I do a lot of volunteer work. And we're just getting along. If they just laid off that tax stuff, raising our taxes, we could swing it on what we get. We don't want a lot of money? What for?

If you can't work, keep going. That's what they tell them at the Y. Keep moving. Get those muscles working. When you see these old people that come in with canes, and this little Japanese, a darling little thing with those canes hooked up to her arms, and her jumping with me and dancing, and exercising with me. This other lady, with a walker. She could hardly walk. Keep moving, keep moving. We keep saying that to each other. And it's doing the trick.

I don't like the way some militants are so demanding. We had to print the ballots in Spanish. For crying out loud, that's an added expense we didn't need. We Italian-Americans had to go through the same siege, and they didn't print them in Italian for our parents. Right? I mean, this is what's burning me up. People demanding better jobs when they don't qualify for them. Go to school and learn like our kids had to do. You think it was easy to pay that money we paid to send our kids to college? We did without things to send them. Why can't these others? You can't hand them everything on a silver platter. And you never appreciate anything unless you work for it. Am I right? I've always felt that way. You hand somebody something, they're not going to appreciate it.

The soul lives forever. I believe in reincarnation. They all laugh at me every time I say that. Am I the only one left to feel that way about it?

I don't think there's any secret about getting through the death of members of your family or close friends. There's a job to be done and you do it. I had to get the undertaker. I had to order the clothes. I had to have my mother's hair done just so, and my father's taken care of. It's a job and you just do it.

I couldn't cry when my mother died, and I haven't stopped since. Every time I mention my mother's name I fill right up today. And she died in 1943. But I didn't cry one tear while she was laid out. I was so busy, getting her hair fixed and all that. I keep busy, that's my secret. You know, there's only two things I'm worried about—my eyes and if I have to stop reading, and my brain if my brain stops working. And if they go, then let me go, because I don't want to live after that. Because one is for reading and one is for thinking. I like a keen mind, you know. They were giving me some dope after the heart attack, and when they took me off it, I said, I'm starting to be a vegetable. I couldn't even think straight anymore. And that was bothering me.

But I have never worried about me yet. I look forward to tomorrow. You know, there's things to be done that have to be done, and I don't worry. I don't sit home and tear my hair out over anything. There's a job that has to be done and you do it. I mean, that's all there is.

# Josephine Davis

*A*t first glance Mrs. Edward Davis might pass as a proper Philadelphia housewife, age 77. Her husband is a prominent labor lawyer in Philadelphia. They have two sons, one a writer and the other a lawyer, and seven grandchildren. Their apartment, in a venerable apartment building in the center of Philadelphia, is more than comfortable and less than opulent.

Seated in her living room, Mrs. Davis is a graceful woman, with up-swept gray hair and fashionable clothes. It is only when she begins to speak of her life that the listener realizes that she has been heavily involved in radical causes.

She was born in Philadelphia in February 1902. Her father was a banker. There were socialists in her family. Her brother was a talented figure in American music, Marc Blitzstein. She attended the University of Pennsylvania until she got married in her junior year. She first became involved in left-wing politics in 1936, during the Spanish Civil War, when she joined the Medical Bureau for Spanish Democracy.

In the 1940s she was on the Committee for People's Rights, defending the rights of Communists in the United States (although not herself a Communist). She worked for the Progressive party in the 1940s, as well. Although relatively inactive during the McCarthy era, she was questioned by the FBI and survived that interrogation. She was on the board of the Thomas Jefferson School, avowedly Marxist, in Philadelphia. She was a member of the Women's International League for Peace and Freedom, which was founded by Jane Addams among others in 1917.

Today she continues to pay attention to politics, to causes, to rights denied, to grievances proclaimed. She donates money and time. She joined the peace movement during the Vietnam War, working alongside young people she admired. She continues to be vigilant today. Her husband does not oppose her activities, although he doesn't share her views. "He is a very good liberal," she says,"and I am a radical."

I was born in Philadelphia, at Fourth and Pine, the new section now called Society Hill, and I was born opposite three of the most famous churches. Saint Peter's was one. I only lived there until I was 8, but I have a very distinct feeling, very distinct picture. I can picture every room in the house we lived in—a big old brownstone, three stories. I remember the gaslight, and I can remember straw being put on the streets, for instance, if anybody was sick in the neighborhood. They would put straw down to dull the thud of the horses' hooves as they passed by. All you had to do was call the police station and immediately they saw that straw was put down on that street. They did it automatically in front of the hospitals. And it was a charming old neighborhood.

We knew all our neighbors. It was a neighborhood of mostly professional people: doctors, lawyers—my piano teacher lived there. And I loved that neighborhood. It was just beautiful. Both sides of Fourth and Pine are churchyards that face each other, so there was a great deal of space there. We lived on a corner of a little street which is not there any longer. They closed it up or made a mews of it or something. In the summer we'd go out to the country. And the country in those days was small towns not more than fifteen miles outside of Philadelphia, or twenty at the most. But to us this was way out in the country.

We lived with my grandmother, who was a banker. She had a bank at Fourth and Lombard. Now, I don't know whether you know anything about the ethnic banks. Well, they were set up primarily to help the émigrés who came over here. My grandmother's bank was never called a bank. We called it the office. And it became a bank later when they actually built a bank building, but at this time it really wasn't a bank building. It was sort of an enormous storefront where they did a certain amount of banking, mostly lending money. And what they did was lend money mostly to Russians and Eastern Jews. Mostly Jews who came over here. They would come over here on forged passports. People would land here, turn their passports over to my grandmother, who would then send the passports back with tickets for steerage passage to the United States. And then these people would come over here, and they would turn that same thing over. This is why the Jews have so many funny names, and why they don't mind changing their name because it wasn't their name to begin with. It was the name on the passport that they used. Rosenbaum's had a bank like that one block away at Third and Lombard—took care of the German Jews. And one doesn't think of the German Jews as having the same problem, but they did. They came over in droves, too.

We lived with my grandmother, and an aunt who was a doctor, and another aunt who wasn't married. She had an office in front. The whole family lived together. We lived with my grandmother's sister whose husband was a poet, and she had two children. We all lived together in this house. Had another much younger aunt, who was then at Cornell. Up on the second floor was the parlor with a piano. And in the evening we'd sit around and somebody would play music, and we would talk. My whole family were Russian socialists. So the discussions were endless. I remember I was only 8, so I didn't really partake of all this. I now am probably plastering a little bit of what happened later on to what must have gone on at that time, because I probably would go to bed around seven or eight o'clock and not be aware of what was going on.

But my great-stepuncle, my grandmother's stepsister's husband, would read his poetry. Everyone who had anything to offer would offer it, and that's the way we spent the evenings. It was a very quiet, leisurely sort of life. We took long walks. We used to love to walk through the graveyards. Well, they were Revolutionary, see, so it was fascinating to see all these famous soldiers and whatnot.

Philadelphia has changed since then, of course. It would be difficult to say politically, because I don't know what the political climate was at that time. I think today it's a city without integrity. I think the whole political climate is extremely tense and dangerous. I think we're on the verge of even more violence.

Oddly, now, Philadelphia is, if anything, more beautiful than it ever was. Center City–Philadelphia was never a beautiful city as such. It was full of row houses, very much like certain sections of London— like the old Bloomsbury section, for instance. Today you have Society Hill, which has resurrected all of the best of Philadelphia before the Victorian horrors came along. So it's all going back to that period long before Victoria, and then above this is another section which is also very modern, with all the new modern office buildings like every other big city. It has a certain amount of big-city charm, if you like that sort of thing.

As far as America is concerned, I would have to say to that that I think it's better. For one thing, we've awakened more people to our problems. I think the whole business with civil rights, starting with '64, has awakened a lot of people to the problems. They haven't been solved, by any matter of means. In some cases, things may even be worse. But I think that's only temporary. I think once you've broken the pattern and broken the mold, it can only get better. And I'm very optimistic. I am an optimistic person.

Well, my father and mother were separated when I was about 10. I was very sick as a child. I was sick for two years, one year in bed and one year in a wheelchair, with rheumatic fever. My brother and I sort of raised each other, rather than my parents raising us. I'm three years older than Marc, and always felt that he was my responsibility from the time when he was 3 years old, and I took him to school with me because I didn't trust him at home with my family. By the time he entered school at the age of 6, he was in the third grade because he'd passed all the subjects. He and I were then in the same grade, so all my life my brother's been in the same class I've been in. The big thing there is really my relationship with my brother, much more than it was with my father and mother. My mother was a very unhappy woman who was mad about my father; she loved him. He was a charming guy. And I guess today he would be considered a playboy. He was the only son of my grandmother. My grandmother saw that every one of her daughters went to college. My father didn't get through the fourth grade, and she couldn't have cared less. She had him in the bank with her because that way she had him under her thumb and he made a good living. Or at least he got what she gave him, and we got what she gave him or what she gave us.

After I got married, my father and I became very good friends. He was a charmer and a lot of fun to be with. But he was no father. He was a great friend to have, but no father. So we became very close. The kids adored him, they just thought he was a lot of fun. But he had no more responsibility. As long as he had responsibility, we were not good friends.

My mother was a very beautiful, clinging-vine type of person. Who had to cling to somebody. And who I'm afraid picked me to cling to. From the age of 12, I just ran the household. We moved to California. We went in the middle of the night actually. My grandmother was being very intransigent at that time. Anything we needed I'd have to go and ask her for it. And I remember I had to go and ask her for two tons of coal, and she wanted to know how much it would cost, and I said I didn't know. And she said, "Well, find out." And that was the last straw. So we went out to California when I was 12. With my brother. And then the letters started. What a horrible thing we were doing to Marc. Marc was taken away from his music and his marvelous music teachers. We were killing an enormous talent. The letters were always addressed to my mother and me as if I were an adult. I got a letter from my father once at the age of 12. It said, "You are old enough now to understand the relationship of man and woman." I was 12 years old. And how you can love somebody and then suddenly fall out of love with them? Well, I wasn't old enough. And so I'm afraid I didn't have a normal family life.

I learned one thing from that life. I told my husband when we got engaged, I said, "I don't give a damn what you do. I'll never divorce you. I'll tell you that—if we have children." In the very next breath I said to him, "The first time you mention money, I'm going to divorce you." These were my two big hang-ups. One was divorce, and the other was the fact that I had to go and ask for this money for a coat, for coal, for anything. And I said, "If you ever discuss money or how we spend it, I'm going to divorce you"—having said I'd never divorce. So very consistent.

My earliest memory was when Marc was born. I don't remember the day he was born, but I remember sitting on the back steps of the house on Pine Street waiting to be called to see the baby and my mother. The delivery was in the house. Mine was, too. But she had a doctor. My Aunt Rose was a doctor and would not let her have a midwife. She wouldn't deliver her. Her boss was then a Dr. Wells, the first obstetrician, I think, in the United States. Certainly in Philadelphia. And that was 1902. That was pretty early on to have an obstetrician. I remember going upstairs. I don't remember who called me from the back stairs. And I went up and saw my mother lying in bed, and Dr. Wells sitting there with a black bag. And the baby over in the crib. And I went over and saw the crib and said, "You brought this beautiful baby. You brought it in that black bag." And he said yes. That's the earliest memory I have.

I don't think I'm a very moral person. Ethical? I went to Ethical Culture School. That's easy. Actually, I think the family was a very

brilliant family to begin with. All of my aunts and my grandmother—
we used to fight like hell. I guess I really liked my grandmother better
than I knew. They were brilliant people and very, very moral. They
were extra moral, which made me as immoral as could be. I mean, I
just went the other way. I'm talking about sex and so forth. I think
people that are brought up in a socialistic family with a sense of what
the world needs would have to have that kind of thing, an ethical sense.
Either that or go the other way. They would get it with their mother's
milk, so to speak. We were enormously well read. I was reading. I don't
remember a time from the time I was 7 or 8 that I wasn't reading
something. Mostly English. Not too much French. And Russian. Because a lot of Russian was spoken in the house, and there was a Russian
background. They spoke Russian. They all could. My grandmother
spoke Russian. My aunts spoke Russian. Mama didn't. Mama was born
in the United States. My father was born in Liverpool. He said he was
born in Russia, but he wasn't. He was born on the way over here.

I think there's a kind of immaturity around. Maybe that's what de-
stroys families today. I don't know what it is. I was like that. I was a
very slow developer. My husband had to put up with a hell of a lot
with me because I was very young when I was married. I don't mean
21. I mean I was a young 21. I hadn't lived. You can't live in a house
where your grandmother doesn't let you out. My first date was when
I was 18 years old, for instance. Well, you can imagine how one lets
loose one way or another afterward, whether for good or bad. My
husband had to put up with a great deal from me that way, and he
handled it magnificently, I must say. Fantastic guy from that point of
view. I was damned lucky. You take people who are mature adult people. It's unbelievable. I don't think I was in my forties as adult as
they are now.

I would say if two people don't get along, the best thing they can
do is get out, because I don't think it's good for the kids. Marc and I
used to sit on the steps when I was 8 years old and Marc was only 5.
Sit on the steps and listen to my mother and father quarrel. It was
horrible, and we'd go to bed just shaking. This is dreadful. Parents don't
know about things like that. They don't know. They think the kids are
sound asleep and they don't know. We were extremely grateful when
it was all over with and we never had to listen to that sort of thing
again.

I do not think that divorce itself is enough of an excuse for a kid to say, "Well, of course if I didn't come from a broken home, you see?" I have a feeling that this is false. Now, we came from a broken home and I would say that it strengthened me in many ways.

I think any kind of inhibition is wrong. I think any kind of inhibition is bad. And I think any kind of inhibition only leads to excess. I think if my granddaughter came home and said she was living with somebody and so forth and so on, I would be a little bit worried about the guy—I'd like to know a little bit about him. But I would have no feeling that she shouldn't be doing this, or anything of that sort. Not at all. I think it's all to the good. I was brought up with a very moral concept. I'd have been scared to death to be caught. I was married as a virgin. In those days one was. That was not one of my problems, as it happened. Boys just didn't go that far. They just wouldn't. I never went with an older man, let's put it that way. I don't think I ever went with anybody who was more than a year or two older than I was. They were just about as ignorant as I was, and we could fumble around from today till doomsday and we still didn't make it. This could happen, you see.

Love is very difficult to define. The first fine fervor is something that's never repeated. I try to evoke it once in a while and see if I can possibly remember that marvelous all-over thrill that you have, which of course couldn't possibly last. And a good thing, too. You would never get anything done. You'd get nothing done at all. What lasts is what's so important, which makes me think that if the kids are smart and they get past this first fervor and begin to find out what each other is about, that could make for a stable marriage, you see? Because marriage is based on a great many things. I would say to a great extent it's a kind of contract. I'm speaking like my husband. But, in a sense, it is a contract. In fact, he's pointed that out to me a few times in my life, you know. Which has sort of caught me up short, and a good thing. Because this is what I really wanted. I might have thought I wanted something else, had aberrations and whatnot. In the last analysis what I wanted was the kind of thing I had: a very understanding, unboring relationship, that goes on indefinitely. I don't know what keeps it unboring. I've tried to figure it out. I said, You know, we don't have an idea in common. We really don't. We don't think alike. Psychologically, we're not alike. If he heard me say what I just said about letting the kids live—he would say, "Jo, how can you say such a thing?" He doesn't agree with that at all. He's a very old-fashioned moral man. Long past interest in sex, but so am I. Well, I'm not, that's what's so interesting, you see. He is, and somehow or other while the body may not be willing, the mind goes on. And so I still am enormously interested. He's not. And maybe it's easier for him, I don't know. But we're not bored with each other. In fact, I once said to him, "I can't figure it out, the only person I don't mind being left alone with is you."

If you ask him that, he'll probably say, "I know her inside out," you see. I don't think it's anything that he's ever tried to put in words. I don't think I've ever tried to put it into words. If Ed were somebody else, if I just met him, I'd probably think he was a dull stick as far as I'm concerned. Of course, he's not. He's far from it. He has a marvelous sense of humor. It's a very deep and sort of delicate sense of humor. It sort of sparks and sparkles. I sort of equate a sense of humor with a sense of proportion, you see. And I think he has that to an enormous degree.

I remember the first time I met him. I had a date with another friend of mine to go to a football game at Penn. Penn-Pitt game, and this guy was a guy who used to come every year and take me for a whole weekend. We were supposed to go to dinner on Saturday night, and he said, "Jo, I hope you don't mind, but I've invited a friend of mine to have dinner with us." And I said, "That's very interesting. You haven't seen me for a year. If you want your friend to come, that's all right with me." I mean, I wasn't in love with the guy or anything. He was very good-looking. That was another thing about me. I never fell for very handsome-looking men, although Ed's a very good-looking guy and was. But looks had very little to do with it. I liked a certain type of guy; it had very little to do with looks, but he had to have a lot of sex appeal. Usually these gorgeous blond men were completely lacking in sex, which I could feel.

Anyway, we went to dinner, and during dinner I met Ed. During dinner Ed said, "Are you going to the football game tomorrow?" And I said, "Yes." He said, "Funny, I happen to have a seat right next to where you're sitting." So we had dinner.

I don't remember this, but Louie—my original date—told me later that from the time I met Ed, I never spoke to him at all. All my remarks were pointed to Ed. I don't know how true that is, but Ed called me the following week to invite me to the theater. And I said okay. He came and he said, "By the way, Lillian Crouse is having a party and we've been invited." Well, I knew Lillian Crouse. She was a lot older than I was; I didn't like her. And besides, she didn't like me. They didn't even know I was alive. I was still a sophomore in college. Ed was a lawyer by then, you see. And I said, "She didn't invite us. She invited you." And he said, "Well, I told her I had a date." And I said, "Well forget it. You go, but I'm not going." I said, "You told me you were coming to take me to the theater." He said, "Well, all right, we'll go to the theater." So we went to the theater. He had to stop and apologize to those people. He had to buy tickets; he didn't have any. We had to sit in the balcony. I was used to sitting up in the peanut gallery with my boyfriends, but not with this big shot. We sat down, and he was very grumpy the whole evening, and so was I. He never called me—this was in October or November. He never called me to thank me for the evening, nothing. I never saw him again until March.

I ran across him on the street, crossing the street, and he saw me crossing the street, and he stopped and said, "What are you doing tonight?" I don't remember whether I had a date or not. I just said I was busy, naturally. I went home and told my mother. I said, "Can you imagine a man expecting me not to have a date on a Saturday night?" Anyway, that started it. In March. We were married June 14. We never were out of each other's pockets. Never were separated for a minute. My mother insisted that we get an engagement ring, I remember that. And I said, "Who wants to bother—I don't want an engagement ring." I hated shopping then and I hate it now. I'd much rather go to the park or something like that. What Ed did about his law practice, I don't know. And what I did about school is nobody's business.

He asked me to marry him not more than a week after we met, again, in March. I went to Atlantic City. I was getting over a love affair actually. And it was over. The guy just decided he was much too young to marry. And I wanted to get married. Well, Ed came down to the shore to visit me. We had dinner in Atlantic City, and then we went on a rolling chair ride at about three in the morning. He told me all about his trip to Europe. Imagine? He made enough money to go to Europe.

Those were the good years. We were married in 1923, and everything was sort of popping then. The guys who got out of law school did very, very well. He was very lucky. In any case, he never asked me to marry him. He said, "Well, maybe by June we can go abroad and I'll show you everything that I saw, as much as I saw." Never asked me to marry him or anything. We just decided on that.

Then, of course, we had the children. I'm glad I had them. They're great kids—both of them. I remember my father and I walking on the boardwalk when I was pregnant with Stephen. And saying, "What the hell are you doing, bringing a child into this lousy world?" And I said, "I haven't the faintest notion except that nature makes me want to have a child." And I did. Really, I was not terribly maternal. Really, I wanted all the experiences there were, and that was one of the experiences. And I wanted it very badly.

My grandmother was an agnostic. My father was an atheist. My mother's family and my mother were religious, but I didn't know my mother's family very well.

I've gone to temple for weddings and that sort of thing. And Ed took Marc and me to a Yom Kippur service years ago. I thought I was pregnant. I wasn't. I was always thinking I was—this was a time when we were trying, so every month I would think I was pregnant.

We went to a reform temple. And Ed said to Marc, "As a musician, you really ought to know the music." And Marc said, "I think I do, but I'd like to hear it. I've never heard it in a temple before." So the three of us went, and Marc said to me, "It's bastardized. They ruined it. It's not what it should be." Then the sermon started, and the guy started speaking about the chosen people. And this was a very wealthy, stuffy congregation. I said to Ed, "You know, I'm beginning to feel sick." Great excuse. And Marc quickly said, "I'll take her out. Don't you bother." Well, there was a restaurant across the street. This was Yom Kippur. Well, we didn't know about that sort of thing. So we not only went to the restaurant to wait for Ed, but we sat in the window. We said we'll be sure to see him come out. And all these people came out and saw Marc and me sitting there eating on Yom Kippur.

So neither of my kids is religious. Ed is religious. I think he believes in God and I think he is truly deeply religious, without belonging to anything. He gave up everything. When we were engaged, I said our children will never go to Sunday school or church, because I'm not going to poison their minds. I was all of 21.

.    .    .

My political activity goes back awfully far. I used to work in radio, and I worked in radio during the thirties. That was a paid job, the only paid job I ever had. We sorely needed it at that time. It was the beginning of the Depression. And I got a job with a small station in Philadelphia called WDAS, which is still around. I was both program director and publicity director. So you can imagine. These were the very, very early days of radio. I was fired from the job because my job was, first of all, to get people on the air. Newspapers would give us no publicity at all. The only way you could get newspaper publicity is if you had somebody so famous that it would make a squib in the newspaper. And so I did very well because I didn't know enough not to. I did marvelously. I'd go to the theaters. And I got Bea Lillie, Fred Allen, Libby Holman, and Clifton Webb all on the same day. By telling all these people that I was a poor little girl just starting out, and how nice it would be if they would come. I knew they didn't need the publicity, but it would be great for me, and I had a car and would be glad to show them around Philadelphia and whatnot. They came, and that was it. I had everybody on. Then I decided, after a whole long time, that it was about time to have somebody political on. So I had Norman Thomas on. He happened to be in Philadelphia. And I got fired because one of my good friends on the *Record*, which was a newspaper in Philadelphia, wrote that what Jo Davis's bosses didn't know is that Norman Thomas is a socialist. And I don't know whether they knew or not. I'm sure they did. It was pretty stupid of them not to, if they didn't. And they said, "Well, that's it. You know, you can't have this." So I lost my job.

I belonged to a group at that time, come to think of it, in about 1932 or 1933, called the League of Women Shoppers. This was the beginning of unionism. I had a lot to do with unions, by the way, also. This, of course, is before Spain. I just don't count that as political. We pulled out about one hundred charge accounts from Wanamaker's because they wouldn't recognize the Teamsters Union on their trucks, and so forth and so on. Another time we were on a picket line at Horn & Hardart's. They had a bakery—a central bakery place at Ninth and Chestnut or Ninth and Locust. And the employees were on a picket line to get the union, also the Teamsters. And so we went on the picket line with them. And the two guys who were head of the union said they needed a lawyer because they were in serious trouble. And I said, "Go see my husband. He's got to take a few free cases just the way doctors do." And that's how Ed got started in labor law. Not exactly. He had had one case before that. He always tells the story as if I got him started in it, which makes a beautiful finished tale, you see, a beginning, middle, and end. He's still a labor lawyer. He likes to tell the story that I was responsible for it. At any rate, I've been involved in causes ever since.

After all I'd seen, I was not surprised by Watergate. I hated Nixon. I always loathed Nixon. Ed was always finding excuses for him. But I was horrified. And I was not as gleeful as most people are, I can't rub my hands with glee about other people's tragedies, and I think it was a tragedy, for everybody, including Nixon and his family.

I never called what I did women's rights. I just wanted to be able to do what I wanted to do. I joined a women's organization, in '58, that was late. I must say I didn't want to. I never belonged to a women's organization in my life and was sure I would hate it. I'd never worked with women before. I don't think I was especially interested in women's rights as such. I've always had a feeling that women should get equal pay and that sort of thing. And they should be able to do what they want and not ask their husband whether they should do it.

It's a shame that so many people hate their work. Mostly men, not women. And I think they do it because they have to. They have no choice in the matter. This is one of the reasons I'm for women's rights. I do not believe in the whole system, that men should make the living and women stay home. I think it should be much more evenly distributed. I'm really a man's woman, much more than I am a woman's woman. My whole life has been tied up with men, rather than women. So I may be the wrong person to talk to closely about that sort of thing. There's no reason why a woman shouldn't go out and work if she can and support the family. If she's a perfectly healthy, strong person and believes in women's rights and so forth and so on, why the hell not?

I think America is in a very bad way. I think many of the dreams that we hoped for even as recently as the sixties and the early seventies are farther away or just as far away as they were then. The antitrust laws, for instance. They had the antitrust laws, so they start conglomerates to get around the whole business of ownership and all the ownership in one hand. Which has only aggravated the matter. I think that we're sort of at a standstill. I want us to be better. I remember people used to say to me anytime Russia did anything and I was labeled a Communist, and they said, "Look what Russia is doing." I said, "I'm not interested in what Russia is doing. I'm an American, and I want the best for America." I don't give a damn what they're doing in Russia, you see. It's not my business. My business is to make this a better place to be.

The whole thing has to be much more equitable. I used to be an ardent socialist. I believed in distribution of wealth. I believed in high taxation. I believed that there should be a leveling off, that there shouldn't be this terrific dichotomy between the enormously wealthy and the poor. Now there happen to be people who are making, literally, millions and squandering it. This sort of thing should be taxed away.

My brother once wrote a song for the CIO called "I Can Live on $25,000 a Year." And that was for the Roosevelt law that nobody could make more than twenty-five thousand dollars a year. Everything else was taxed away, and the rich people had to give up their enormous homes and servants, and live in the garden, in the cottage. The gardener's cottage. We had friends who actually did that.

I think that if you go to the Soviet Union and you see how excited people get about earning ribbons, you see that there are other sources —power is a great incentive. Now, that's a danger, I admit. If you don't have the money incentive, you probably will have a power one. That's when danger comes in, to my kind of thinking. So I no longer think that way. I don't prefer either. I used to think I knew the answers. I no longer know the answers. I used to think I knew the answers because I figured that an equitable distribution of wealth would put the powers, the railroads, and so forth in government hands, telephones, all the utilities, in the hands of government. I forgot all about power and bureaucracy, and how dangerous they can be. And now that I see the dangers I don't know what the answer is.

We have a tendency to think in clichés. And the most difficult thing, one of the things you learn as you get older, is to stop that kind of thing, even if you have to stop thinking. It's just as well to put your mind at rest and say okay, you know, this is the best we can do. And that's about all you can do.

I admired Roosevelt most. Wilson, although I was fairly young. I was 15 when he was around, but I thought he was great. They were thinking men. They were men who thought about the common man. They were people who thought in terms of rectitude and good government, in spite of their mistakes. The fact was that Mr. Wilson was a fairly weak man, I suppose, as a President, but a very learned man. And I admired his Fourteen Points, which, by the way, we, the Women's International League, were partly responsible in helping him formulate. We had gotten together fourteen points and some of them were used in his Fourteen Points. When I say we, I wasn't there at the time. I was 12 years old, or 14 years old at the time.

I didn't like Truman. I didn't like Kennedy. I didn't vote for Kennedy. I was scared of Kennedy, and I was scared of the guy who was running against him. Nixon. I wouldn't vote for either of them. I'm not a hero worshiper.

When people retire, they stagnate. What are they going to do? If anyone wants to change his job, give up his job and do something he's always wanted to do and didn't have time to do it, that's great. I would say these people are in the minority. They think, if I retire I'm going to read all those books I've never read. Well, you cannot sit and read books twelve hours a day. It can't be done. This is also true of people who think they have certain talents. If they have such talents they'll come out long before they retire. If they should be doing it and find themselves not having enough time to do it, you see, then that's the kind of person who should retire. And do it.

There have been several times, I'm sure, when I spent sleepless nights wishing I hadn't done certain things. There was one thing that I remember that had to do with my son Kit. I'll never forget that night. That I regret. We always had the problem that our sons always came to me rather than to Ed for advice, for one thing or another. Especially if it had anything to do with sex. And Kit must have been about 16. He was a very attractive 16 and very grown up. And he told me that he was going out on a date with a black woman. And I said okay. And I gave him no advice, said nothing, nothing to him at all. And he didn't come back till morning, and I never went to bed at all. I just sat up wringing my hands, realizing what I should've said. You see, he's always been brought up to believe—and this is a mistake one makes—that everybody was equal, black and white are all the same, and so forth and so on. And he was out to prove it. Well, one of the ways you don't prove it is sleeping with a black girl. You don't have to be liberal to sleep with a black girl. Plenty of illiberal people have done that. And what I wanted to say to him was just that. "By the way, when you're in love with a girl, just understand that you're not doing her any favors. Also, you want to be damn sure it's safe. Aside from anything else." Well, I realized that I did it out of a kind of vanity of my own, that I had raised him well enough and schooled him well enough to know that he would do the proper thing. And I just let him go out. And then he came reeling into the place, looked up, and said, "I need taxi money." So I got him taxi money, and he paid the taxi and he came upstairs, and he said, "Go to bed." I said okay. So I went to bed, and the next day I let him have it. Well, then he told me that the girl's brother came in and threw him out. I said, "You're lucky you weren't killed." And I blamed myself for it. "Because how smart do you think you are doing a thing like that? You feel nice and liberal now? You've had a black girl. It was just a terrible thing to have done to her." And I felt that was my fault.

My point about that is, that's not a mother's business. The point is that I did this—I made it my business. Actually it was none of my business. Once he told me about it, what I should've said is exactly how I felt, but I wanted Kit to like me. I wanted Kit to still think I was a great gal. So I never told him what I should've told him, that I disapproved. I did. Not because she was black. In the environment in which it was being done. You know how many years ago that was. That was probably the thirties or the forties, something like that. And the climate was very bad. And in this kind of climate you make your position clear. Then he could go out and do whatever he wanted. But the point is I didn't, and I didn't for my own sort of self-aggrandizing kind of thing.

I think so much of life is unfair to so many people. Simple things. Misunderstandings. I might go in the office and somebody might say something to me about why weren't you here yesterday, you know? And I'll say, "I don't know, I just didn't come in." "Well, you know you were supposed to do this." And I say that's very unfair. Right away I use that term, and that is naïve. But that gets me very angry.

You know, I've come to the conclusion that very few people think. They think they're thinking. What they're doing is ruminating the way cows do, you know, except they don't have cuds. I deliberately went to bed one night. We had a blackout, the lights went out and I was reading, and I wasn't sleepy. This is a fate worse than death, as far as I'm concerned. So I said, "Jo, get yourself together and just don't panic about it." There must be some self-sufficiency. Now, where is it? I would start thinking about something. You know, the minute I put my mind to it, my mind was as blank as a white sheet of paper. I couldn't think of a thing. The most horrible thing.

And yet I am an optimist. Yes, I am. Because I do think that there have been certain small gains. I wouldn't be working right now unless I believed that. One works primarily for a sort of sense of well-being that one has within one's self. That's the primary reason. I think that I do believe that at least one can say one has tried. One has made every effort, has bent every effort to help. And there have been tiny little glimmerings, and those glimmerings are worth it, because without them you would have nothing.

Maybe that is my faith. I think I have enormous faith in human beings. I really do. I really do, or I wouldn't be doing the kind of thing I'm doing or wouldn't have been doing it for so many years. I think they'll come out great.

I don't believe it's easier for religious people to face death. Maybe it is. I must say I wish I did believe about death. But they suffer too. People who believe. Having none, the only future is the future of your work that you leave behind you or your children or whatever, and that's all. I don't know. I don't deal with it very well. My mother died, and that was a sort of easy thing for me to accept because she'd lived with us for about four or five years. She got sicker and sicker and died when she was 87. So one didn't have a feeling of great loss. She had quite a fulfilled life. But my brother was killed at the age of 58. I've never been able to accept that. I was devastated, and I must admit I think something went out of my life at that time that has never been recovered, never. I used to care about lots of little things, unimportant things, like what I ate or what show I went to see, or whether we took a trip or not. I was easily disappointed if something didn't come true that I had been planning on. That's all gone. It's a whole dynamism out of one's life. It isn't that I suffer the way I used to about it. In the beginning it was horrible, because we were very, very close. And for him to die so horribly and to die at 58. All of it was in the cards, as well, unfortunately. I don't handle that too well. I handle it on the surface very well. But I avoid confrontation. For instance, when Leonard

Bernstein had the memorial concert for Marc, I was in the Soviet Union and I didn't even go. I deliberately saw that I was out of the country so I'd have a very good excuse for not going. Because I knew I wouldn't be able to take it.

I never seem too scared about dying, never seem to care about it very much. I'm much more worried about living to be very old and sick and a burden to myself. I don't give a damn about being a burden to anyone else. Let's be frank about it. But I just hate the whole idea of that kind of thing, and I just would like to not wake up one morning.

# Dr. Herman Karlen

*The* customary way to become a psychologist is to complete grade school, high school, and college and then go on to obtain a doctorate. Usually, this is done at a relatively early age. That was not the case with Herman Karlen.

He was born in February 1902, in Putnam, Connecticut. His father was a wood-turner. His parents were immigrants without the skills to earn much money. They raised five children—in Putnam, in New London (where they lived on a farm), and in Bridgeport. When Karlen was in the seventh grade, he was forced to leave school to go to work. He worked on several jobs in different places, including an uncle's hardware-locksmith store. He met his wife in 1928, when she visited Bridgeport from Philadelphia. They were married and moved to her hometown. For many years Karlen worked in the wholesale book business, earning a decent living and supporting his wife and two sons.

In 1956, at an age when most men are casting a dubious glance at retirement, Karlen decided to alter the course of his life and to compensate for the inadequacies of his youth. He passed his high school equivalency test and entered Brooklyn College; he spent much of the next few years commuting to it from Philadelphia. Along the way he discovered the work of William James—it was to become, along with the theories of Jung, pivotal to his future. He got used to hearing his fellow students call him "the old guy who never made it." He got his B.S. in 1958 and phased out his business two years later when he added a master's in social work from the University of Pennsylvania. He persisted until he found a job at the Philadelphia Psychiatric Hospital, working all the while toward his doctorate, which he got in 1964. He entered private practice as a psychologist the same year.

He sees twenty patients weekly in his practice, is active in a local mental health clinic, and conducts group therapy sessions. His youngest patient is 15; his oldest, in the late sixties. He specializes in marital and sexual problems and in depression; he avoids psychotic patients ("They're not predictable," he says). He practices hypnotherapy as well and has taken an interest in biofeedback. He works—often discarding his jacket and tie—in a small, casual office that adjoins his own apart-

*ment in a building he owns in central Philadelphia. His joy and curiosity persist, whether he is talking to a stranger, to a patient, or to his wife. "There is always another step to take from where you are," he says.*

I remember that we lived in Connecticut in a kind of ghetto among a lot of Polish people. And we lived in a house, in a frame house. And we were very careful. There were four of us, boys one year apart. And whenever we went to school, we went together. Because if we didn't go together, two of us would get beat up. So we used to wait. We lived in an anti-Semitic neighborhood, and very often we would forget that there were enemies outside the fence. I think my parents were very intimidated people. And they taught us all how to be intimidated. And if we had company to visit us, I remember we got shunted off very nicely, and we were very shy.

I felt very confined, very restricted, and very ashamed of my parents. Very ashamed of them because my father didn't know how to deal with life. If somebody persecuted us in school, he came for a showdown at the school, and he was put aside because he wasn't too articulate. He was right. He was trying to protect his children because they were being, not really persecuted, but put upon. And he came off second best. My mother was a very pretty lady. On the other hand, very articulate and sort of lively. She might as well have not come here. You know, my mother finally decided she was going to learn how to sign her name, and we didn't know this. She went to night school a few times to learn how to sign her name. She lived to 86.

My father would have liked to be part of this thing, but he was too formal to know how to go about it. He was very rigid. I never hated him for preventing me from going to school, because if I had any sense, I'd have gone myself. I tried. I did not know how to do it then. And I realize that things happen when you're ready. But I think there was a whole compression chamber on top and it kept everybody down. You went to the shop and you worked and you were told what to do. If you ever did get out of line, there was always somebody to suppress you.

My father had the feeling that he had married the wrong woman, that he was very unhappy with her. He tried to leave her for a while, put us on the farm. That didn't work, and they came back together again. But he died of cancer a very unhappy man. My mother lived on and on and on. Was very unhappy, too. Many times I was the mediator in trying to keep them together, but I was so ashamed of them. I thought to myself, Gee whiz, life is nothing to write home about.

I'll never forget that up until 8 we stayed in the neighborhood and never got to center city for any reason at all, because my father worked in the shop nearby and we never had to go into center city. There was always that gauntlet. Like going to school. I remember the first day I went to school. I was in a panic. And I think they took me home because I was too much in terror. They took me home. And school remained a very intimidating place. I think I would try to stay in, because when I went out during recesses, I'd get beat up. So the back line is all repressive. I had to shed some of that continuing feeling of being put down all around. I remember once that my grandfather went to school with us to protect us. He had a nice, beautiful, handsome white beard. But he didn't know that snowballs could be pelted. So he took us to school, then finally he left, and we all got pelted with snowballs. And we were scared.

There was no kind of Jewish community at all. Besides, my father was busy working. My mother was raising a family of five kids. They didn't seem very happy. Now I remember once when an uncle of mine came to visit and he wanted to take the kids out. So he took me to the theater, and I still remember the light surrounding it, off and on, off and on, a series of lights burning around it. And there were people who were dressed up, and I thought to myself, We better hang onto Uncle Barney. And I hung onto him, and we saw some lights on the stage, and music, and I was utterly intimidated. We were kept very well sheltered. However, there was an interlude of three years when we lived in New London, Connecticut, on a farm. We went to school there, we went to Columbus School, and it was in an Italian neighborhood. I had some friends there, a few, but we were like a clique unto ourselves, we four brothers. I remember my brother Harry graduated first—he went right to work. And then I was next, and I had to go to work, which I resisted very much. I refused to do anything until I realized that I had to. And then my brother Sam went on to high school.

I went to work for my uncle at that time. And there were streets. Main Street. Elm Street. Golden Hill Street. And you had some department stores. Well, I almost avoided it all. It was like I shut it out. This was not my life. And at that point I think I began to do a lot of reading. And most of the reading I ever did I think I did between the ages of about 14 and 20. I was influenced by my uncle, who was a scientist and a socialist, and I read the Russian literature of Tolstoy and Pushkin and Turgenev, and I almost memorized all of Shakespeare. And if I have any method of speech at all, it has to do with the reading that I did then. I was very impressed with Shakespeare and began to take notes. I think I was copying the good parts of Shakespeare, and I found myself almost copying the whole thing. I was ashamed of it later, but I couldn't erase so much work. I kept it.

Years later, my wife found it all. And began to read it. She said, "Why don't you throw away the books we have on Shakespeare because here you have it verbatim?" Finally I destroyed it. I realized later what I was trying to do. I was trying to find the substitute for the words that I needed to go on. Shakespeare was my whole life. And then the Russian literature. I discussed it with my uncle, who was quite literary. After my father died, we picked up some of his things and we found some rejection slips. He had written some poetry and sent it to the Jewish newspaper. We didn't know he did it. Also, we had an aunt, who wrote for the Jewish newspapers at that time. Was looking for literary talent. But not me. I felt cornered and trapped in Bridgeport. And every weekend I had a chance I would go to New York. I don't know what we did sometimes—we'd have parties. I'd go with a friend. I remember my brother Sam went to City College, we went to visit him. I remember he took me to my first opera. He was very sophisticated. I was absolutely amazed—all of a sudden the world began to open up a little bit.

I had to wait such a long time. I consider myself kind of a late bloomer anyway, because here at 26 I was sort of unsophisticated, and then waiting until 54 to finally say, Hey there's another world, there's a second half of life that can open up. And I have the feeling that if I have anything to do, it's to let people know that there's something else they can do, whether it's 24 or 64, there's something more they can do.

Compared to my childhood, the world is infinitely better, because the name of the game, as far as I'm concerned, is hope. And when people come to me and they say they're on medication, Valium, Librium, or whatever they're taking as an antidepressant, I say, "Well, I think medicine is for crisis, and if you're feeling very poorly, I think you ought to take it as is prescribed. But I think the only way to get over feeling depressed is to have something to look forward to. So take your medicine while you may, but try to find something else. Because the medicine is until you get rid of that anxiety, until you feel free to exercise."

I think the world is a more open place. A lot of it is very superficial, true, but I prefer openness and the open stance and the great hope, even with all the mistakes, to the kind of deadly quality of everybody being suppressed. When you hear that kids are against the institution, and they want their rights and they want to have some say, some input in what's going on in their school, it's good. At the University of Pennsylvania, not blacks, whites sat in for forty-eight hours. The school finally gave them some privileges. How wonderful!

When I was in school I felt I better make it while I can because that's my only hope. And I'm so pleased with people who have the guts to try to do something. They say I'm going to make it, I have enough sense, and let me do something for society or for a cause.

I was very much influenced by my uncle, my father's brother. He had the hardware and locksmith store, and I went to work for him. And I think his influence, his ideals fixed in. For instance, when prices of stock were going up, if he bought a dozen tools at a buck a piece, then he would sell it for $1.40. If a salesman came in and said order two dozen next time because the price is going up, he would sell out the old stock at the old cost. And I said, "Listen, the price is going up." He would say, "Because we paid less for this, you sell it at the old price."

Money was not the important thing. It was relationships, and he had a lot of influence on me. In fact when I left, I wondered if I'd have someone to talk to if I wanted to discuss something. We had a beautiful relationship, but I was glad to get away from it because I felt as though somebody had a noose around my neck and I really wanted to get to New York. Then I figured Philadelphia is not too bad. It's not far from New York. And I got caught in a whole string of things which lasted for a long time—all kinds of variations, twenty-five or thirty years before my head cleared.

I think I always had a feeling of inadequacy. As a child, if company came, you went into the other room to get out of the way. And I had nothing to offer. Fortunately I married a woman who grew up with a sense of superiority. She grew up with a sense of being special, and she's never lost that. She still thinks she's special, and she is.

The family is crumbling because parents don't have very much to offer and they walk away. And one of the things that I talk to people about is that maybe you ought to have some kind of contribution, that everybody should make a contribution, and when you are dealing with your children, I think you almost have to help them become parents because eventually they will become parents. And that way they will be able to give what you give.

And I think people have very little self-esteem. I think it's the key to so much depression. I think of my own lack of self-esteem and I think I had to go through a whole syndrome of school to get rid of my lack of self-esteem. And it's quite as simple as that. I still remember when I got my doctorate and I had my office in the Medical Arts Building, and I'd be waiting at the elevator and somebody would say, "Good morning, Doctor." And I would never turn around. So for the first six months I thought "Doctor" couldn't mean me and then, yeah, it must be me. So I had the self-acceptance of a low-grade person, didn't have much to offer. And I still have a residue of that, occasionally. I get intimidated. If you're not careful and relax too much, you can get intimidated. And I still have it. I know that I can deal with groups, small groups. But if I have a large crowd to address, I have problems, still do. And I know exactly what it is.

Self-esteem enables parents to set an example. In other words, some kind of pride in family, that we are somebody. I am somebody, therefore you are. And if you don't want to accept what I am, do it with some sense of your own worth. Because you can be the best carpenter in the world, you can be the best ditch digger in the world. So you must have some self-esteem. I think that parents have to do that first because that's what children are watching.

Oh, everything is better about sex today. It's more open. There's more of a chance of more people beginning to find out what's wrong or what they're ashamed of. What they think is so personal—suddenly they find it's everybody's problem. Thank God it's more open. People come in and see me who have been married for thirty years. And they begin to talk in a way that tells me that nobody ever told them anything.

They could be so happy together. They really don't know how—it's really pathetic. You know, If I tell my wife so and so, she'll laugh at me. Or, If I tell my husband I feel this way about this thing, he's going to think I was out with another man. That kind of thing.

There are so many clichés about love. I think it's a twofold thing. I think first you have to trust yourself and then you trust yourself with somebody else. And being able to say "I love you" first, and not to say "I love you, too." But being able to reach out verbally or nonverbally and say, "You're fine. I love you. You're fine. I trust you. I love you." In other words, the commitment of one person to another almost in an impersonal sense. And in a personal sense you say this is who I am. And I will take my chances that you won't downgrade me. The giving. The giving. I think that has to do with relationships.

I don't think marriage is truly endangered. The only substitute for marriage, which is a one-to-one relationship, is with many, and nobody with any sense of self can really do this for long. You really need one person. So that I think marriage is still the only way—even common law, living together doesn't seem to do it. People find out.

Certainly, I think they have the freedom to say I'm not going to do what my parents did and I'm not going to live a life of silent desperation like we're supposed to because marriage is bad and sex is bad, and this is bad. So people take chances. And I think it's all right for people who don't get along to get divorced. And maybe make it better the second time.

I left my wife for three and a half years and went into therapy. And I remember the last session we had. I got very angry with him. You sit there like a dummy, and in those days, twenty years ago, I paid him twenty-five dollars, now it's fifty dollars. I sit here and you don't help me. You sit there and you take notes. I feel like I'm talking to myself. Will you spend the last five minutes talking to me? So he said, "Okay, okay." And he said, "In the last session you mentioned the word *family* sixteen times." But I already knew something was happening. My brother had died, left an estate, and we were already beginning to get some money. And I thought to myself, Who do I want to share this with? In the meantime, I'd been living separately and every woman I met wanted to marry me. Every woman I met was like my wife. I thought to myself, I got one of you. I don't need you. I have one of you. And so I remember how that came to pass. After I'd been gone for three and a half years, she gave me a hard time. She said, "Are you coming back for the children?" I said, "Yes." I was trying to be honest. I don't think I was as sophisticated as I am now, didn't understand as much. I think I would've handled it differently. Anyway, we got back together again, and this is years ago. But I learned a great deal about me out there alone, which I never would've learned. I don't talk about it, but I think I learned that everybody needs some kind of an anchor. And I think that all the terrible separations are not that unholy or terrible, because I do think that people find out who they are. So you take your chances and you build your own strength, and you try to remember that if you learn how to cope and take responsibility for who you are, then something different happens. And taking responsibility is one of the hardest things for people to do—responsibility for what they do, what they don't do.

When I first met my wife, I felt very good about her because we were both reading either *The Forsyte Saga* or *Of Human Bondage*. I was 26 and she was about the same age, and all of a sudden there was a meeting of the minds, and then we began to write letters. A courtship by mail. I remember being very intellectual and using all the fancy words I could use. She saved them for a long time, and then sometime she would read excerpts and she'd say, "You're a pretty good letter writer. Why do you think I married you?" We visited back and forth. But I think it was mostly a courtship of writing.

I wasn't ready for my first son, Mark, until my second, Arnie, was born, and when Arnie was born, I almost adored him. And people began to notice: "You sound like you only have one son instead of two." And I thought, Gee, how horrible. I discovered—and he knows this because we've talked about it—Mark at about 15 or 16. I suddenly discovered him and I realized what I had missed. But Arnie was fantastically precocious. To give an example, he was always running in and out of the house and we had one friend who really was crazy about him, and every time he ran through the doorway, she tried to grab at him. Finally, he was careless. She grabbed him, pulled him over, and rubbed his face against hers and said, "Don't you like my skin? I use Camay soap for my skin." He looked at her and said, "For a pan like that you should use Brillo."

Once he was running in the hallway upstairs and he slipped and almost fell down the stairs. I said, "Did you get hurt?" He said, "I just hurt my anterior buttock." He was about 6 or 7 when he did this. So we were all intrigued. But you see, Mark had his own precociousness in different ways. But Arnie was obvious. It's very hard to resist that kind of thing.

I was better with them later. Not as kids. I remember times when I would take a walk with one of them and we'd look into cellar windows and imagine what's in the house. But I think I was a little too stiff with them. We are more accepting of each other now. Mark and I will spend hours together. And Arnie and I will, too. And the four of us will spend a lot of time together. It's grown. It's better. See, my feeling is that relationships can grow as parents become more aware of what's going on. My wife was always aware of this. And she would handle it—she handled it by herself. She loves them. And I have to have some really different kind of rapport with them. I'm a lousy grandfather. I don't know how to bounce little ones—when they get to be about 16 or 17, then fine, I can talk to them. But as children I don't know how. And I tell them so.

There are many things that I wish I had done differently. It took me a long time to get over the desire, when I was living alone for three and a half years in New York, to discover everything about sex. And I wouldn't be surprised if a great deal that I know now I discovered in those three and half years. I didn't know it before. Maybe I felt very guilty about that, but I never discussed it with my wife. She wanted to know everything that happened, and I said I can't tell it all.

I have been afraid. I thought I had cancer when I was thirty because there was a lump in my back. I remember the doctor keeping me in his office. Also when I had cataracts in 1948. I was sure that I might die. If they slipped and I was blind, I would kill myself. And I remember preparing ways of destroying myself. And I find now that everybody who has cataracts does the same thing. Since then, three people came to me and told me they went through the whole idea. They were going to kill themselves because they didn't want to live blind.

Five weeks in Zurich, where I went to the Jungian Institute, was a very traumatic time. A very deep experience. I met some of the old coterie of Jung's at the institute. I had a sense that I had been bottled up and all of a sudden the whole world was mine. I have a little bit of that left. The whole world is my nugget. I can go anywhere that I want to. And I realized something else, that there were a lot of clay feet, those people who were really on top and were giving lectures had jealousies and played politics, and they lost, and they won. And they seemed so petty, and I thought, Gee whiz, they're just like me. They're like that. And why am I climbing up there because I can be just as petty and small—I am. I don't have to pretend I'm that great. It was very odd. I realized that all of a sudden the things I was looking up to were the things that everybody had, and if I was going to be a more complete person, I didn't have to go anywhere. And I stopped really going to lectures again.

When people talk about anxiety and panic, they really come back to those things I understand. The only person who understands anxiety attacks is someone who's had one. I've always said it's impossible to understand how disorganized you can feel when you really get like that —you totally need someone sometimes. A husband doesn't know. A wife doesn't know or the children don't know. Don't try to tell anyone how it feels. They can't know unless they've had it. And just find out what you have to do with it. Because the only thing you can do with it personally is learn how to live with it, and then you survive one, you survive another, and you survive another, and as time goes on, you realize that everybody's doing the same thing in a different way. Just surviving. Learn to be a survivor.

I think I have gained so much from the people I have seen, and the sense that the way to get love is to give it, and the way to get acceptance is to give it, and the way to have a relationship with somebody is to take a chance and offer yourself and say that's what I think. If you're brash, you're going to get some answer that you don't want if you're not careful. But the more open you are, the more you get back. You don't need everybody to love you, just a few people.

Sometimes you get the feeling that the women who are very active in women's rights aren't very attractive or what they have to offer has always been misunderstood. And they're angry at what men want, because men want more than just sex. They could want a relationship and their women are saying you've got to toe the mark. When I listen to women's-lib talk, I turn it off and go somewhere else because I know what they want. Now if they think it's a political forum—like abortion, where they're really finding out for themselves and humanity in a sense —I like them. I guess I've gotten to the point where I like strong people and strong women. I remember one of the things that one woman told me, that if you are emancipated, you're not afraid of women. Strong women. So I said, "What does that mean?" She said, "You really should be more afraid." And I think she had a point because in a sense you're no match, because it's not that they're equal. They're different. I think women are different, and I think you have to accept the difference. A man, I think, is a fool to take on a woman and fight her, because he may win the battle but lose the war.

When women say they want to have equal rights, I say sure. I think they should have equal rights and money. I think they should have equal rights—there's an awful lot of women who didn't have to join women's lib, who controlled everybody they wanted to and they still do. But if you think there are a lot of women who really don't know how to live their lives, I guess that's good for them. It's like trying to help the women who get beaten by their husbands. I guess there should be people who protect these women.

There comes a crisis—usually it happens in the thirties and forties when people who have been corrected by their parents or whatever in life, they've gone to school, they chose a profession they thought they chose, and all of a sudden they're facing law and medicine and they say, I'm unhappy with the thing. What should I do? So I say, Step back from yourself and let the process of individuation really happen in the middle of life. Not middle age, but the middle of life somewhere. And as you step back, you say, What did I ever love to do? Not what I'd like to do—what would I give up? What would I give up to get what I want to do? And I say, In the first place, never do something quickly. Do it slowly and do it in three stages.

First, thinking, and then talking, and then doing. And don't go from thinking to feeling to doing. Meditate about what you're going to do, and sit back and discuss what would you like to do, and don't do things suddenly because the impulsiveness will defeat you.

So I would say think back, maybe hold on to what you have. I held on to my book business until I felt as though I could earn enough in the book business, and then I dropped it. When I went to get a job at Philadelphia Psychiatric, people came and said, "Don't you have your books?" I was then selling bound books to schools and libraries by mail, mostly by mail. It wasn't dynamic enough. I missed the human contact. And I suddenly found out that I love to influence people. And I tell somebody, Wouldn't you like to be more influential? I feel very influential. Here I am talking, and all of a sudden you're listening to me. That's a good feeling. That's the reason I work, because I get a lot of feedback. Why don't you find out something that you love to do just as I love to come in to work every morning. Sometimes I don't want to, but I know that it beats staying home and watching TV. And besides, there's a lot of excitement going on between human beings.

I think I've been very lucky in the sense that although I waited a long time to do what I wanted to do, there is something unerring about what I did, because it finally came together. It's almost like saying all's well that ends well.

I'd rather live in America than anywhere else in the world. You know, I feel very comfortable. I am more comfortable with a devout Catholic in Philadelphia than with some holy Jew in Israel. I feel I have more in common. I would make more sense and be better friends with anyone—with a Moslem, with a decent Arab, than I would with an Israeli or some religious Jew I didn't like. We have a kind of politics here, which is shameful. But I think it's always gone on, and people are being exposed and they keep right on doing it. And I realize the ruthlessness of people.

I was intrigued by Kennedy because, by God, that man really was so comfortable in front of people and taking them on. Roosevelt, Wilson —I remember Wilson and I thought to myself, My God, what a nice kind of person to have as professor at college, an intellect. He's not a dese-and-dose guy. I remember being pleased with him. But Eisenhower was a chump. I think about Roosevelt, and I admit I was very impressed by his looks and "My friends, you are my friends"—that bullshit. I was really taken in by him. I liked Kennedy. I admired him. I thought to myself, Gee, I wish I was six-two. I wish I had a million dollars. I wish I could leave a million to all my kids. I wish I could be—you know, you lucky bastards. I wish I could go and look at how that dynasty was built, by the old man who was ruthless as he could be.

I am not patriotic. No. Goddamn it no, not patriotic. Kind of pleased or grateful or thinking that thank God it's a good place—I'm lucky.

When somebody comes to me and tells me that he's been asked to retire, I know what I do. I cry with him. Get out of it. Do something. I don't care what you do—I'll help you. Do something illegal. Work. Get a part-time job. Work. Don't retire, you die. Because you're waiting to die.

When I lived in Bridgeport, my brother came to me and he asked, "What's your business worth?" How much would I sell for? I said ten thousand dollars. He said, "Why don't we lock up and just go away? We won't tell anybody, just go away. Just lock up, and just pay the rent and just don't say anything. See what happens. Let's take a trip to Europe for two weeks." He wanted somebody to go to Europe with. He was single. And I got pretty excited. I didn't answer. He finally said, "Forget it, you don't have any imagination."

Years later, he came here and he said, "I'm making money hand over fist. I don't know what to do with it, and I think family is important." He invited me to come in. I stayed for a year. And I think if I remained with him I'd be a multimillionaire now. Because when he died, he was a multimillionaire. But we fought most of the time. And I finally said, Let me get out of here. I don't want to be here. And I came back. Then I discovered my own family, and I have the feeling that- I'm happier now with my family. I talk to people about how family is so important because you can directly influence people by just being. You don't have to do anything, you just be.

It makes me angry to hear some chauvinist saying, "I don't like Polacks. I don't like wops and I don't like Jews." It happens in group therapy. Of course, everybody laughs, but I get furious. And it's almost like calculated anger. You have no right to do this. You have no right to talk like that. You don't belong here. Who the fuck do you think you are? That's what I do. Getting really angry. I think I've learned—I think I internalize my anger. I get angry and I internalize it, and I get depressed. Sometimes it's disappointment. Sometimes it's frustration. Sometimes it's being contradicted. Sometimes it's a sense of futility.

I don't think I have explosive anger. I don't think I have unreasonable anger, or the kind of fury that you can't control. I don't have that kind of feeling. I think I was always afraid to be angry for fear that I might really do something terrible. I internalize it because I don't know what else to do.

For me the flow of ideas has never stopped. New ideas. I'll tell you what happened recently, and I think it's only fair to know. I'm a little surprised and shocked and annoyed to find out that I get tired. I'm wonderful in the morning, until noon. Around two or three o'clock in the afternoon the energy runs out and I would like to stop. I remember once, this goes some five, six, seven years ago, and a guy was coming into the clinic and he wanted to see me at lunchtime. And he said, "I'll bring my lunch and you help me." And at one point in the conversation I was talking and then the telephone rang and I answered the phone and came back. He said, "You know, Dr. Karlen, that I'm a hypnotist." I said, "Are you really?" He said, "You know, about a half hour ago I put you to sleep." I'll never forget that.

I think I started out below bottom and I had to reach up to touch bottom. I think if I started off and somebody said, "You go to school, and get some"—we're back to it—"self-esteem." I feel comfortable with young people. I trust them. I like them. They're bright. I wish I were like them forty years ago. But maybe I couldn't be. I think if I had been a therapist at 40, I'd have been a lousy one. I think I needed what I have—and there's a kind of a justice in this world. And when people talk to me about how Mozart died too early, I'm not so sure. I think everybody did what they could—if they had more to give, they would've given it. How much can one do? And look at us living endlessly—we die of ennui. So I feel satisfied. I think that's the greatest gift I have gotten. I was a slow beginner, a late starter, but I'm happier now than I've ever been in my life because I know I'm going to die in the middle of some project which is new to me. Death? Ignore it. Mostly you're going to join them. I don't get depressed at all. I sit and meditate. I've gone to a lot of funerals.

I feel if I have contributed anything, it is saying, Hey, it's possible never to stop growing. And I am glad that I can do it instead of saying it. And I think maybe I have some influence—see that's what I mean about family influence. It is the thing that you finally do with your life that makes sense. I'm pleased with myself.

I have some work to do. I can't let my life be cluttered by being unhappy. I'm sorry if some die when they're too young, but if they die in their seventies, I think—Well, it can happen to me, too. Maybe I'm one of the lucky ones. Besides, I'm busy. I don't want to clutter my life with tears. I think I can get very emotional. I remember when my sister died. I was told over the phone. Her husband called and I screamed at him. I yelled and screamed, and there were tears, but not sobbing.

I don't think about death very often. I think of it more than usual now because my brother Sam who was just 75, a year younger than I, has leukemia and he's down to 118 pounds, and he's taking it so cheerfully.

I'll die—I try to prepare myself sometimes. Yeah, you can't live forever. I'm going to die, but I try not to think of it. If I feel lousy, I think, Gee whiz, is it now? And then I feel better, and I'm fine again. I eat something and I feel the energy come back and I feel fine and happy.

I'll tell you, I get a lot of feedback from my patients, and I think I am so lucky that I've gotten into something that if I go to work in the morning, no matter what I feel, there's someone who will walk up to me and say, "Dr. Karlen, don't you feel well?" I say, "Why?" "You're not smiling." Mostly, I'm so intent on my work I don't go for coffee breaks. I've been the oldest one every place I've been. I'm a father figure. They'll all come in and tell me about their bad marriages and bad love affairs. And who to marry and who not to marry. And who they are sleeping with now. And why don't you get rid of him, and don't, until you find a new one. That kind of thing. It goes on all the time. It's enlightening.

# Leila Danette

*L*eila Danette is short (five feet) and sturdy. She has the demeanor of a teacher and the elocution of an actress. She has been both. She was born in August 1909 in Jacksonville, Florida, in a poor black family that battled back against its poverty. She got through the eighth grade in Jacksonville and then moved to Baltimore to live with a cousin and finish high school. She enrolled at Howard University in Washington, D.C., stayed a year there, then got married and dropped out of college. A year later, at her mother's urging, she returned to school; she eventually received her B.A. at Morgan State College in Baltimore. Her first husband died in 1929. By then she had become an elementary school teacher and was able to support herself.

She began to take courses in drama at Catholic University in Washington. She met a "gambler and sportsman" and stayed with him for fourteen years. "I didn't need to work," she says about those years. She did continue to teach on and off, however. She managed to get her M.A. in speech and drama from Catholic University.

She was teaching speech therapy in Washington, near the Arena Theater, when she got to know director Edwin Sherin. Sherin was casting The Great White Hope and persuaded her to take a role in it. That was in 1968. She came to New York with that show and stayed until 1970, then went back to Washington to teach for a year—and to qualify for retirement benefits. After that she came back to her Harlem apartment and the world of acting.

She has played in The Little Foxes in Toronto, Indianapolis, and Syracuse. She has appeared on television and has done commercials for McDonald's, Polident, and Golden Griddle Pancake Syrup, among others. She keeps in motion, racing to auditions, interviews, and classes (acting, singing, piano). She now lives in a high-rise middle-class fortress —alone in a studio apartment strewn with the signs of her life, from plants to an electric piano—amid the decay of a midtown, west Manhattan neighborhood. She never had any children. She has few fears. Her advice for protecting oneself in New York is simple: "I watch out for sneakers. Guys in high heels can't run fast. I carry a collapsible

*cane and I can develop a limp if I need to. When I do, I just limp along*
*and sing 'Swing Low, Sweet Chariot' at the top of my voice. It works."*

Remarkably, I felt that Jacksonville was a very nice place, and
I had nice friends. And I had a very religious family, and we
had many opportunities—in fact, I guess that was where I first got
my little idea about being on the stage, because we used to have to
go to something that they called at that time the BYPU—the Baptist
Young People's Union. They used to have programs in church. And
at that time my mother saw to it that we went to church and Sunday
school. We went to the morning service. And then something would be
going on at four o'clock, then the BYPU, then the night service. I think
after I got to be about 14 or 15, I don't think I went to church for
about ten years. I had had my whole share.

As I remember Florida, I even remember some of the little people in my classes. I wouldn't know where they are or anything about
them anymore, because I've been away so long.

As a child, you see, I knew that Jacksonville was a very wide-open
city because there were things that my mother wouldn't permit me to
see or hear. But Jacksonville was like the New York of Florida. It was
the meeting point for everybody. If you were going to Miami, you
came into Jacksonville first, and then you went to Miami. But the train
always stopped in Jacksonville. One of the big things in that childhood
period that I remember very distinctly was the fact that my godfather
was the ticket taker at the movie house. I'm sure there wasn't but
one. The black movie house. And so I could always go to the movies
without paying the fee. So I went to the movies practically every
day of my life. Now I can't bear hardly to go to a movie. But back
then I went to the movies practically every day of my life. And that
was one of the big social things. Then I had to take piano lessons,
which I didn't learn one single solitary thing from. Altogether, it was
happy.

We were poor, but there was always enough to eat. And my mother
had a business, and if we weren't in school, we would go from school
either to home to Grandmother or we would go to the business

where she was a milliner, and she was also a hairdresser. I can remember even as a little kid helping her shampoo hair. I'd stand upon this stool and wash the ladies' hair and get them ready for her to straighten their hair. Because this was in the beginning, when they were just beginning to use hot irons on people's hair. Madame A. Leila Walker was the millionairess at this time. Of course, we only knew about her. I only knew about her in childlike terms.

But I would say—certainly not until I went back many years later, was I conscious of the large pockets of poverty in Jacksonville that were there then. In other words, it didn't matter to me when I was a child.

I would've called Jacksonville a sophisticated place at that time. Like I was saying, it was like the gateway to the rest of Florida. And they had the places where they gambled. And I'm sure they were there because my mother said you can't go down a certain street. You must not go down that street because that's not good. That's a bad street. Things like that.

Lots of unpaved streets. Lots of sand streets. Streetcars. No cars. My father—my stepfather—bought a Hudson Super Six, and we were the talk of the town. We really were, you know, like way out there. The Hudson Super Six was something, and my grandmother never would get in that automobile. We moved in Jacksonville from one house to the other. And my mother had to hire a horse and buggy because Grandmother was not going to get in that devil's wagon and ride anywhere. So certainly, it was much slower then, with a lot of religious influence in the community.

I was about 6 years old when one of the sheriffs in the city of Jacksonville went into the red-light district, and there were all kinds of stories told about what really happened. But anyway, that sheriff was killed up in the alley behind this red-light district. And I was about 6, and they lynched three men—three black men—supposedly connected. And there were no witnesses, so no one could know whether these three men were those three men or not. And I remember having Grandma say, "Put out all the lights," because they dragged the bodies right past our house. And I remember we were cowardly afraid and huddled into the corner with all the lights out. And that's one of my very stark remembrances.

Nothing happened to my immediate family. I don't remember any incidents. I remember my mother coming back and saying she had seen a black man cleaning up in the store, and she told him not to go behind that counter when there were white salesgirls back there. Because all one had to do was to scream and he would be lynched. This was just a story that I heard. But I was aware of the fact that there was bigotry—I knew that I could not eat where they ate. I knew that I had to go to the black movie theater, and I couldn't go to the other movie theaters. This didn't concern me, though. You know, it wasn't a terrible dynamic. It was just a fact of life, you know. Yes. We were all segregated. We were in an all-black school, yes. I didn't have any white friends.

I think it has changed since then with some individuals. Some, and I qualify that "some." I might even add, few. I don't think Archie Bunker is a myth. And I know that with myself I would say within the last twenty years I began to take off my mask if you were white. Because if you were white, I was not Leila. I was what I wanted you to think I was.

I think it was after I matriculated at Catholic University that I changed. I was the only black student in the drama department at that time. And I began to see a different light and began to sort of feel, although even at that time it was an extenuating circumstance, that I had to do, I had to be good. I had to do the best—I didn't want a mark any lower than any other person in the class because I was black and there was that kind of impetus there. But I did begin to form individual friendships that let me loosen up. That let me feel that I didn't have to put on a façade.

I think through the media, and I'm talking about the public media— the television, the radio, which are very powerful influences in our civilization—I do think that there is more knowledgeability and frankness about racial differences. And that isn't only black and white, that's the Caucasians and the Orientals, the whole bit. The Indians. And I think for the first time, because we're not confined just to books or just to reading, therefore the first time, people are more conscious that differences are only superficial. I don't think this is as much true as I'd like to see it. And I don't think it's where it should be. We have to live one to one, right? And we're caught up in a society that has some very false gods, you know. Such as we live where money is the only power. And whenever that happens, the human ideals become subservient to this god of theirs. And we lose a lot of the values that are native human traits. We lose in the subservience we have to the fact that we've got to have money, money, money, money. One thing we lose is our regard for each other. We put people in mills. We grind them up like they're fodder, to make money, you know. It's all about making money. As much as I love my new art, the art that's new for me, being an actress, I know that I'm just a factor. It is not my work. It's how much money I can produce or how much money I can make. What's the box office to me? Has nothing to do with my ability to portray or to reenact an experience or a circumstance. And that's characteristic of our society. And I think there's some societies where this is not true, where you find more humanness. More awareness that certain other things are important, such as the mind, and such as the soul.

I was very fortunate. We were a very closely knit black family. My grandmother had twelve children. My mother was the youngest child of twelve, and she was sort of the focal point, like she was also the focal point for everybody who ever got in trouble, like the other sisters' children. I remember influxes in our house of those children who had gotten in trouble somewhere else. And they would ship them down to my mother. And she was also the center for the grandmother, fortunately. One of the bulwarks in the black community is the grandmother. Nobody has really emphasized this very well. If it wasn't for the grandmother in the black community, we just could not exist. We could not exist. My grandmother was the true matriarch. I never saw my grandfather. He had died long before I was born. My grandmother was physically an invalid, but a very powerful personality. Believed in truth, and—I'll never forget—she had coal blue eyes. And if you told her a lie, which I was very capable of doing . . . I always had a vivid imagination. I really didn't think I was lying, but I'd make up a story in a minute. And at that time it was considered a lie. Now they would be promoting it and say, "Oh, this child is going to be a creative artist," and one of those things. But I got a whipping because you just didn't tell a lie—you told the truth. And I remember these blue eyes of hers that would stare completely through you. And you would get so nervous and start shifting until then you'd finally just break down and tell her what was really, you know, what really happened.

My father had died when I was 2 years old, and my mother had married again. So to me she was the only authority figure. The family didn't approve of the second husband, and so I was given to understand by the other members of the family—my uncle and my aunts and everything—that my father was not there. The only person there to obey was my mother. So she was always the authority figure. I don't think I ever took to authority too well because I always had my own way to do things. And so I was always a little leery. My mother was not my sister or anything like that. She was my mother and I respected her as such. And she lived to be 91, and she never saw me with a cigarette in my fingers. I smoked. But she never saw me with a cigarette, you know. In the bathroom, back up behind the bed, in the closet, or somewhere. But I never had the courage to come in and just sit down and take a cigarette out in front of my mother. So that's the kind of relationship we had. It was never a mother-sister relationship. It was always mother-daughter. She was the authority figure in my life. She was somebody that was beautiful, but I wouldn't want to be like her. No, I wouldn't. I could not walk the straight and narrow path. I wouldn't even want to.

I remember things like this, for instance: I guess I must have been around 2. And I never had any store-bought clothes. My clothes were all made by hand with beautiful little tiny stitches. And I remember, it must have probably been my second birthday. I loved where my mother had business, I loved to go to the other businesses all the way around, and everybody would make love to me and everything. And I remember one man that I was particularly fond of because he was the undertaker and he had the big car, you know, the great big car. And he would pick me up and take me riding in this car. And I would be gone for just, you know, hours. And I remember this birthday they dressed me all in red. I had a red dress. I had on red shoes, and I had red socks and everything. And when I came into the undertaker's parlor, he just said, "Oh, my little red bird," and picked me up and Mama didn't see me the whole day. He just took me everywhere he had to go in the car. And I was tickled to death. That's one of my early memories.

I'm not really a sports person, but I like physical activity. And in college, the guys on the football team were always my epitome of romance. During college I can remember going to football practice because my guy was a halfback or a fullback or something like that. So I always liked the spectator sports, you know.

And as a kid I loved to dance. I used to take dancing in high school and wasn't too bad either. I always wanted to do the ballerina pirouettes, but I was always doing the gypsy shake dancing or something. But I liked all of those things.

Family training: that's where you get your first ethics. And if you don't get it there, I think it's very hard to get it anywhere else. I mean, those do's and don'ts that you had even though you may defy them. If you've been exposed to them. Like, for instance, I really believe this as a person and as a human being, that what is done in the first five or six years of a child's life is going to govern that child's moral life the rest of his life.

Families are too loose now. And I think that's one of the reasons why we're having an educational problem. In fact, having been an ex-teacher, I saw it fall apart, you know. Like you've got to see it. Then the parents expected the schools to take over the part of the education, the actual education and the training. And teachers have not been trained for that, and they get the child too late anyway. And so it is with many of our today problems, many of our adolescent problems, many—I have spoken with parents so often. When children do things that you know are wrong, they are only testing. And parents in their new liberality don't give them the bars they're looking for. That's why we have to send children to psychiatrists and we have to give them special treatment. They want bonds. Everybody has to have some bonds. You talk about freedom. As black people we've always talked about freedom. *Freedom* is a very tricky word. Because there is no such thing as freedom; once you're born into a society, you have to be governed by that society. And that has to be true from the baby right straight through. He has to come under the social development in his home.

And whatever he comes up, that's going to be the product of heredity and environment, you know. I feel that many of the problems the adults are having have been because of the failure, the fall-down of that family unit that used to be so much tighter.

I personally feel that birth control and abortion are some of the best things that could happen because they've always been going on, some kind of fashion. I think having been a young girl and knowing what it has been to have an abortion and the danger you had to go through. I remember once having a whole package of poison in my pocket-book because I could not bear to feel that I would disgrace my family by having an illegitimate child. And yet I had no way—I had no source of advice even. I obviously solved it because I had a family doctor who was closer to me than probably anybody else, and he realized what dire straits I was in. But I mean, certainly you should have that privilege. I mean, I don't think children should just be miscellaneously brought into the world as a result of just pure sexual pleasure. I just don't believe that. I think it's a burden on the nation, a burden on everybody. You just should not have those type of children. That's all there is to it. I absolutely believe it. The way I believe that love and need go together. The word *love* has been so distorted by so many different kinds of connotations, mutations, which are true of our English language. I would like to have something that happens between two people a little bit more definitely defined. Now, love to me is the feeling—is the need of one person for another person in some kind of way. It can be emotional, it can be physical. It can be aesthetic. But it has to be based on you have something I need, and you need something I have. And we share.

I think it's very difficult to be married today. I think it's very difficult. I think sometimes it's more difficult than at other times. I advise any person in the theater against marriage. It's better to live together because you already have a mistress. Now I don't know that that's true, and I can't speak for other professions. I'm only speaking from what I know. I think maybe a teacher or a person engaged in a nine-to-five job can probably deal with marriage better, because they're already on a routine. They're already going to something and coming home to something and getting up to something, and dealing with problems. I think maybe they can do it better. But in the arts, I think it's particularly hard.

I still remember my first marriage. I had been to church and I stopped by some friends' house to just say hello after church, to visit. And he came in, also visiting. And we were introduced, and I was with my best friend, who is still my best friend. And so he offered to take the two of us home. And we gladly consented because he was driving a car. And so both of us told him where we were going, you know, where we lived, and I thought he would take me home first. But he didn't take me home first. He took her home first. So that gave us this little time to ride home alone. But it was just casual conversation and he did take me to my door. And it was so funny. In doing this trip, we had gone down one of the main streets in Baltimore, Churchill Avenue, the black community at that time—lots of the better class of people lived there. And I hadn't been in the house an hour . . . Oh, and he had a convertible which made it even more exciting, and the top was back. It was in the spring; I think we were on the Easter vacation from school. And somebody called up ny mother and said, "Do you know I saw your daughter in the car with that Clarence Small, and you know he's a married man." And my mother called me on the carpet. I said, "I didn't know he was married, Mother. I didn't even ask him that." But it was a big to-do. So I was forbidden, which was like waving the red flag. So I think about seven months later we got married. Ran away and got married. I can remember that first year. I had to leave school. So I was definitely going to have this baby. And I did everything that they told me you did to get the baby. And nothing happened. And at that time it was probably just the fulfillment of that female instinct, you know, to just have a child. And my husband had tuberculosis. We finally discovered it. First we thought it was just a cigarette cough, and unfortunately, the family doctor laughed it off. One of those things. But it became increasingly worse. And I think after we got the positive diagnosis, we went through sort of an emotional trauma. Anyway, he decided he would go to a sanitarium—a Maryland sanitarium. And I think we went one month, and I discovered the next month that I'm pregnant. There's no possible way. I'm the only bread-earner. The baby would be exposed to tuberculosis. I had no alternative, you know. So it was the abortion. And I think that to me was rather traumatic—at that point, because I could say here for a change, I married, I'm legitimate. I can have this baby, and I'm pregnant. And so I gave that up with a little degree of regret maybe. But now that I look back on it, I don't have any regrets, you know. I still don't have any regrets. Because I know some people are meant to be mothers and some people are not.

Some things are meant to be. I have a very firm belief in what I consider my religious self. I also believe at this point in my life that your spiritual self is just as important as your aesthetic self, your physical self. You know, like we train everything else, and we give everything else some due. Well, I think you've got to do something for yourself spiritually. Either you must develop some form of worship, some form of belief that's satisfying. You know. It can take any form with me. Now you know, you would rather worship Buddha. That's your business, if he represents that to you. I think there are some things from other cultures that are just as important as the things in our culture. But I think every person within themselves must do something for their inner spirit. If not they are bestial.

I need that kind of support at all times. I can feel down at times. But I know that some people that I know have them worse—periods of depression. And to me I have my own spiritual thing that deals with that because I know that today is transient, and tomorrow is another day. And I know that if nothing happens today or whatever happens today, it won't happen tomorrow. Tomorrow is an entirely different thing. So all I have to do is get over this day, you know. So there's no sense in being down and out about it, or worry about it. Maybe I don't feel good, but I'm going to feel better tomorrow. So as they say in *Annie*, there's always tomorrow. And tomorrow, tomorrow.

I became a Catholic convert some years ago. My husband was in the sanitarium with tuberculosis. I was the only breadwinner and my mother had had a house with several apartments. I lived on the second floor of this apartment house. That's where I lived. I could not afford much—I could just barely exist. The Protestant Church had become dissatisfactory to me because I found that I wasn't getting enough time to spend with my own spiritual self. I was always wondering if that minister was believing what he was saying, or if what he said agreed with me. I had no time to sit with my own spiritual self. So I went to a Catholic mass and the thing that impressed me the most at that particular mass was that nobody concerned themselves about what you were doing. If you didn't stand up at the right time, nobody noticed it. You wanted to stay on your knees and pray, nobody noticed it. You were not conspicuous. It didn't matter whether or not you had on a new coat or a new hat. You didn't have to listen to any-body talk for hours or anything like that. The music was soothing, the atmosphere was pleasant. And fundamentally I think I like the pomp and splendor. So far as I'm concerned, when I physicalize my spiritual-ism it must be in the surroundings. I like the pomp—I like the priest dressed in his robes. I like the statues. Beautiful. And I like the candles, and I like the paintings. This all goes with my spiritualism, with the physicalization of that spiritualism. So that's why I found at that time Catholicism was very satisfying for me. And it wasn't easy—

it took me a long time. I went all through that, and it wasn't until the man I lived with in Washington got cancer and I realized he was dying, that I really became a member of the Catholic Church. And that period just after his death—it was a complete solace for me. I made the novenas. I was terribly maladjusted for the first time in my life.

I don't say this to many people because it's always such a point of disagreement, especially when you say it to people who have not had any money or had very limited money. During this period when I was with this man, I had unlimited money, and when I took him to Mayo Clinic for his final trip—I think I had ten thousand dollars in my bosom just to go with. And they took a look and said there's nothing we can do. And the ten thousand dollars would have been followed by any amount of money. And there was nothing they could do. And for the first time in my life I realized that money was absolutely, positively nothing, because I would've given all of it and anything else that I had to have kept him alive. So that made a whole revision in my life, so that when it came to giving up the stability of being a teacher and going into the theater, I was absolutely prepared for it, because I know it's all transitory dust.

I think I neglected my health for a long time. I only did the things that were pleasant for me. But as the years grow on and you reach each birthday, you say, hot dog, I'm lucky, I made another one. After you get over the period of saying, Oh God, I'm getting older, and I'm not doing anything. What's going to happen to me? Then you get to the point where you say, Oh Jesus, I made one more. So right now I'm very conscious of my eating habits. I'm not so conscious of my health habits that I don't indulge in some things that I like, because I think that's due me. For instance, I know that meat is not good for me, but I'm not going to turn into a vegetarian at this point. I try not to eat large quantities over periods of time. I try to space it with the chicken and the fowl and so forth and so on. But if I have to have a roast beef, I have a roast beef.

I have a physician who's really a very good friend and I usually go and have a one-year's checkup—you know the one they give from the insurance. I have the checkup. I really believe that the body, if it's taken care of, will be okay. One of the things that I think we're into in this generation is this constant medicine and these drugs and everything. I really think that's so bad for everybody concerned. I don't say if you break your arm, you shouldn't have your arm set. But I do think that a lot of times we rely on drugs when we just don't need to, if we eat right and take reasonably good care of ourselves.

The actress who is very important to me, very, has been a great influence on me, is Helen Hayes. I remember two times that I had the lights turned on in the movie house because I had a complete breakdown in my emotions. And one of them was Helen Hayes doing a movie called *The Sins of Madeline Claudette*, and I've seen it a couple of times on reruns of silent movies. Anyway, this girl becomes a prostitute in order to send her baby through life. It's a silent movie. And when she comes to the office as a diseased old woman—on her way out—she goes in the office of the man she loved and they want to put her out, and she finally gets a chance to just sit in his chair. And by this time I had such an emotional buildup with all of this coming, that when she sits in the chair, I just scream "Ahhh!" as loud as I can. Of course they turn on the lights in the movie because they don't know anything, and the ushers are running down the aisle and I'm just screaming and crying and lying there. So I've let movies out in my day.

I haven't had that kind of reaction so far as plays are concerned. I like the theater much better than I do the movies. I guess that developed later though, although I always wanted to do any kind of acting. Theater is really my best love. But I don't know that I've seen a play that really shook me enough. Now I think I'm always very critical. I'm trying to find out if the author wrote well. I think that's what removes me from having a play just hit me altogether. I have a tendency to sort of dissect it rather than just enjoy it.

I've never been active in politics. But I know that I must vote. And I find people say, "What's the need of voting?" Well, I think that need to vote came out of that early existence when I knew you could not go to the polls and vote. And I must vote, you know, like when I lived in Washington, I would get on this—because Washington has no vote. But I'd get on the train and come home for an election and vote. Yes, back to Baltimore to vote. And it wasn't, I guess, until I moved to New York that I really gave up my Baltimore political affiliation. I can't go out and stump, you know. And I'm not even the kind of individual like when Martin Luther King was marching on Washington, I wasn't there—I didn't want to go out and march, but I wanted to get you some cocoa and some coffee and some champagne and a drink and everything, you know, because you went. I wanted to serve you. Even when Watergate happened, I didn't see anything to be alarmed because I know that happens. I know that's happening. I think that dollar will make anything, you know, happen. I mean, all of the low things, I don't think any form of government can prevent. Like every once in a while, they'll come along and catch somebody and make a big example of him, and all of them are doing the same thing. That's why they hated Adam Clayton Powell so. When he went to Paris with his secretaries, and they were mad because this was a black man doing the same thing they were doing. You know, it had nothing to do with Powell using the city, the state's money, the government's money. You know? It was the fact that as a black man he was not supposed to do that. But it's been going on. They've been doing it all the time. He sat next to them when he was there.

Women have rights, yes. I think financially, yes. But I want the door opened for me. I don't want to go to war. I want my husband, if he's able, to go out and provide for the family. I'm not particular about him cooking. That's my job. And I'm sorry, I'm just of that nature. I don't mind my man helping me with the dishes and I don't mind him fixing his main, his *pièce de résistance*. But I don't want him to feel that he has to get breakfast, dinner, and supper because I go to work.

It's not like the civil rights cause. I felt it was so necessary. I was very proud because I had lived through a period when I knew there was very little unity, especially among black people, which had been intentionally done—the segregation of the black race was a part of the whole slavery idea. That's why they broke up families as soon as they came on the shores, to see that there was no unity. And because we had been subjected to that kind of training, and environment, it was very hard for black people to come together under those conditions. And when they came together under Martin Luther King, I was rejoicing because we had made one big step. One big step.

I think the changes are very visible. I haven't had the opportunity to go back South since I left some years ago, but I have had friends who say if you really want to see the changes, that's where to see them. It has been done very smoothly with no upsets. And they tell me it just works beautifully, you know, in the schools and the churches and everywhere.

I've worked. Teaching was a necessity. Teaching was the economic reward for the years and the time and the energy that I had put in school. If I had been economically secure earlier, I would've been an actress from the beginning. But an actress would not have paid any bills. And then I had another conclusion, that acting was not a very nice profession, not in my family. Teaching was. It was almost a compulsion. In fact, there were times when I actually could not do it one more day. One thing I think was that there was a structure in teaching in which you were under a principal, under a supervisor, under a— could you say the power? You know, under the power structure. And the power structure came to me or wrote to me, and told me what I should do. And if they came in my room and I wasn't doing what the structure said was the right thing to do—I remember a great contradiction I had with them because I guess I know communications well enough to know that you cannot ignore phonetics if you're going to teach reading in the English language. Because phonetics is hard enough to learn. And they took phonetics out of the schools. In order to teach it, I had to close my door, shut the windows, and do it almost as a secret. And if I was caught, I would've been called upon the carpet.

One of the frustrations was that I never knew at the end of a day when I had poured my whole energy out from nine o'clock until three, whether I had reached anybody or not.

Acting is very different. It has a very personal reward. A very personal inner reward that has nothing to do with the final production. For instance, when I'm working, my rehearsals are as important to me as a performance. I heard actors say, "Well, I'll give it all in performance." But I give it all, all the time.

After you have spent these grinding hours, the reward is when the audience does say, Yes, sir, you did it all right. We like what you did. That's always sort of like the whipped cream on top of a cake.

If you can't get that feeling from your work, I guess my first reaction would be to say just stop. Do anything else, or just stop. Get your head straight. Make up your mind what you want to do, and go for that. Certainly life is not worth . . . I mean, I think of all the years that I got up and went to school. Now I'm not going to knock it, because

I lived well, you know. I was a part of a social situation that was rewarding, even though I was rebellious. There were moments when I could read, I could come to New York and go to the theater, and I could do things—I could travel. And I had two months off in the summertime. But I don't know that I could do a job that was just absolute drudgery, you know.

I remember one summer I was getting some extra money, and I worked packaging peanuts in a factory. I think I worked a month and I was just going crazy. I couldn't do that. No, and I wouldn't. I don't think any money can pay you for that.

I don't want to be anything else but an American. Number one, I haven't traveled that widely, but those few places I have been don't match up. I want you to understand that I don't think other places are far behind. I think because they have a different culture and go at a different pace, I think they're just as satisfied as I am being an American. But I think the place where you're born, the place where you grow up, is it. Like right now today, if you came in and you say, Now here is your passport, here is a piece of land, you will have servants and a house, and you can go back to Nigeria. I would say, Thank you very much. I don't want your passport. I don't want a house in Nigeria. If it was forced upon me, maybe I could go to Nigeria and make an adjustment. I don't want to go to Nigeria. I don't want to go—this is where my roots are. And this is where I am, and I have no more in common with those people in Africa than they have with me. I don't know anything more about their habits than they know about mine. And I would have to make that kind of adjustment. I'm not willing to do it.

So I have to deal with the American Dream. To my mind that dream goes back to that materialistic thing that I think is the demigod that hangs like the sword of Damocles over everybody. I know that there's good and bad, but I'm really not terribly concerned about things. Because in America or in the world, I know that they're there and I know the problems are there. I have a theory that a lot of the troubles we have are a matter of communications, just a matter of communications. I think if we could communicate, Israel wouldn't be after Arabia.

But I as an individual feel that there is some kind of divine plan that works these things out. And I'm not terribly concerned. I mean, I don't run around raising my hands because the younger generation is different from my generation. They're just different. But I saw the flower children come and I saw them go back into society and do just like everybody else. So I just think we get all upset for nothing. I don't have that. I just don't have that. And every once in a while a President comes along to reassure me. Franklin Delano Roosevelt for the first time made me feel that there was a President there who knew I was there. You know? He was the first—it was the first time that I felt here was a man who was for all of us. He wasn't just in the White House. And then John Kennedy was sort of the epitome of what a President should be like. He had the charisma. I liked him to be my President. I liked what he said. I liked what he did. I guess, too, I like fundamental actors. He was one and so was Franklin Delano. Diplomatic actors. That's what they were.

When I retired—and even now—I loved it. Let me see. This is my eighth year since retirement, and I have not gotten over how beautiful it is on Monday morning; in fact I try to make very few appointments. If I have to get up early on Monday morning, it's really because it seemed to me that I had been getting up on Monday mornings all my life. I was the most happy person in the world to not have to get up on Monday morning, and go nowhere, and talk to nobody about anything. Listen, I have not gotten over it, and it's been eight years. I still look forward to Monday morning. Somebody says, Well, can you do something nine o'clock on Monday? I say, Do I have to? My retirement has been the most beautiful part of my life. For the first time, actually, I don't care how much money I have. I don't care how little money I have. I can do exactly what I want to. I can almost say exactly what I want to. I can certainly think what I want to. And to my mind I have been fulfilled. Everything I have done, all the mistakes—everything was the making of me as I am right here today. And the only way I learned or became what I am is because I went through it all. No, no, I wouldn't take one thing back. Everything had its purpose.

I believe in constant growth. I believe that anything you do at any point, you do to grow in what you're doing. And I constantly try to do that. When I'm not working professionally, I try to take professional courses. Right now I'm very much into learning how to sing, and along with that my teacher insists that I learn the piano, which I never learned when I was a child. But I'm very conscientious. I practice. I even have a keyboard that I practice on at home. So I think that you should be constantly growing, you know. I don't see how anybody because they retire can come home and sit. Because there are courses you can take. There are places you can go that you've never been before. There is the time. I don't understand that element that says you must come home and disintegrate.

I just lost a friend who had cancer. And who had lived very broadly and widely and did everything that a man was supposed to do. And his wife was my best friend all the way through school. I was there when they got married. I went to see him just about two or three days before he died. I was thankful when they told me that he'd passed away. Now I'm very sorry for her because I know she's got the aloneness to deal with. But so far as my friendship for him was concerned, I know it's better for him. You know?

I think about my own death. But it's not distasteful to me. I think the reluctance to talk about death is very foolish. I think that death is something that is inevitable, and so far as my life is concerned, now for a number of years, it's only today. That's all that I'm really planning for. Today.

# Robert Inglis

*Unlike some men, Robert Inglis was happy to retire. In the course of a long life of hard work he had saved some of his best dreams for* ❧ *the end. Inglis and his wife, Mary, to whom he has been married for more than fifty years, live in a modern brick ranch house in Oxford, Maryland. They had the house built to their specifications in 1965, a year after Inglis retired after forty years with General Electric in Philadelphia. The life they lead is the life they chose to lead: They enjoy the comforts of their house, set beside a creek that brings forth crabs and oysters. They are active in Presbyterian church affairs, in the Izaak Walton League, and other organizations. They have a son, a daughter, and seven grandchildren.*

*Inglis was born on September 25, 1903, in Scranton, Pennsylvania. His mother's family came to America from Wales and his father's from Scotland. Inglis and his sister grew up in Scranton, where he attended the public schools. In 1923 he entered the Bliss Electrical School in Washington, D.C., but soon left to go to work for General Electric. It was eleven years before he went after his college degree and it took him six years at night to earn a B.S. in mechanical engineering. With it he was able to go from construction electrician to manager of quality control at his GE plant.*

*Inglis is a strong, muscular man (five feet eleven inches tall, 230 pounds) with a round, smiling face, a gray crew cut, and large hands. With them he repairs cars, works around the house, improves his land, does electrical and carpentry work at his local church. He is known and admired in Oxford, on the eastern shore of Chesapeake Bay, even though he has not lived there all of his life. He represents to his family, friends, and neighbors a kind of basic American type: conservative, reliable, helpful, loyal, strong.*

Scranton is a center of coal mining, and it is mainly built in the valley through which the Lackawanna River runs. It cuts the city into two pieces. The mountains go up to the east toward the Poconos, and to the west there's a fairly good rise—you wouldn't call it a mountain, but then that slopes back into the valley and then the mountains go up. So it's situated right down in the mountains. It had been a very progressive city. They had one of the earliest streetcar lines. They had their own gas-generating plants for lighting and cooking purposes. The coal mines offered very lucrative employment. We had very good schools. And then we had the mountains back of us and the woods for recreation. We had good electric line service from Scranton to Wilkes-Barre, along which there were some very interesting places to go.

The Boy Scouts never wanted for a place to hike or camp. I know that there was a beautiful mansion up on the side of a mountain, and once a year we were invited there for a jamboree. This was one of the highlights of the fall season. We did take a lot of long bicycle rides, trips, and a lot of camping activities.

I haven't been back there much. The last time I was there I saw quite a lot of change. Well, first of all, in the old days the industry there other than coal was limited to silk mills. And there wasn't much more than that. There was a small operation that made silk stockings. There was another place that was called the Scranton Nut & Bolt Works that did metalworking. Outside of that there was not too much. Well, when the mines started to slack off and the miners had a strike in the middle of the winter, and forced a lot of cities like New York and Philadelphia and other places to change to oil, then the level of activity in the mines went way down. And people were in bad financial condition then. So they started to encourage industry to come in. And they have had some success to a degree. The General Electric Company went in there and opened up a plant. And several other companies went in there to make use of the excellent labor market. Because the people there are good workers. They were people that were trainable and did a good job.

I would say that Scranton as a whole went through a really tough period when the coal mines slacked off. Since then things are very well stabilized. I think that while a lot of people left Scranton, those that remained there have been gainfully employed and economically are well-to-do.

In my childhood we were in the early years of the development of the electrical industry. It wasn't too many years before that that they were experimenting with higher voltages of transmission, better efficiency in transformers and motors and things like that. The development of fascinating innovations in the use of electricity. That's when Steinmetz was with the General Electric Company and Whitney and a lot of those early pioneers were then living and working.

Well, I would say we're better off today. I would say that the average person in this country, even though we say we have a lot of poor, they don't know what being poor is. They've never tried to work in the coal mines in the wintertime when there was no work. The mines were shut down for one reason or another. We had no Social Security. We had no alternative income. And if you didn't have it and couldn't get it, you had to beg for it. We had an awful lot of poor people there. I mean poor—destitute. How they survived was to a large degree based on their willingness to work, to do anything. They didn't sit back and wait for the government to feed them. They got out—even if it was just shoveling snow or digging a garden for somebody who could afford to pay them a little bit, and they worked for very little.

Then, too, a lot of things that they did they weren't paid for in cash, they were paid in kind. We had a large garden, grew a lot of stuff. My mother canned a lot of stuff. We always had a barrel of apples and a barrel of potatoes in the cellar. These people that needed something got it if they were willing to work for it. And so they would do menial tasks, anything. And we were not wealthy. Somehow we struggled through. And everybody helped everybody else.

The earliest thing that I can remember when I was just a little boy was Mother standing me up on the kitchen table. She had made a velvet suit for me, with kind of puffy sleeves and then bloomers. And she was fitting that on me. You know, I never forgot that because I was so proud of that suit. I liked it, and Mother made it for me. Of course, she made all of our clothes then.

Well, for one thing, we never owned our own home. While my father was living, we never owned our own home. My grandmother owned it and we rented from her. My father was born in Scranton—in Taylor, just below Scranton, a suburb of Scranton. My father's family originally came from Scotland. My mother was born up on a mountain west of Scranton. Her father and mother came from Wales and they immigrated to Canada and then down into the coal-mining region because Granddad worked in the Welsh mines. So he came down there as a mine foreman.

Mother was a mountain girl. She was limited in her social contacts because they lived up in the mountains. But they had a lot of friends and she was a very active girl. My father was apprenticed as a plumber and tinsmith. And this was work that he thought he would enjoy. But as time went on, opportunities in that field were limited, and so he went with this electric line that ran from Scranton to Wilkes-Barre, as an electrician. And he had done some studying on that. I think correspondence school or something like that. Dad was a very athletic fellow. Loved ice-skating, baseball. I wouldn't say that he ran the family as such. I don't ever remember there being a question about who was boss. It was a very enjoyable childhood as far as I'm concerned. True, we were very limited in what we had. Today, when I see what the grandchildren have at Christmastime, it scares me because we got one major present and a lot of other things which mainly were clothes. We got a stocking and that had an apple in it and an orange and some nuts and a few candies, and that's all. That's all.

I remember the first thing that I had was a windup train, you know. Dad bought this little set with just a little ring around it. And since he had tinsmithing experience, he made tracks that went all over the room. Made the tracks—a beautiful job. And he made all of the stations and houses, out of metal. He was very clever with his hands. He could do most anything.

Mother was a very outgoing person, and she always had a willingness to help somebody else who needed help. She always found time to make friends and be friends. She would share anything she had with other people. During the war she took a course in practical nursing. Father died in the flu epidemic in 1919. After that, Mother then went with the district nurses' association. And she did nursing all through the city, wherever they had their stations. People would come in with their children and all, and they would counsel and guide them and help them. The last place she worked was down in what we call the Jewish flats. This was down in an area of the city that was right down at the base, right near the river. It was a big area. And it was not a predominantly Jewish settlement, but there were a lot of Jewish people who had settled there, and many of them that I went to high school with lived there or came there. That is where Mother really enjoyed that work. She said that the people who came there were delightful people to meet and work with and to help. And this was a big part of her life.

Behavior was something that was impressed upon us by my parents, strict discipline. We were taught what was right and wrong. We were also taught what our responsibilities were to other people. That is, we were not an entity unto ourselves. We were part of society, and being a part of society, we had a responsibility to take our place in it.

We learned morality mainly by day-to-day conversation, relating things that happened in and around us that were wrong, what children did that were wrong. Breaking a window, doing that, and the effect it had on other people. Why don't we do something constructive instead of some destructive action? These came about by daily counseling, discussions about right and wrong, examples of what you should do or what you shouldn't do. If I came in the house with something that didn't belong to me—"What is it?" "I found it." "Take it right back where you got it." That was that. We didn't bring anything into the house. We didn't "find" anything. I've seen boys find something with a grab, you know, and parents never do anything about it. Where that kind of permissiveness crept in, and a boy could get away with it, he wasn't apt to feel conscience-stricken if he stole something. And I knew that, and I didn't want to be like that. I have gone through five-and-ten-cent stores, and have seen my cousin and some other kid snitching this or that and putting it in their pockets. I have no part of that. Soon as I saw it, I left, I'd meet them outside. I didn't want to be involved in that.

From the time I was old enough to go off by myself, I went into the mountains. A lot of us boys went up into the mountains. We had trails and we had our places. We had a cave up there, and we stored it up so we could stay there in the winter on a cold night. As I grew older, of course, I got into activities. I played baseball—sandlot baseball, sandlot football, ice-skated. A lot of ice-skating. We had little hockey leagues where we played ice hockey of a kind, but it wasn't like you have today. Nobody got hurt and nobody got a punch in the lip, or anything.

When I got into high school, I was working, because of my father being dead. I started at eight in the morning and went to one, instead of nine to three. And then I went to work. At two o'clock I went to work in a soda fountain. I'd work there until eleven at night. And then I walked home. There were several boys who worked near each other.

We'd walk home. We'd walk to school in the morning to save five cents. About three and a half miles, at least that.

I'll tell you: If you ask me about my own family and my children's family, they were as close-knit and as happy at home as we were when I was a kid. And we were close-knit. We were never out all night. By nine o'clock we were in the house, even when I was in high school.

You have to develop a sense of family responsibility in everybody. The mother and father and the children. If you try to raise them in a controlled atmosphere, then you've got to set the patterns. You've got to set examples for them. And you can't expect the children to be conscious of their actions if the mother and father are not conscious of what they do. What they say, how they say it, their discussions—political, social, and all—the whole pattern of family development is basically the result of everybody being honest with each other in the family. Also, if the parents were wrong, the children would know it. And our reaction to their feelings would be known to them. I've seen both my son and my daughter raise their children. They were all accountable to the family. There wasn't the permissiveness that you see in a lot of families today. Permissiveness in children. Let them do what they want to do and give them everything they want. No matter what. Never make them understand the value of a dollar. These are things that have hurt the family. Another is that the mother and the father have become disoriented from the children in that they have their parties, their cocktail parties, their social time, and this takes too large a part of their life, instead of being home with the children. The children are pretty much excluded. They're home, they're with baby-sitters. You know, some of our friends do some baby-sitting around, and you wonder how the kids grow up. Here's a family with three children. This baby-sitter has been over there—they're like wild Indians. They don't pay any attention to her because they don't pay any attention to their mother.

You can see the failure of the parents in young children. They don't make discipline stick. "Don't do that." It goes right on. "I'm telling you now if I have to tell you again. I'm telling you it's going to hurt." The kids go right on, and they never get whipped.

We were at my niece's. They have two children. The little girl is a doll and she's real good. The boy—he just goes his way. They tell him he's not to do this, he's not to do that, he's not to turn that electric organ on full blast while they're trying to talk. You can't tell him. And after I sat there for a while and I listened to this, and his father promising to break both his legs and nothing happened, I went over and pulled the plug out of the wall. And I said, "Okay, boy, you've had it." He doesn't like me.

I'll tell you this, all the sexual craziness stems from permissiveness. The seeking of enjoyment and pleasure that are not offered by the home. If the kid's in the home, he's at the television alone. And it never stops. But he gets tired of that and he wants out and so he goes his merry way. And he's never punished for not being punctual in coming to meals or coming in at night or anything. They just get to go their merry way and do their thing. And then they get involved with drugs and things like that. Not all of them, but enough of them, enough percentage of them to make it evident. And then, of course, they also become involved in sexual relationships to a degree that would never have happened years ago. Because they have some safety. The biggest thing is that all of this stuff is blown up, you see it becomes front-page news every day. The media, the same way. And they display a lot of this in movies. Well, we didn't have television when we were kids. We had little radios that we built ourselves that you put earphones on and listened to KDKA and WSM. Those were all clean fun things.

The safety I mentioned is a good thing in this respect, that if you didn't have it, you wouldn't know what to do with all your unwanted children. That's about the size of it. This has been one of the things I think that has kept the population in some kind of control. Whether we have the pill or not, the kids, the way they're schooled and the way they're brought up at home, they would get into trouble. And so what? Instead of an occasional pregnancy, you'd have a whole mess of them.

Let me take my own feelings about love and lay them on the carpet. When I was at school in Washington, aside from some puppy loves in high school and all, different associations, I did meet a young lady down there that I was very much in love with. At least this is what we both thought. And we planned that someday we would get married. But several things happened.

First of all, the financial reverses that hit her father. He lost his job. And this threw the whole family into a tailspin. And forced this little gal that I knew to make a decision—she had finished high school, and now she had a responsibility to go out and help the family until the younger kids got out of high school. And so we sat down and talked it over, and she explained that, well, that she had a family obligation and she just didn't want to tie me up. And I explained to her that time was not a factor, but she decided that she was going to break off. And we did. And I think that probably was the best thing for both of us. At least we both knew where we stood. Then I met my wife through a friend. And we courted and started going together. And we would be invited to parties together.

The first time I met Mary, we were in a young people's group of the church on Sunday evening. I asked her if I could take her home. And I was an outsider. I just happened to be boarding in the house where the group's party was held. She looked a lot younger for her age. Nobody seemed to be with anybody else, and I said, "Well, is somebody going to see you home?" And she said, "Oh, yes." She had a boyfriend. Well, I didn't even see him around the place, but he was there. And we're still very good friends. Anyhow, it must have been a month or six weeks later that Mary and I were asked to be on a committee to do some planning for this young people's group. And we were to meet at her house. So we met there. I was the only one there. Nobody else showed up. So I took her to the movies. And then from then on we saw each other quite frequently. Eventually we became engaged. Now, there I feel was a situation of mutual admiration and respect, and a deep feeling that we wanted to spend our life together. Now this is what I think is the outcome of love. Not a perfect splash of passion, you know. And then cooling off. But a realization that this was our life.

We had common interests through the work in our church, and through our friendships there. We had a lot of nice associations. We started our home. And then the children came along. And I feel that we had developed a deep desire to be with each other. And we looked forward to the coming of our children, and we enjoyed our father-and-mother relationship with them as they grew up.

It's basically a part of life to reproduce. Just to reproduce indiscriminately, you see, is not a part of nature's plan, in my opinion. Human beings have developed over the years a deep understanding of parental responsibility. And children do not develop as fast as kittens. They need the help of the parents for many years, until they're able to take care of themselves. And puberty doesn't come very young in human beings. And so this means that you've got at least fourteen or fifteen years of responsibility there. It's a part of my life that has meant more to me than anything else I can think of.

I recall that one of the big things for the kiddies was when we would go out to a restaurant for dinner. They looked forward to that. And they looked forward to making their own selection of what they would like to eat. They were taught table manners at home. They were taught how they were to act when they were out, and they were just little goddesses, that's all. God and goddess. They just were perfect. We always enjoyed taking them out.

I can remember at Christmastime, when we'd have our Christmas tree and we'd have our little Christmas get-together where we'd open our gifts. These were big times. But then Christmas was more than that to them and to me because we had aunts and uncles and cousins, and we would all get together at Christmastime, and this was a tremendous time of the year for us.

I can remember taking them ice-skating. I bought them little runner skates, and Mary and I would take them ice-skating. We'd take them to the movies and all. Those were little family moments that you never forget.

Both my mother and father were people who went to church every Sunday. We went to Sunday school. We were taught our role in the church and the history of the church and all the background. We knew what Christmas meant and what Easter meant. We knew what all of the different church activities meant to us. My mother and dad were active to some degree in church work. Not as much as we are today. But nevertheless, when we had dinner, grace was said. We were thankful for our food.

We were also taught that part of Christian living was clean hands and a clean mind and clean clothes. Cleanliness. This carried through in our life. Both my sister and I grew up knowing it. I became associated with the Boy Scouts, and she was associated with some of the girls' groups up at church. It was always church-oriented. I never got involved with a group of fellows who hung around the corner. This was just not allowed. If we wanted friends, we brought them home. They were always welcome there. And if we went to somebody else's home, we had to say where we were going to be and when we were going to be home. So our schedule was regulated.

So most of these things that we were associated with were religiously oriented. There's a lot of personal satisfaction, you see, in following through with your religious beliefs. And associating with people who, like yourself, are church-oriented. And whose activities and associations are the kind that you're proud of. I have refrained from joining some organizations—this was back before I retired—because I felt that the biggest part of their program was drinking, having a bar and going in there and sitting around and drinking. This I shied away from. Not that I'm against drinking as such. I'll take a drink myself. But I didn't think that it should be that much a part of my life.

As I grew older, I did have some problems with health. The biggest catastrophe was that I fell and fractured my hip, and it took quite a while to pull out of that. It's just like everything else. It's all in a day's work. You've got it, so you've got to live with it. You may just as well be happy and let it go at that. To sit down and cry about misfortunes is a crime. When I had this misfortune, the fractured hip, when my wife came into the hospital, I was sitting there with a big grin on, and I said, "Hi, sweetheart." Well, she was about ready to cry. And I said, "Now, look, tears ain't gonna help anything. We got it. We gotta live with it. And that's it. And I'm going to get out of here as quick as I can."

When I was a younger boy, I remember I had a little altercation with another lad, and I beat the liver out of him. I never forgave myself for that. I was bigger than he was, and it was just one of these flash things. Somebody says something or somebody says you said something. Bang! And I was awfully quick. And I beat the liver out of him. And after that, I had remorse. I felt awfully sorry about it. And I figured, Well, he'd have done the same to me if he could. I didn't feel happy about doing that. And so I apologized to him and I told him that that would never happen again. It wasn't that I was afraid of my strength, really. No, I don't think so. My dad always taught me that fear was man's worst enemy. And a lot of things you fear never happen anyway. So he said you can't think and act sensibly if you're wrapped up in fear. Fear is something you're going to have to control, and this is something I have preached for many years.

We've been to Alaska, Hawaii, Germany, Italy, Austria, Switzerland. All those. We've been to Portugal, Spain, Morocco, Mexico, Puerto

Rico. Well, the standard thing is it broadens you. I understand, it means it broadens you literally if you keep eating. But it has been a tremendous experience for myself and my wife to go to these places and meet people who live in different environments and see how they manage in those environments. We were up through Alaska and we went clear up above the Arctic Circle, a 90-percent Eskimo population. And you could see that they were prepared to live in their environment because they had dogs by the hundreds. And they had dogsleds. And they had snowshoes hanging up. You saw fish drying on the rack. And you saw these people shuffling along, and then you realized that we couldn't exist in that kind of atmosphere. We couldn't. But the one thing that brought this home to me, and one of the reasons why I was interested in getting up there was that I met an Eskimo woman down at the arena in Philadelphia, ice-skating. I was teaching an Eskimo how to ice-skate. This girl came from an island up there, and they were taken off the island during the war. An explorer who went up there brought her and her family down here with their dogs, and their array of everything, for exhibit at Gimbels in Philadelphia. She just lived here for a while, just during this Christmas period. So anyway, she said she had never seen an American home at Christmastime. And I said, "I'll come down and get you." So I did. She came out, and she talked to a whole group of young ladies from the missionary society. She told in detail all about her homeland and her father, who was then 80. And he was straight as a ramrod, and he was quite an unusual person. She said that all of their things were left right on the island, everything they had was there. And when they go back, they'll be there for them. Other people will take care of them, and nothing will be gone. If a dog dies, they will make a record of it. But nobody would take anything that belongs to somebody else. I remembered her story and when we had a chance to visit Alaska, we went.

I can think of individuals who have strongly impressed me. One of them was Professor Bliss. He taught one of the largest Bible classes in Washington, D.C. His class met in a theater, and I went down there many times. He was head of the electrical school I went to. He was one of the Edison pioneers. He worked with Edison. And every day we had a session—not preaching but how to live and how to live right. It was a philosophy on good living. He talked about all the prerequisites for a good life. Honesty in dealing. Love your neighbor. Don't do something for somebody else just to get paid for it. Always feel that you are your brother's keeper. You see somebody going astray or needs help, step in and give him a hand. If your help is welcome.

I've always felt that women already had rights. And I always felt that my wife, to begin with, at home, had a right to discussion of our plans and programs, our finances and things like that. I felt that I couldn't be dictatorial because that would rob her of her rights as a mother, and in her home. Now, when you talk about women in general, I feel that they ought to have equal rights within their capabilities. I mean that if a woman has the capability of becoming a good engineer, then there is no reason why she should ever be excluded from the engineering circles. I happen to know a daughter of one of our good friends who studied engineering when I was at Drexel, and she became an engineer.

I know a number of women who became doctors, and they became doctors when we were just people. They became doctors, and they went into the mission field as doctors.

If my wife went and applied for a job that she had the qualifications for and they told her they wouldn't hire a woman, that would upset me, but only to this degree. If it was a job that I would want to see her working in, it would bother me that she was excluded because she was a woman. But if it was a job that I didn't think she was capable of handling because of certain things, or there was danger involved in it and all, then I would not object.

I probably am as much pro–civil rights as anybody could be. I grew up in an atmosphere where we had Polish and Slavic and Lithuanians and Welsh and Irish and Scottish and German and everything else. We had a smorgasbord of nationalities right in the coalfields there. I had a colored boy playing on the football team with me. We never made anything of that. We were all friends. We were all good sportsmen, too. Nobody ever called a friend of mine a dago, you know, with the idea of being slurry about it, without getting a punch in the nose. We had everything.

I never could condone slavery, as such, although it was past my time. I had a man working for me one time and there was some kind of colored fellow did something—rape or something like that. And he was bitter. He said they ought to have open season for them like they have for rabbits. And I said, Well, it's all very well for you to talk like that, but don't forget that these people never came here on their own volition. They were dragged here in terrible circumstances. Many of them died getting here. They were brutally treated. And they by and large were just what they were, slaves. They didn't have the right to make decisions for themselves. I said, I can't condone that kind of behavior. And I can't forgive at all the white men who ever became a party to it.

I suppose that there are some people who will never be satisfied with anything. In my industrial experience, you see, I ran into very, very few people who were dissatisfied with their jobs. Now there were some people who would rather do something else. And I kept close to my people. My door was always open. They could come in and talk to me if they had any problems. I was on the floor. I didn't live in my office. I was on the floor.

Should you just work for the sake of the dollar or should you work because you need the money to live, and you enjoy your work, too? I would never want to work just for the dollar, at things I didn't like. No. I was very fortunate in enjoying all of my industrial life. There were some things that were bothersome to me at times. But that's all part of the work. But I enjoyed going in in the mornings.

I'll tell you how I feel about America. These little things that come up from time to time, like Watergate and some of the other scandals and some of our congressmen getting into trouble with gals and things like that—these are all passing things. If you start to look at your country from the little nits and bits, then you can get damned dissatisfied. But if you've read your history, you've seen how we started, with a bunch of trees and some brush, and how we have grown into a mighty industrial complex, you realize the tremendous technical advances that have been made. Then you have to be glad you're here. And I think we've got a wonderful country.

I don't think that we're as philosophical as we ought to be, in many respects. But I'm not a liberal radical. I'm not even a liberal. I would say that I was a very careful conservative. I don't think that we are very philosophical when generations of people are born and raised on welfare. I do not believe that that's the right way to do it. They ought to be working for something and not sitting at home and getting money to spend in the beer hall and letting the kids get a square meal at school instead of at home. Now, this is not good philosophy. It's a degree of liberalism that is stupid, in my opinion.

I've seen many Presidents. I go back quite a ways. One President that I was sorry ever was in there was Woodrow Wilson. I think that was a mistake. I think that he was a college professor with a lot of long hair, and he couldn't see through the hair. That's about the size of it. And his handling of the German threat was bad. But then a lot of other people made mistakes on the other side of the water, too. There were several Presidents that I had a lot of respect for. I think that Teddy Roosevelt was one of those dynamic individuals who get something done. And he had a chin that would stick out far enough to get it done. I think he did a good job. I think Herbert Hoover was an excellent man. But he got gummed up in the political infighting, and a lot of the things that he could've done were denied him because of just what we have today—a Congress and a President and they're always at each other's throat. I liked Ike. I thought he was very good. He had the experience in life of handling large groups of men, and I think that he had the executive capabilities that I liked. He didn't get everything done that he'd like to do. This is where the breaks are. There's a lot of flat motion in this area. But I'll tell you, one fellow that I had a lot of respect for was Kennedy. While I didn't vote for him, and I wouldn't vote for him if he were running again, I was right in his corner when he told the Russians you get the hell out of Cuba or we'll put you out. Now this indicated a degree of intestinal fortitude that commanded respect.

I recommended retirement early to a number of people. I have seen some men who if they went out before 65, they would just go to pieces. I don't think they would survive very long. And I wouldn't recommend early retirement for those. But I have recommended early retirement for people who I felt were reaching a climax in physical endurance. And that sometimes indicates some degree of mental instability. I thought that they'd be so much better off if they would retire early.

I had worked it out long before. And I was very well prepared for it. In 1953 they reorganized the plant and they split it up into these separate divisions and brought in what they call professional business management types. It wasn't quite the same to me. I come home then, and I told Mary that I was going to retire when I'm 60 years old. I said, We're going to make plans now to do that. Bob and Jean were married, and I said, Now we've got that off our back, we've got our house in good condition. We've got a new car, we've got this, now we're going to start working for ourselves. And we started our investment plans, and we knew exactly what we were going to do—we were going to come down here to Maryland.

And then we started working with drawings. Friends of mine would bring me these architectural drawings of homes all over the country, and we would study them, we'd go over magazines, and finally we come up with a composite drawing of our home. We didn't want anything pretentious. We wanted to live on just a normal scale. But we knew what we wanted.

So I taught Mary how to lay out her dream house. And then after she got the basic plan laid, then I went over and I started to edit it. I'd say, Well, now if we make this this way, standard wallboard will do this, and standard timber will do that. And we worked it out, what became a study in economics. So that we could accommodate our basic plans to a respectable economic base. Then I made up the working drawings. By the time we were ready to talk to a builder, we had all these plans. And when I sat down with him, he said, "Where did you get these?" I said, "Well, my wife and I drew them up." So he offered me a job. He said he needed a man on the board and wanted to know if I'd go to work for him. I said, "No way." We had our plans made, the transition was painless.

Instead of going around the plant on the last day of work, you know, going around and shaking hands with all those hundreds of people, I did my daily rounds and I saw most everybody that was in my organization there. My replacement was in an office. Two years before I retired, he was there and I was on special assignment. I gave them plenty of time to be ready for it. And after I had done my morning's round, I went in and saw a few of my old friends, sat down, and talked with them a little bit. Then I just quietly walked out.

I have an awful lot of respect for tools and how to use them. And I've had people around here who have borrowed some of my tools and they abused them. Burn them out. Then they bring them back and hand them to you. And this is the one thing that I can't take. It grinds me a little bit.

Another thing that really angers me as much as anything is to see anybody abusing a good piece of equipment. An automobile. See a jackass get out there when the temperature is down about ten above zero, get out there and start roaring before it has a chance to get any oil in there. Now this is bad. And another thing that I can't take is anybody abusing an animal. I can't do that. I love them.

I think that the next generation will do much better than we did in many things. But not all things. There is one thing that I don't think the next generation will be prepared to do, and that is to learn to manage on an economy that is going down. I don't think that they'll know how to face the kind of thing. They've never had to do it. They never had the Depression. A lot of these people coming up now never knew what the Depression was. They never knew the impact of economic failure. And in that area I think they're going to have trouble. In other areas, I think the intellectual capabilities of our young people are going to be much higher than today, and, of course, in my generation it was much higher than before. And that's to be expected.

I have a granddaughter who is the brain. She's the tops. The best in everything she does—athletics or anything else. She couldn't see finishing high school when there was nothing more for high school to offer. So she left high school in her junior year and started college at the University of Alabama. Now she has been in advanced studies down there, and this one professor says to her, "I don't see your name on my senior list." She says, "I'm not a senior, I'm only a freshman." He says, "What?" "Oh, yes," she says. He says, "You're so far ahead of all the rest of them." And so this is what it looks like for the future, the next generation.

Being of Scottish descent, I think that basically Scottish people look at the realities of life as they are. Somebody's going to live and somebody's going to die. I don't fear death, and I'm not concerned about it. I'll live my time out and that's it. I don't feel the emotional distress that some people feel. I've seen them go emotionally crazy because of somebody dying. And you go to one of their funerals and they get hysterical. You don't see that at any Scottish funeral. You never see that. In all my family life, you know, as a boy and all, I could never remember any hysterical emotion as you will see in some kinds of people.

I think that everybody ought to live the best life they can. Now, for some people it depends upon their ideals. If they have low ideals, they're going to live low, that's all. If their ideals are high, they'll live high. My own feeling on the matter is that when I die, I'm sure that I'll feel that I have lived a good life. I've enjoyed life. I've had some of the comforts of living. I've seen some of the distress that economics can have on people. And more. I have a friend who is starting to pull out of a bad case of alcoholism. I have stayed by that fellow for the last couple of years and he is beginning to show some signs now that things are going to straighten out. I feel that this is part of my Christian duty, to help a fellow like him. I help neighbors around here if they've got a problem. Just a few hours ago we were over to see a fellow who couldn't get his truck running. Two garages couldn't do anything. And I went over there and I knew what was wrong, and we worked it out and it's running like a top now.

I live day to day. We don't live for tomorrow as such. We don't go too far in the future. You don't know what it's going to be. All we have to do is to try to maintain some stability in our finances so that we can pay our bills, eat well, and just enjoy life.

# Marjorie Bitker

$M$arjorie Bitker, a woman of understated elegance and intelligence, likes to sit at the window of her duplex apartment in Milwaukee, look out at the calm of Lake Michigan, and talk about her life. It has been a productive one.

She was born in New York on February 9, 1901, the only child of a credit manager from New Orleans and a Brooklyn-born mother. She spent her earliest years in Harlem, on 131st Street between Lenox and Seventh avenues. She attended the Horace Mann School and then Barnard College, from which she graduated in 1921 as an English major. She got her master's in English from Columbia shortly thereafter and began a career as a writer, doing newspaper features and poetry. In 1922 she married James Jacobson, fresh out of Harvard. They had three daughters, while living first on Long Island, later back in the city. During the Depression Marjorie Jacobson worked in a department store. As the economy failed, so did her marriage; she divorced her husband in 1942. That same year she was remarried, to John Mayer, a widower with three children, and they settled in the venerable Beresford on Manhattan's West Side.

In 1945 they moved into a building on East Ninety-fourth Street; a few days later, Mayer died of a heart attack. She was left well off, but alone for the first time in her life. She worked in book publishing—as a copy editor, then an editor: for Farrar, Straus, and Company, G. P. Putnam's Sons, and David McKay. She taught writing at Hunter College; wrote for The New Yorker, The American Mercury, and other magazines; and opened her own editorial consultation service. In 1957, while on vacation at Martha's Vineyard, she met a lawyer from Milwaukee; she married him and moved to his hometown, where she has lived ever since.

Her life is a full one. She plays tennis, swims, walks. She keeps in touch with her daughters and her grandchildren. She contributes book reviews and articles to the Milwaukee Journal. She is at work on a book about her childhood. Recently two novels she wrote years ago were issued in paperback, Gold of Evening and A Different Flame. She *reads extensively, loves music, theater as well. She keeps in touch with the world. She enjoys remembering the past without being rooted in it.*

When I was about 18 months old, we moved from 131st Street down to 124th Street, between Broadway and Amsterdam. It was called Elmore Court, 541 West 124th Street. It was in the neighborhood of Columbia University, and I believe is now Morningside Gardens. And I remember the whole block very well. There were a lot of kids on the block, and I learned to roller-skate there. And one of the little girls that I played with was Fanny Halberg, whose father was a Swedish engineer who came to complete the subway. He worked on the part of the subway that emerges from the ground at 117th or 118th Street. And I remember Fanny and her little brother and I were treated to a preview of the subway. We went all the way down to the Battery and then up into the air. I remember that very well. It was a very family-oriented neighborhood. A lot of Columbia professors lived on that street. And Fanny and I used to play with our dolls. I have a complete baby book, incidentally.

My mother kept my baby book since I was an only child. She hadn't any other children to bother with. She kept my baby book from the day I was born until the day I was married. And it is such a period piece. You just never saw anything like it. All the costumes, bathing suits, stockings, terrific.

Well, anyway, when I was 5 years old, I guess it was, I went to kindergarten at a school which was only a few blocks away. But I also remember that in the good weather I used to be taken to Riverside Drive, either by my mother or by our general houseworker. We had a maid by the name of Hannah who had never worked for anyone else. She came to my mother when she was about 17 or 18 years old. And I really never liked her very much, but she adored me. She used to call me "Honeybunch." And every time she said "Honeybunch" I would quiver. She would take me to the park, and I remember she had friends on 122nd Street, which is where we went into the park. One set of her friends ran a little tintype store. And it always smelled of the acid that they used to develop the tintypes. I had a picture in my baby book of Hannah and me in the tintype store. And another hangout of hers was Grant's Tomb. It's still there. I remember Grant's Tomb for several reasons. One is that she had quite a little flirtation going— Hannah did—with the custodian of the tomb, whose name was Colonel Burnside. I don't think he was a colonel. I think he was a self-made colonel. But I remember playing stoopball against the side of the tomb and also roller-skating madly around it because there were no curbs. And my mother would say, "Where are you going today, dear?" And I would say, "To the tomb." Which was a very normal thing for me to say.

I also remember my Flexible Flyer. There's a wonderful coasting hill down the side, across the drive from the tomb. I remember doing that. And in the summertime I was among the first little girls to wear middy and bloomers. And we used to have a little coterie of kids that would roll down the hill in our middies and bloomers. And we used to have charades and play statue there. And at that time there were still horses on the bridle path occasionally.

There were some private houses. I remember the Doelger mansion— the Doelger brewery, I think it was. And then there was the Schinasi house, which is down on 107th Street that is now an adjunct of Barnard, I believe. It was white marble.

And then another thing that I remember very well, there was a very darling young woman, Diana Rice, I think. And she used to ride a motorcycle all by herself, clad in pants. And that was, you know, way back in the beginning of the century. And I also remember the Iron Steamboats. Every summer we'd take the Iron Steamboat to Coney Island. We felt Coney Island was not very chic. We went to Luna Park. My mother thought it was nicer. My mother always liked things nicer. But I remember best the taste of Durkee's salad dressing, which we used to have on our sandwiches. I haven't tasted it since then. And, let me see, my father was a great sightseer, and my father used to take me to different places on Sunday mornings. We really covered all the wonderful museums. We went to the Bronx Zoo. We went to the Central Park Zoo. We went to the old aquarium down at the Battery. Of course, we took the subway. I'm sure we took the subway to the aquarium. I think the first time we went under the river to Brooklyn, because my grandfather lived in Brooklyn, that was an adventure. And when I was very little, I remember we used to go to visit my grandfather, my mother's father, who lived on Bergen Street in Brooklyn.

And we used to take the trolley car and then the ferry and then another trolley car.

I remember the horse-drawn trolleys because I had orthodontia, although it was called straightening your teeth in those days—and our dentist lived near Mount Morris Park. And when I was old enough, I would be allowed to go by myself, along Saint Nicholas Avenue, which was a diagonal street, and there were horse cars there. I remember that. But I remember best the fact that the dentist had a little girl by the name of Aline, and she had a whole set of Elsie Dinsmore books. And I wasn't allowed to read them at home. So I would leave early, and my mother would say, "You don't have to go so early, dear." And I'd say, "Oh, well, it's so nice out," or something like that. And then I'd go and catch up on my Elsie Dinsmore. I think my teeth were all right before I finished the set.

I think for people who were middle class like ourselves, almost everyone had a maid in the house. We were not at all wealthy. We got by all right. But we always had Hannah in the house. So that my mother was able to get away. She never cooked anything except once in a while a chocolate cake, or some salad. But Hannah did everything. Hannah cleaned. We had a cleaning woman in, too. And now no matter how well off people are today, there just isn't any service in the house, so that women have to do everything. I think women have a much tougher time now as far as physical labor is concerned in spite of the labor-saving devices.

America has become motorized for one thing. It was very rare to have cars in those days. My uncle had a Pierce-Arrow landaulet, and that was the first car in the family. Formerly, he had a summer carriage and a winter carriage, and the horses were named Caesar and Cicero. I think the motorization of America is one great difference. And of course, the fact that people without very much money can travel and do travel. Travel is much easier now. But I think the great difference in people's lives, aside from the electronic age and all that sort of thing, is the gap that's developed between parents and children, between the generations. Seems to me that's one of the most important things that has happened.

I obstructed myself. My parents didn't marry until they were fairly old. My mother was 29 and my father was eleven years older. So that I grew up with old parents. And my mother was so delighted to have a child, she doted on me. I remember being doted on. She would come to school and dote in the kindergarten and in the first grade and so on, and it really embarrassed me as a child. She always made my clothes. She wanted to see if my skirt was hanging properly. And the teacher finally had to ask her not to come because it upset the class.

I was embarrassed by being the center of attention at home, and I loved going to other people's houses, where there were other children to play with. And in my class in school I developed very strong friendships, which sometimes my mother encouraged, but sometimes she didn't. And she was always in cahoots with the teacher, because I was always a very good student and a model little girl, very well behaved. And I really got very sick of that role.

My father was very scholarly. He was a Shakespeare scholar. He loved William Cullen Bryant. He could quote Alexander Pope by the yard. And he grew up in Harlem. There was quite a little subculture in Harlem. He belonged to the Rowing Society and the Shakespeare Society. And he used to read to me. He read me poetry, and he also read the funny papers in his Morris chair. That was a big deal. And he was very proud of the fact that I began to like to write stories myself.

I have no idea who set the rules. But I remember once I was spanked with the back of a hairbrush for telling a lie which I hadn't told. So my mother said, "You do it, Cecil." His name was Cecil Alexander Marks. And so poor Cecil had to go into the bathroom, put me over his knee, and he didn't spank me very hard. And they were both crying. All of us were crying. That was the only time.

I think my father was the least successful in an economic sense. He was the only one who stayed North. The rest of his family went back South, to New Orleans. Except one brother who worked for the Customs House in New York. My father was very scholarly, always was the historian or the secretary of any organization that he belonged to. He was quite introverted. But my mother always regarded him as the perfect gentleman. And his habits were exact. He always smelled of bay rum. And he would take exactly forty minutes in the bathroom in the morning, and his breakfast would be ready. And he would come out looking just beautiful, with his collar and his tie. He always was immaculately dressed. And he carried a cane. And when we didn't go to museums and things, then we would call on different relatives. We had stacks of relatives in New York, and he always looked wonderful, with his cane and his derby hat. He kept on working until he was in his eighties. He founded the credit men's association for the cloak and suit industry. And he always felt socially far superior to the people he worked for. He was very conscious of family. And he was a very proud son of the American Revolution. The family had come to New Orleans in time for the Revolution. They were Sephardic Jews. And I think they came via Jamaica to the South. And that part of the family stayed in the South. I think my father's branch of the family came from England. There was a slipper in the family. I don't know who has it now. Worn by a Jewish lady-in-waiting to Queen Victoria.

My mother was the youngest in a large family, and her mother died when she was born. She was very pretty and rather plump. She loved to eat. And she was giggly. She was brought up by her three older sisters. They took her in turn. When my grandfather married again, it was against the wishes of the three sisters, and they said they wouldn't want my mother brought up by "that woman." So they did it. And she spent a good part of her life in Owego, New York. Not Oswego, but Owego, which is in the western part of New York State. One of her sisters—Aunt Gussie, married to Uncle Robert—had a big house there at 15 Park Street. It was a lovely little town. Not even a trolley car there. It was a railroad junction. And my mother grew up there, and she was really kind of a country girl at heart. I think that was the part of her life that took, because she was a middle and older teen-ager when she was there. And she was very sociable. Had very nice friends, and was always greatly in demand for sewing circles and things of that sort. And by osmosis she drifted to the Spanish and Portuguese synagogue down on Seventieth Street and Central Park West, where she headed up a sewing circle. And she did that until she was too old to enjoy it anymore. She also worked for the draft board in World War I, and had a plaque which she was very proud of. She was a very good housekeeper.

I really have total recall. It's terrible. I remember playing on the stoop of 541 West 124th Street with our doll carriages. And I had a wonderful big doll given to me by my father's oldest sister, who was like a mother to him because it was such a big family. And she gave me this lovely doll with real hair, which I named for myself. And this was the pride of the neighborhood. I remember a lot of things for that block. I remember having what they called a water blister on my heel, because I wore barefoot sandals. And my mother went into a panic everytime there was something the matter with me. And she borrowed a baby buggy, although they called them go-carts in those days, from a little boy called Virgil, whose father was a professor at Columbia. And I had a yellow powder called Dermatol on my heel, and I was wheeled around and I felt terribly ashamed. I must have been 4 years old at the time. I also remember there was a Miss Smith who had been watching me when I was playing in Riverside Park. And one day she approached my mother and said, "I've been watching your little girl. She is very expressive. And I would like to do a series of pictures of her for *Good Housekeeping*. I'm doing a series called Small Cruelties to Children." So by golly, she did. I still have the pictures. They're in my baby book. I had to sit with my chin on the table. And try to eat with my arm, very uncomfortable. I was dragged up onto a trolley car with a step that was too high, by my armpit. And I remember that very well.

And I remember I must have been older, but not old enough to be in school. I had a cousin—I had a lot of first cousins—and this first cousin was a doctor who had just gotten his M.D. His name was Clarence Bandler. He had opened an office on 102nd Street near Broadway. And he didn't have very many patients. So my mother and I would sit there like shills, you know, hoping to attract customers. And one day I was sitting there looking at a magazine and there was a terrific explosion in the street. I remember it very well. And then there were terrible screams and yells, and down the street there staggered a workman bleeding. He had been working on the street sewers or something, and the dynamite had exploded. Well, that was Clarence's first real patient. He dashed out into the street. I think I might be afraid of loud noises anyway, but that explosion really did something to me for life. I really start like a deer whenever I hear anything like that.

It seems to me I learned from both parents that one of the most important things was education. And also I think by reverse I dreaded being conspicuous. They wanted me to be conspicuous, and so I hated to show off. But the things that they taught me, that to work and to work for something that I believed in, was important. And I think that was the best thing I ever learned from them. I also learned, in reverse, not to dote on my own children.

My father was a great walker, and so was my mother. And as she grew heavier and became older, she wasn't able to walk so much because her feet hurt her so. And that was really one of the great crosses she had to bear. I'm still a tennis player. Although I have a torn cartilage now. And I can't play without a knee brace and it slows me up. I used to be very fast. And I learned to enjoy small towns, because the one time I visited Owego when I was 11 years old, I simply loved the quiet and the neighborliness of the town. And I think that's one reason why I like Milwaukee so much, because it's like a small town in a certain way. Although it has a million and a half population.

I think everyone in New York is an island. And the only thing I ever belonged to there, aside from Barnard Alumnae Association, was a little sort of public relations group. But here, of course, my husband has been a public character for a long time. And he's been very active in all sorts of interreligious and civic things. So the fact that he was interested in public service oriented me towards that.

I think I followed the rather strict code of my parents. I was really quite a prissy little girl and the one time when I stepped out, I became friends with a whole group who were very silly. This was in around the sixth or seventh grade in school. And my grades dropped. But I was having a wonderful time for the first time in my life. I really had some friends who were very close to me. And we had secrets. And my mother stepped in and broke it up. And I skipped a grade. That was how we did that. I never had any desire really to overstep the moral code of my parents. My father was the most upright man. If he walked off by mistake with a dime, he walked a mile to return it. That was the sort of person he was.

The family unit, as it existed then, is hard to find these days. I do think that part of it has to do with advances in technology. That women can get away and still do their housework. Also I think TV has a lot to do with it. I think that children get ideas from TV. In the old days you went to the movies, and that was an event. It was a thing like going to a stage play or reading a book. It didn't have very much relation to life. It was a treat. But now, children are exposed to TV all the time. Not only as targets for advertising, but also suggesting behavior. And I think that may have something to do with it, too.

I think it begins earlier, the fact that women are out of the house more. I always had a nurse for my kids. Even though we didn't have much money, there was always someone with the children. They weren't left to themselves. But my daughters can't afford that. The children are left by themselves a great deal, much more than they used to be. The mother is not a presence in the home.

I'm writing a book, and it's called *Teachers for Lunch*. And it is about exactly the period that I was referring to. It's about the early days in New York, when the highlight of my school year was having the teacher for lunch. And I remember exactly the way the table was set. The menu was nearly always the same. And the teachers loved to come because Hannah was a very good cook. And the teacher was looked up to. And now the teachers are not—at least very few. I think an awful lot of little girls that I knew used to invite the teachers for lunch. And then the children would be sent out of the room, and the mother would discuss with the teacher how the little dears were getting along, etc. I was talking about that the other day—I gave a little talk at the local Jewish community center, and later on we were talking about the attitude of children towards teacher. And they don't have the teachers for lunch anymore.

Believe me, in the days of the flappers, that was a sexual revolution. They were just beginning—the Scott Fitzgerald generation, and the John Held generation. The girls would park their girdles in the cloakroom, and quite a few of the girls who were in my class at college were very risqué by standards then. I think I was just beginning then. I think it was the result of World War I, probably. That was at the end of World War I.

In some ways, I think the pendulum has swung too far. I do. I really feel that sex is a private affair, and that what you do is nobody's business except your own. And if you choose to step out, okay, but let's not send off skyrockets about it.

Love is a very deep-seated feeling. It depends on what the love object is. If it's a love for a child, it's one thing. A man and woman— well, I think that it can't really be defined. It's something that you feel very deeply. You have a feeling that even if you know the person that you love has faults, you forgive him because you love him. And it's something that you don't know anything about until you go through it yourself.

In a successful marriage you have to be very sure that both people are grown up enough to understand the main fibers of life. Speaking of my own experience in my first marriage, we were both very young.

I was 21 and he was 22. And we were both babes in the woods. And he had never done anything, except work for his father. And I had never done anything except a little writing. And it was a stupid marriage. Nowadays we would've just lived together, except that I was so shy I wouldn't have done it.

I met him when I was 14 years old, and I was invited by my Camp Fire Girl leader to a house party down in Woodmere, Long Island. She was newly married, and she had a friend who had a niece just about my age. So the two of us were invited to this house party. And she asked a few boys who lived around, and Jim Jacobson was one of them. He was very handsome. Blond, handsome, athletic. He was just a few months older than I. And that was the first time I met him. Then when I was older, just after my freshman year, I took a job as a sort of day-camp counselor in that area, and he was home from prep school some-where—and he was even handsomer. And I remember meeting him for tennis. We both played tennis. He was a very good companion. We had a grand time together. He was crazy about me, and I think that was it. Well, we kept on being friends. And the year I graduated from college, which was 1921, he went abroad. He had graduated from Harvard, and he went abroad with the Harvard Glee Club as a sort of post–World War I gesture. Franco-American . . . and I was given a trip abroad by my parents. We got engaged in Paris. It was very nice. In the Bois. And then I got cold feet because I didn't think I loved him, and so we broke it off. And then I didn't see him for a long, long time. And then we got engaged again. And my parents were very much in favor of him. I had a few other beaus by that time, but they were pushing for this. Yes, we had a fairly long history. And we were very happy for quite a few years. I think probably the Depression did us in. But we did have our daughters. Emmy was my first baby. I thought I never wanted to do anything at all in the whole world except take care of that baby. And my mother-in-law insisted that I get a nurse. "Get a nurse, I don't want you washing the diapers—my daughter-in-law." So I did. I enjoyed all the children. I loved having the children. And after the first one, which was difficult, the other two were very easy, and I always had plenty of help in the house.

The children used to love to go swimming when we stayed in Long Island for the summer. We used to go swimming. And I remember the first one, of course, the one that makes the biggest dent. And Emmy talked very early and walked very early. And she was really a very unusual little girl. She was terribly bright. And she used to say very funny things. And they were all very different. And I enjoyed the difference. And one of the difficult things about splitting up was that the youngest was only 11 when it happened. But they discovered that the only stipulation was that there would be no custody. Wherever the children wanted to stay and it was convenient, they could do so. And that's the way it worked out. Well, I had a lawyer who had been through this himself. And he said this is the one thing he would recommend. And it worked out very well. I think I'm closer to all of my daughters than most mothers are to their grown-up daughters.

I had a bout of religious fervor. Part of it was just conformity, and part of it was need. There was a Jewish quota in the Horace Mann School. And it was a very small quota. And most of the girls that I went around with went to church and to Sunday school, and I felt quite deprived. I had taken Bible lessons with my little cousins, one cousin older and one cousin younger. The teacher was Miss Hadassah Levine, every Friday afternoon, and she would teach us Bible. And I don't know whether it was Miss Hadassah Levine, or the fact that the other children went to Sunday school and I didn't. My father was a complete agnostic, even though his brother-in-law was a rabbi in New Orleans. And my mother had been brought up as a Presbyterian in Owego because there were no Jews in Owego, so all of my Aunt Gussie's family went to the Presbyterian church. And I was weaned on all the Presbyterian hymns and so on. So anyway, I wanted to go to Sunday school. My parents talked it over, and they consulted Uncle Ben who was a pillar of Temple Emmanuel. And I did go to Temple Emmanuel, and immediately won prizes for Hebrew and a medal and so on and so on. I really felt the religion very deeply until the rabbis got into the act. I identified with the history, the Bible, the ideas—and the psalms I can quote by the yard. They're wonderful, and I still think about them. But when the rabbis got into the act, it seemed to me those particular rabbis gave me the creeps. One of them had a style of delivery that was like Moses on Mount Sinai. He thundered and then he whispered. And the other one had an oleaginous voice. That's the only way I can describe it. I was very sensitive to sounds. I am interested in music. And I think sounds have always had a great effect on me. But I think it was the feeling of their hands on my head when they blessed me. I just didn't care for it. I did belong to the

Temple Emmanuel Junior Society and had a few boys from there call on me. My mother was glad I had social opportunities. There was a little boy called Elwood Feldstein, who was in love with me and had me down to meet his parents. And another little boy called Elsworth Solomon came to call on me on his roller skates. But nothing took, and I left the fold.

I think I am back more now. My husband is very unreligious. He's very pro-Zionist and always has been. He's always belonged to all the Zionist organizations. He's a political Jew. I don't know what else you'd call it. But he does not believe in going to temple. And I have deep religious feelings, but I think they were more influenced by Bertrand Russell than they were by any rabbi. Once Bertrand Russell came to Barnard and talked about his book A *Free Man's Worship*. I think that had more effect on me than Temple Emmanuel. And then I had one very good friend who was a liberal Catholic. This was when I was a young married with three kids. Her name was Dorothea Claflin. And she was a Carroll of Carrollton—you know, the people that founded Baltimore. She had been born Dorothea Carroll. And I was reading Sigrid Undset's *The Burning Bush* at the time, and I went to a few masses and to a few services and so on. And I was tempted. But then that was all—I believe now that all religions are true and no religions are true. I think it's just a matter of concept, that's all. That's how I feel about it now. But I relate to the Jews.

I don't need a great deal of sleep. That's premise number one. I've always needed exercise, and I've always played tennis or roller-skated or done something like that. I won tennis tournaments. I was the Barnard tennis champion. And when I first moved out here, I didn't know what to do with myself. I had very nice in-laws, but after all I was new in the community. So I joined the Jewish Community Center and there was an exercise group. Every Monday and Thursday at nine thirty. And I went to it, and we played badminton. Then I discovered there was a tennis group, and I joined the tennis group. And I played indoors in the winter, and outdoors in the summer. And until last year I was a member of a tennis team. In fact, I was the oldest living member, and we won. But this darn cartilage separated.

Anyway, I take walks when I can. And I'm going to start swimming, because I don't think I'll be able to play tennis unless I have an operation, and that's dumb at my age. So I get up very early in the morning.

I'm up at five o'clock every single morning. That's my working time. And I read and work at my desk in the morning. And then, if the weather is decent, I take a good long walk and that's about it.

I have been afraid. I was afraid once when I was taking a plane trip. I was terrified before my first plane trip, which was a perfectly lovely trip from Boston to New York in the moonlight. And there were clouds and it was like going over snow. So I soon forgot to be afraid. Then there was the trip I took to meet Emmy at a dude ranch. And the flight to Bozeman was very good. And then we had to take a little plane, a one-motor plane through the Rockies. And I was simply terrified. And sitting next to me was a girl who was green in the face. And I said, "Are you frightened?" And she said, "Yes." And I said, "Is this your vacation?" She said, "Yes." I said, "What do you do when you're not on vacation?" She said, "I'm an airline stewardess."

And coming back on that same trip, I was alone. And when we left Chicago, the captain spoke and he said, "I want to warn you, we are expecting quite a lot of turbulence." So on my way back to the facility, I said to the stewardess, "Ha ha, turbulence. This isn't turbulence." She said, "Madame, I don't think we've had it yet." And I've never been on such a flight in my life. The plane was quite empty and there was a man sitting across the aisle, and he was terrified, too. Thunder, lightning. And they couldn't land. They couldn't land at what was then Idlewild, and they went to Newark. They went to Allentown. They went all over the place. And this man came over and sat next to me and he said, "Are you frightened? I'm frightened too." Okay. Well, he told me the story of his life. He was a refrigerator salesman. And he said, "If we get down, will you have dinner with me?" So I said, "Yes, I'd be glad to if we get down." So we sat there shaking. I've never been more frightened in my life. I can't remember ever being as frightened as that. Except sometimes in the park here, there are incidents. They break windows and things. And I don't care for that.

In a way, I think wanting my divorce was the worst thing I ever did. Because it involved so many other people. It was right for me, but I was terrified of hurting the children, and I think I did. Well, they were on their father's side, so to speak. And it took a great many years until they realized the reason for it. I wasn't guilty exactly because I had to do what I did. But I was afraid they would never really be close to me again. But that fear has now been dissipated. Aside from that, I can't think of anything terrible I've done.

We have traveled a lot. I love it. I have a brand-new frame of reference for anything that's American, for one thing. For instance, my husband has been on a UNESCO commission for a long time. And that took us not only into far-flung countries but also enabled us to meet people who are part of those societies. And that was very good.

In Nairobi we had a letter of introduction to the rector of Kenyatta University, a big university. And he was a handsome fellow who was young—he was only in his early thirties—and who had been to the Sorbonne and to Oxford. Most civilized. And he gave us an hour of his time and showed us around. And he was of the Kikuyu tribe. And I asked him, "Do you ever see your parents back in the village?" He said, "Oh, yes. They don't come in to the city to see me. I put on my blanket and go to see them." And I mean, that's such a wonderful thing.

The very first play I ever saw was called *The Top of the World*. In fact, polar exploration had a great effect on me, because that was the time of discovering the North Pole. And one of the books that influenced me very much as a child was called *Anighieto, or the Snow Baby,* which was the story of Admiral Peary's little girl who was born near the North Pole. And it's just been republished, I noticed. It affected me because I had seen this play called *The Top of the World,* which was a musical, and my father's sister, Aunt Kate, who is like a grandmother to me, took me and her grandchildren to a theater that was on Columbus Circle. And we had box seats. I still remember it. And every year we used to go to the Hippodrome when it had live performances. And the thing that scared me for life, because I had already been exposed to that dynamite accident on 102nd Street, was called *The Battle of Port Arthur,* and it was a re-creation of the battle. And they were shooting Japanese, and they fell over into a big swimming tank. And they carried me out kicking and screaming. I remember that. And every time there's a pistol on the stage, I react like a child and cover my ears.

I adore the theater. And when I lived in New York, I went to everything I possibly could. The opera, too. I'll tell you a wonderful thing about the opera. When I was a little girl in school, there was a child in my class by the name of Carol Truax. And her mother was a lawyer and a widow who had a friend who was the manager of the Metropolitan Opera. The old one, downtown. And she had a box every Saturday afternoon. And Carol would invite her friends to go to the opera with her. And I think I saw every opera in the whole repertoire of the Met. And it conditioned me for life.

Music has been important to me from the time when I was about 4 and heard a band play Chopin's "Funeral March" at Grant's Tomb at the end of a Decoration Day parade up Riverside Drive. I went right home and played the melody on our Sohmer upright. I began taking piano lessons at the age of 6 and continued, by choice, beyond college, even into studying composition. When I moved to Milwaukee in 1957, I met a woman about my own age whose "thing" was music, too, and we've been reveling in four-hand sessions once a week ever since. If I wake up at night and can't get back to sleep, I play all kinds of music on my inner stereo.

Books? I don't remember Bertrand Russell's A Free Man's Worship very well, except that he felt as all scientists seem to feel now, at least most of them, that whatever intelligence or creativeness created the universe, galaxies, the world, was something to revere and had much more meaning than any kind of denominational god. I've just been reading the same sort of thing in the Jacob Bronowski book which is marvelous. I don't mean The Ascent of Man. No, I mean The Origins of Knowledge and Imagination. Absolutely marvelous. Well, he says very much the same thing, and he refers to Bertrand Russell a great deal. It isn't that they are agnostic or irreverent. But it's personal as far as one's self and one's fellow man are concerned. It is a cosmic feeling about whatever it is that made the world and the stars and everything go.

The Forsyte Saga certainly influenced me a great deal because—and this is personal again—Galsworthy talked at Barnard. He came and he spoke to the student body. And I remember him very well. I don't know whether I'd like him so much now. It was toward the end of the war, and he came over for Anglo-American relations, I guess. Very gentle and not particularly distinguished. But ever after that, everything he ever wrote had a special meaning for me. Because I'd met him.

Poetry probably had a more direct influence on me as a young person than anything. Mostly the Lake District poets. I wrote a great deal of poetry, and won a poetry prize when I was in school. Keats has stayed my very favorite one. And then at Barnard we had a marvelous course given by an Englishwoman named Caroline Spurgeon, who was an expert in Shakespeare and all poetry. But she had a special seminar that you had to qualify to get into. And this was in the romantic poets. And I was steeped in that for a whole year. It was just wonderfully revealing, and I've always had a great feeling for that particular period. And Shakespeare. I think Shakespeare was one of the dominant influences in my literary life in school. Because I cannot bear to write the sort of poetry that people write nowadays. Even though now my lines are somewhat irregular, there is more form in the way I conceive poetry to start with. And that is the influence of Miss Helen Bartlett Baker, who was our English teacher at the Horace Mann School. Matthew Arnold was one of her great pets. And we were exposed to Alfred Noyes, who wrote "The Highwayman." Anyway, poetry has had a great deal of influence on my life, and I have a good library of poetry.

I was very much in favor of women's suffrage. And also I think that women—as far as brain power is concerned, imagination, arts—are very competent. I feel that as in so many revolutionary movements, the pendulum has swung too far, and this is all black or all white. Because I don't know whether you're aware, there is a foundation here called the Johnson Foundation in Racine, which my husband and I have been connected with from time to time. And they had a seminar on Women in the Arts, and I was asked to go down there to cover it. This was to be a kind of personal impression, a summary of all the talks and the discussion groups and so on. And I was simply appalled by the excessive views of the people who participated in that discussion, because they seemed to me to be cutting their own throats by going so far in their views. And as far as lesbianism is concerned, I don't really care at all about what sex people prefer, as long as they are discreet and don't pound the pavements and wave flags about it. I feel they are trying to go too far in extending the time for the final vote on the ERA. It isn't quite fair to extend it, although I hope it is confirmed somehow. I'm in favor of the ERA. It's their tactics. It's the tactics I deplore. I think Betty Friedan did herself more harm than good, but then she seemed to have backtracked a little bit too. The militancy affected me.

I'm gung ho for civil rights. In fact I once started a piece that I never finished, which had to do with the fact that my father would move from his seat in the subway if a black person came and sat next to him. I remember the time when I was first married, I had a black cleaning woman whose name was Ethel Trott. She came in once a week to our apartment. And I never called her Ethel. I always called her Mrs. Trott. And how she loved me because I called her Mrs. Trott. And little by little, the conditioning of my childhood has evaporated. And in this community there are quite a few really remarkable blacks who are pioneers for their own people. And have gained quite a toehold in the community in general. Two of them are good friends of mine, and there's no ill feeling at all on either person's part. That feeling of holding back or treading softly because something that you say might be taken the wrong way. None of that at all.

I know a great many things that FDR did were, let us say, brushing the law aside a little bit. And although I think that he was impressed with his own personality and his charm, and so was everybody else that didn't hate him, I think his objectives were admirable. And, also, one admires his courage in overcoming his handicap to become what he became. And there was something about his style, his voice, his handsomeness, that really got to me. But every President that I've known since I was a little girl I've regarded with great admiration and respect. My father was that sort of person, and I think I took my attitude from him. He was a dyed-in-the-wool Democrat. And he used to talk politics with me a great deal. So that everyone from William Howard Taft, right on down the line—I remember standing on the corner of 125th Street and I think it was Lenox Avenue, there was a big electric sign, to see whether Woodrow Wilson was going to get elected. And he was. I admired Woodrow Wilson, even though I realized even at the time that he had slipped badly during his second term.

As far as retirement goes, I think people should decide for themselves. My father kept on working until he was 82, at half-time. But at least he felt needed. And I think if my husband didn't go to the office every day, he would fall apart. It all depends on the sort of person you are, I think. I'm very glad not to have a regular job. But I'm glad I have some skill that I can use at my own pace. I think it's very important for people to develop some sort of avocation that they can use in their retirement years. Not so long ago I met a woman whom I used to know and I was asking about her parents, and she said, well, her father had been forced to retire at age 62 or 63. And she had dreaded what would happen to him. But, he was quite a good carpenter, and carpentry had been his lifesaver. The days weren't long enough for him. He was making things and giving them away to people and having a perfectly wonderful time.

I'm still learning, and some of it has to do with moving from New York. I had gotten the beginning of it in Martha's Vineyard. It was that as a citizen your voice counts. In New York you don't have that feeling, really. I never had it. But in Martha's Vineyard, Roger Baldwin, who's a very good friend of ours, formed something called the Town Affairs Committee. Which meant that the people who owned property but were not voters could have at least a voice of recommendation in the affairs of the town of Chilmark. I was the secretary for Roger. And I learned that it's important for everyone to speak up and learn the facts first, and then speak up on the basis of them.

Well, Milwaukee is a small town in a sense. And I do not hesitate to call the police or my alderman or my councilman if there's something that I feel is really wrong. And I've become a better citizen. That's one thing that I never would've done if I'd stayed in New York.

Milwaukee is a wonderful place. I really love this city. Years ago when I went to the public library downtown my wallet was stolen, and I had to borrow money to get home on the bus. And all my credit cards, driver's license, everything was in the wallet. So I called the police, and they sent a very nice young blond policeman up to the apartment. And he couldn't have been politer. And he asked all the right questions, and he was walking around looking at different things, and he said, "You have a very fine collection of art here." And I said, "Oh, are you interested in art?" And he said, "Well, mainly ceramics." So I said, "That's interesting. Do you have a studio?" He said, "Yes, a friend and I have this studio together here, and we go to Sweden every summer, where we take lessons." Well, you know that couldn't happen in New York.

One of the things I have learned here is that you get to know the tradespeople. You get to know how other people live much more than you do in a bigger city. That's one of the dimensions that's been added. For instance, the man that we buy our liquor from, Dave Kohler. I have an eastern accent, they tell me. I don't mean a New York accent. But they know right away I'm from the East. So I call up in the morning and Dave answers the phone. And I say, "Hello,

Dave." He says, "Hiya, Midge." I mean, it's so wonderful.

And one day at this wonderful market owned by an Italian family. They changed their name, I learned, from Balastrieri to Sendik because when they first came, someone said, "Send it," and it became Sendik. And that's their name.

You know, here you communicate with the tradespeople. There's a little cleaner in our part of town who is a Czechoslovakian refugee, and when she heard that I'd been to Prague, I became her friend. And the checkroom girl at the club is a Yugoslav, and we talk about Dubrovnik. I have really enjoyed getting to know people that I would never have gotten to know in New York.

I have encountered so many deaths, drawn out and sudden, that I am not particularly upset by the thought of anybody dying. The death of a child, yes. And the death of my son-in-law, who was a brilliant young mathematician. His whole life aborted—that was terrible. My second marriage was a two-and-a-half-year idyll, a true love match. It was terminated by the completely unexpected death by embolism of my husband on a lovely June afternoon just ten days after we had moved into a town house. No death after that incredible twenty-minute horror can frighten me. But you don't deal with it. You accept it. I keep thinking, Well, you know, I'm 77 years old. I shouldn't be doing all the things I'm doing, but I'm doing them. And if a plane crashed tomorrow and I was in it, I would think as I went down, Well, it's been very interesting.

# Dr. Huai Ming-wang

*D*r. Huai Ming-wang was born in Shansi province in China on March 29, 1892. He was one of nine children. Confucianism played a strong role in his early life. So did the law. He attended the law college of Shansi, and in 1919 he came to Northwestern University in Chicago to study law here. During his American stay, which lasted for three years, he became a Christian. Back in China, he served as professor of law at the provincial university, as a judge, and as president of the appellate court. He became commissioner of education for Shansi province, while continuing to teach law. In 1932 he was named president of the National Shansi University (a post higher than at the provincial university), and was speaker of the Shansi provincial assembly until 1949, when the nationalist regime began to fall to the Communists.

Dr. Huai fled to Peking, then to Nanking, Shanghai, and finally by plane to Taiwan. In 1952 he decided to return to America for good. He reentered Northwestern's law school with the help of the school's dean, who had known him during his earlier visit, and completed work on his doctorate in 1955. Shortly thereafter he settled in New York. For six years he worked for an old friend at the Bank of China on Wall Street; then, in 1961, he retired and became an American citizen.

After his first wife, the mother of all six of his children, died in China, he remarried. His children remain in China. He cannot return to visit them, and they cannot leave China to join him. The Chinese Communists, he says, "are very strict." Although he knew Mao Tse-tung and other Communist leaders during his years in China— and despite the fact that some of those friends have urged him to return—he prefers to remain here. He now lives in a well-run nursing home on Manhattan's Upper West Side; he comes and goes as he pleases.

He is an active man and a thoughtful one. In heavily accented English, he can discuss his life and his fervor for appreciating life, which derives from his devotion to both Confucianism and Christianity. There is no conflict in the two, he says. "Usually I carry things with my hands. Confucius gave me a car. But I had to push it. Very hard. But better.

*Jesus Christ gave me the motor. Much better. If Confucius were alive, he wouldn't oppose that motor car. He'd want one for himself."*

Since I first came here, in 1919, there have been changes. One of the things that changed was, especially, the peace and order. Security. Quite a difference. When I first graduated from Northwestern, I came to New York. I took a course at Columbia, two terms. During that time, the weather was hot, so I went to Riverside Park, slept there all night, afraid of nothing. I lived near there, then. Now I can't go out. I dare not go out. I will not go out after nine o'clock, on the streets. So many robbers. It's quite different. The customs have changed. I was discussing it with some professors. The first time I came, in the streetcars or the trains, people would give the seats to the ladies. And why have they changed that system? The professors started laughing. I guess because the ladies are stronger than before. Many things change, you see.

The peace and order and social security is changed so much. Other things, like scientific developments, are improved. Improved very much, very quick. In other countries, the government gives oppression. Only the professors can study this and study that. But in this country it's free. And the professors work so hard toward invention. They do the work themselves. Without pressure. One thing you can notice, the Nobel Prize, that's the real picture. The Nobel Prize winners—many have been from this country. Many winners, all from this country. That's a very clear picture, you see?

When I was young, I read all the classical books. I read Confucius. I can still speak on it. I can repeat all of it. I follow the Confucius teachings. Most of the people in China follow Confucius teachings. Of course, we have Taoists and the Buddhists—also they dominate. But the fundamental philosophy of life is Confucianism.

My parents were primary school teachers. My uncle was the principal of a grammar school. When I was young, I really didn't think of myself as being that. When I had gone to law school, I saw myself as being a lawyer and judge. I made my decision.

Confucianism is not a religion. It's a pure philosophy. Classical philosophy. Mostly ethical. It's not in the Western concept. It's not mystical. No. Mostly, Confucius' teachings are ethical. In everyday life, we keep contact with human relations. Fathers and mothers. Sons and daughters. The brothers and the neighborhood, and then the government. Step by step. Confucius had a very good philosophy for that. How the mother and father take good care of the children. And how the children should honor the mother and father by being obedient. Maybe too much obedience, but still obedient to the mother and father.

You start with love—father, mother, neighbors. The basic thing is to start from yourself, from your mind and your heart. You must have your conscience enlightened—they call that enlightened. It is purified and not involved with dirty things. And how to do it—that is something very philosophical. You check yourself. A good writer once wrote, Confucius said that the measure of man is man. Not God. You check yourself. Through your conscience. You deal with people who have trouble the way you want other people to treat you. If not, you are wrong. The measure of man is man, that doesn't mean God. Really, Confucius never said a word against God. Even he has an idea to stick close to God. And sometimes he prayed. He prayed to God. He always prayed, but he never taught his disciples to pray. Because Confucius was such a person who knows that when he says something he must know for sure. If he does not know for sure, he does not say it. He would not teach his disciples to pray. Why is that? If prayer is good and he did it himself, why? Because he's not sure. He tried. Confucius was looking for God. He knocked at the door but never got it open. So he's not sure. So that's why he would not teach his disciples to pray.

Exercise to me is very, very important. That's why I still do exercise. I have a friend who is a very good fighter and he learns exercises from me. I've done that many years. That exercise is not from Confucianism. It is from Taoism. Chinese philosophers get involved with Confucianism, Taoism, and Buddhism. The exercises I do are from Taoist priests. Taoist priests are very similar to Buddhist. Every day they keep quiet, meditation, keep absolutely quiet. And gradually the quietness is not enough. The quietness becomes action, that's the exercise. Even though you're moving, it's still the same as meditation. Very quiet, very quiet. You don't move so much muscles and bones this way. They call it the internal exercise. The intrinsic energy. That's the translation of the term. Everyone can do the same—you sit for a long time, the center of your body should be warm. That is a kind of electricity itself, electric energy. Your body is not moving. Your body is absolutely quiet. You can hear something from inside your body. This warm feeling is moving. How it moves—we don't know. But nature knows. There are different channels where energy moves. What is a channel? I don't know. Nobody knows. But nature knows. That warm feeling, moving, moving goes down. First there, then to the back of the spine. It takes several months to do that. Then it follows the spine, that energy, through the spine, up, it follows the spine up, up, up. Then it is moving, moving. Then you must let the tongue touch the roof the way an electric wire connects. Then that energy goes down, down, and comes back. It circulates, circulation goes around and around. That is the start of my exercise. I get it done in about three months. Some people in only one month, some people in one or two years. Everybody is biologically different.

I want to tell you this: The Chinese have a good family life, but a big family is not good. It has many troubles. Confucius said to maintain this family relation, be harmonious. Most teachers teach that, but really it's very difficult. Living together is good, but you can have many troubles. Father, mother, and the children must love each other. But the brothers and sisters are different. And your brother's son and your brother's wife are always together with you and that causes many, many troubles.

I'll tell you a true story. In the T'ang dynasty there was a family who lived together, many generations living together. Big family. The people encouraged that. Such a big family, if they could live together, that's good. Really many troubles. Then there was an emperor and he said many generations living together is not easy, and he called this man to the capital city to have a talk with him. And he asked the leader of the family, "How do you maintain this family, living together so harmoniously?" The man used a pen and wrote one word. *Patience.* He wrote that word a hundred times.

But patience causes problems. If you don't say a word, you keep it in your mind. Some people get sick that way. Patience is a limitation of your freedom. You want to say something, but you dare not say it. You keep patient. You can lose your freedom that way. So, really, I don't like big families.

When we talk about a family now, we're not talking about a family like those in old China or India. We cannot have such big families now. Everything's changing. Even in China, the Communist system doesn't like that. Don't allow it. Family has only husband, wife, and children. That's all. When the children get older, they get married and they must move out. The old Chinese system—even when they married, they still lived together with relatives. That's why you had so many generations in one house.

Love is a good word. But now that good word has almost become a dirty word. Love is so important. Even many churches have a sign that says, GOD IS LOVE. When many people say love, it's very easy for them to think of love as a man making love to a lady. They misunderstand that. There is a Chinese word. The word means man. This means two persons. When two persons live together, one must not only think of himself, you should not think only of yourself. Human love starts there. When the Chinese talk about love, they use that word. A strong "like," the "like" is very strong. It is the basic philosophy of Confucius—that word. That's what I told you—the measure of man is a man.

You make love today without having children. Yes, I know that. Well, that's a limitation. There should be a limitation, of course. If everybody used that method, human beings would perish from the earth. You need limitations. But those drugs have side effects, might cause cancer, you see.

I am a father. That's human nature. Everybody loves his children, especially his own children. That's human nature. Of course, I love my children. There's no question about that. That's very natural.

When I was young, I was so obedient to my father, too much. Then, children had no freedom at all. But here in this country there's too much freedom. That is why we have so many juvenile delinquents. Chinese people with big families have many troubles, also, but they take care of the children. Children are mostly obedient. I was a judge for many years, and I never tried a case of a juvenile delinquent. The juvenile court—we didn't need it, there's no such thing. The parents take care of that.

I got information from a magazine about a juvenile-court judge, an old man. He was in juvenile court for many years and he retired. He knows so much about juvenile delinquency. He says he heard in Italy there were very few juvenile delinquents. He didn't know why, but he wanted to figure it out, so he went to Italy for a few months to investigate. When he came back, a newspaper man asked him what he had found out. He said the children are mostly obedient to the parents and the teachers. In this country, in America, they call it freedom, freedom, freedom. But it causes many troubles. This country has so many juvenile delinquents, so many persons murdered because of freedom. Freedom has caused the system to be almost bankrupt. They abuse freedom in America.

There are many things I did I am sorry for. I didn't like to do it, but I did it. Like smoke. For thirty-five or forty years I was a heavy smoker. At least two packs a day. I tried to stop several times, but they had no such an invention—nothing to tell me that cigarettes cause cancer. I never heard that. But I knew it was not good, so I wanted to quit it. I tried several times. The first time I tried for two weeks, but after two weeks I smoked again. Then for one month I didn't smoke. I didn't smoke for a month, and I was thinking to myself the month's almost up and there's only two more days left. And the next day I got up early, and first thing I smoked. I could not do it by myself. Even after I became a Christian. I was baptized as a Christian, but I still smoked. One of my pastors said, "No, you should not smoke. That's not good—a Christian to smoke." I argued with him. The Bible did not teach one not to smoke. I could not find such words in the Bible. I looked in the Bible and I found drink wine, drink whiskey, because Jesus Christ himself drank wine. Wine makes people drunk and nervous. Smoking does no such thing. Smoke will not make you nervous. It's quite different. If Jesus Christ could drink wine, I thought I could smoke. Even when I write poems or articles, if I hold a cigar or cigarette, I can write better. And Bismarck, the German politician, he always had a cigar. He could write good poems and did many wonderful things. So it will not hurt me, I said. My pastor said, "I will not argue with you. You speak like a lawyer. Promise me one thing. I don't urge you anymore not to smoke. But tonight, you go back and you have a prayer. Ask God—don't ask me—ask God if smoke is all right or not. If God gives you guidance to smoke, it's all right.

If God says smoking is wrong, will you follow God's guidance?" I said, "I must. I must. If God gives me guidance, I will quit it." He said, "That's good enough. You do it. You let me know." I tried it, that night I tried it. Before going to bed I knelt down and prayed for a long time. Usually I pray only a short time, but now it was a longer time. I asked God whether to smoke was right or wrong. Very clearly God gave me an idea that smoke is wrong. I said, Well, I have to quit it. But I still think, Is it my idea or God's idea? Next morning I tried again. I prayed. I got the same answer. Smoke is wrong, very clear. Since that time I quit altogether. I got God's guidance that smoke was wrong, so I quit it altogether. I never smoke.

Other things. When somebody criticizes you, you use very bad words. You cannot stand that—you get mad. Many of these things are not easy to conquer—it is not easy to stop. But with God it's all right. I had many of these troubles. I prayed to God.

I was baptized a long time ago. In 1920. The first time I came here as a student. I was baptized as a Christian in Illinois, in a church there. In China some friends introduced me to the church. I attended the service, the prayers. I did that, but I wasn't baptized. Then, in America, I was. It gave me a better life. I have hope.

When I came to this country, the second time I came to this country, I worked in the Bank of China, in New York. My former superior had been the governor of my province for nearly forty years. Very good man. I worked under him, and afterward he became the prime minister of the Nationalist government. I liked that man and he liked me. I got the news that he died in Taiwan. And naturally, I cried. I felt so bad, so bad. But I had to live my life on. Well, the crying is an emotion, only for a short time. Not too long. After an hour or two hours I stopped. After a time I gradually forget the crying. But I still think of him.

After the death of my father I felt so bad for several months, for nearly half a year. Then I got better. That's also a natural feeling. I think everybody has that feeling, some with much tears and some not so much. Natural feeling.

Confucius did not teach anything about the next life. But the Bible, the Bible does. That is something nobody can prove. But some people believe it so much and you cannot disprove it. I believe it, because the Bible says it. Many things I cannot explain. Many things in the Bible, even as a Christian, I still cannot understand, I cannot accept. Many passages in the Bible I don't believe. Like in the beginning God created heaven and earth, according to the Bible, from that time up to now is seven thousand years, a little more, and Noah and the ark, and only the things he took on the ark survived, all the other living things died. Really, that's not true. From Noah's time up to now is around six thousand years. But now the scientists make it very clear, their proof makes it very clear that for many, many thousands of years, millions of years, human beings were here. So that is not true. Many things, especially in the Old Testament, I cannot believe—I must tell you the truth. I even tell my pastor I don't believe it. But some parts I do believe, I really believe.

I believe in these two, Confucius and Christianity, there's no contradiction, not at all. We can be together. After I was baptized, a friend of mine criticized me, "You're from a family who all read Confucian philosophy. How could you become a Christian?" I said, "It's a long story."

# Alexander Schneider

*A* brief biography of Alexander Schneider could say, simply, that he is a violinist. That would be like saying that Willie Mays was a baseball player. It could, as one program for a concert at New York's Avery Fisher Hall did, call him a conductor and violinist who "has performed at all of the world's great music centers." Or it could, as the entry in Who's Who in America does, go on for thirty-eight lines and still omit much about Schneider's life.

Yet Schneider, a strong, proud, opinionated, and temperamental man, does not act like a titan. He lives unobtrusively in a small building near lower Fifth Avenue in Manhattan, surrounded by wholesale firms of all sorts and old office buildings and warehouses. It is his building (he rents the ground floor to a small company), and he has lived in it for more than nineteen years. It is a comfortable home, neither opulent nor ostentatious. Schneider himself greets visitors in gray flannel slacks, polished black loafers, and a bulky wool sweater. His semi-halo of gray hair, his glasses, and his ready smile combine to create an image of kindness and charm.

He is charming, and it is a charm that grows out of his vast and fascinating experience. He was born in Vilna, Russia, in 1908 and studied with the same violin teacher who taught Heifetz in Vilna. He began on the violin at the age of 5½, when his father decided that the family needed a violinist to join the pianist and cellist already among his children. The father was a locksmith and an amateur flutist, and his passion for music was transmitted to Alexander. The family left Vilna when Schneider was 16; they traveled throughout Europe and, in 1932, came to the United States. Schneider has left it often since to perform, but it is his home. He has become a citizen.

He has become a worldwide performer. He was a member of the Budapest String Quartet and a guiding force in the work of several other notable quartets. He has taught at a number of universities. He has conducted many of the major symphony orchestras throughout the world. He has directed many music festivals—in the course of which he worked closely with Pablo Casals, in Puerto Rico and in France—and *he has performed at many. He has won innumerable awards. He was the first violinist to perform all of Bach's unaccompanied violin works in a concert series. "My purpose," he has said, "is to get young people to learn how to make music. When you make music, it has to come from your heart, from your soul, or it has no meaning."*

*He has been married three times, and at present is single again. He has not had any children. His children, he feels, are his students. Throughout the world they pay tribute to him, in words and in the music they play with a passion that he encouraged or inspired. They, in turn, have helped him stay young.*

When I got here, I thought America was very strange, of course. I spoke very few words of English. I remember the first thing, an uncle of mine was then alive, and he lived on Long Island somewhere. He had a little house there, a very nice house. It was winter, and he picked us up—my brother and myself. And, of course, he insisted that we don't stay in a hotel, that we go to his house. Every day we went to the Great Northern Hotel because two of my colleagues were staying there. Every day we used to go in, and my uncle would send us off with his son to the Long Island Railroad, to land at Pennsylvania Station, go to the hotel, rehearse there, and then his son used to pick us up to go back home, because he was afraid somebody would take us away or something like that. It was really very strange.

Well, it was all incredible. As a matter of fact, Long Island looked a little bit like Vilna, the house you know. And of course arriving in Pennsylvania Station was overwhelming. And getting to, my God, to Fifty-seventh Street. I remember, particularly, looking up always at the skyscrapers and getting a headache from looking up. And I was really a little bit afraid, I must say. It was too much, you know, coming from Europe. I mean, the whole movement was incredible, the pace. And then during the intermission between two rehearsals we had each day, we used to go and have a sandwich—a beautiful sandwich. At that time there was on Sixth Avenue a Jewish delicatessen that had wonderful sandwiches of chopped liver, I remember, on rye bread. And the whole amount for that chopped liver sandwich was exactly fifteen cents, and coffee was five cents. And that was a great lunch. Later on, the most important thing was a milk shake. That was one of the great things which impressed me at first in America.

Rehearsals and then concerts. And in '32, that was the first year I was here, they closed up all the banks. We didn't have any money to travel. So Uncle sent us with his private car, his son was driving. And we toured, with the instruments, with the luggage, in the little Chevrolet—I'll never forget this, traveling in winter. It was very bad. Going to, I remember, Cleveland, Ithaca. Especially I remember that. That was, as a matter of fact, Cornell University, that was my first contact with students. Eating at a cafeteria and seeing how they worked. And paying for their education by serving. And it was really extraordinary. I was very impressed by all the young students. And they wanted to learn, all of them. And their interest in music—you couldn't drink coffee by yourself. Somebody would always come to you and talk to you, ask questions, wanted to know. To learn something. I had the feeling all of them wanted something to learn about music.

Meanwhile, I was learning English. The best learning for me was going to the movies. That was the best because there you could really learn much more than by reading. You see, because the sound was very important. Also, menu reading. I mean, anything where you could read something was very important, of course. Then, of course, we were usually invited after a concert to some private house, or if you played at a college or a university, you were in contact with professors and students. And usually they spoke German or French, some knew Russian. I could at least have a conversation, which was pretty difficult because in English I couldn't.

New York was much cleaner then. Oh, definitely. It was much quieter. The movement was really beautiful. And walking was the greatest pleasure. That was something I never forget. I loved to walk. I had the great pleasure of knowing the city, learning. And of course, in the summer we used to go to the park, always, you know. It was the most wonderful thing, going to the park. There was a certain time, I would say a few years ago, when it was pretty difficult in New York to walk at night. Now I am not afraid anymore. You know, it is really much better, I think. I walk very often, you know, and walk home here, from midtown.

There's only one city—that's New York. There is really no other city in the whole world for me, which has everything you really want, you know. And you can be absolutely secretive—nobody would even know that you are in New York, and that's also beautiful.

Of course, I wish it would be cleaner, like it used to be. That's one thing that really bothers me. And, the people are so introverted now, they don't talk. But the whole world is that way. Brotherhood doesn't exist anymore. Everybody is involved in himself and doesn't care about anything whatsoever. Frightening.

Maybe it's our fault, that we didn't give them enough opportunity. I don't know. It is very sad, I find. Really very sad that we don't have this human connection like it used to be. They don't have it even in the arts. I mean, even with France we don't have any more of this. I remember during the war it was fantastic how, you know, we were all together. Artists, it was the most incredible life. I remember that. Now everybody is separated. Everybody works by himself. You see each other by accident in Paris or in London or somewhere, but not in New York.

Don't forget, I was born in 1908, so you see right away there was the war when I was 6 years old. In 1914. Already the war was going. And that was terrible. I mean, it was much worse in the second, the real, the big war. But it was terrible during the first war because we didn't have anything to eat. It was really awful. Education could only be at home because all schools were closed for four years. There was always war, war going on. Everything was closed. So the only thing you could learn was at home, from your parents. Well, I learned a lot. And the most important thing I learned is discipline and respect. They taught me that. By beating me up. It was not like today—psychoanalysis, doctors. They didn't exist at all. If I didn't do something, well, I knew that I would get it one way or another way.

I do feel that I would've become the biggest bum, really, if they wouldn't have—both of them, Father and Mother—kept with this discipline. The only thing I was interested in at that time was playing soccer. Only soccer and then, later, billiards. I was absolutely crazy about those two things. Nothing else was interesting.

Luckily, you see, my father was an amateur flutist, played a little bit of flute. And music was for him the most important thing alive.

And naturally he wanted his children to be only musicians, nothing else. And well, the first one—the oldest one, my sister—he started with her on the piano. Then my brother, cello. Then there was no violinist, and I didn't want to do violin, I wanted to play the piano. I always went to the piano. And he said, "No, no, we have one pianist. We need a violinist." And so that's how I started the violin.

The other brother, who is in Toronto now, he tried with him and the instrument didn't work because he wasn't musical. So my father was disappointed. My father took him to the factory, and he became a very important locksmith, so he's doing very well.

In Vilna in those days they were all involved, not only in religion—in philosophy, in science, in everything. It was extraordinary—it must have been, while I was a child there. For my father and for all the others, it must have been an extraordinary life. A Jewish Renaissance. But we were all versed with the pogroms.

I remember playing in a café in the winter, to attract people. That was during the German occupation, I remember. And the pay for that was I could clean up everything that was left on the plates, that I could take home. But there were other kids on the street who would beat you up and take it away from you, because they were going to bring it to their parents. You see it was awful, the first war. Terrible.

My mother was a very strong woman. She had to do everything. Imagine, to take care of four children. And everything was gone—there were no maids or anything in the house. She was really responsible for everything going on, because my father used to work from six in the morning until six in the evening. And then come home exhausted. He would eat and go right to sleep again. And he would only ask if I practiced, and sometimes she would tell him that I didn't, so I would get it from him, not only from her.

The two things which I'm grateful to my parents for are discipline and respect. Those are the most important things. I really still feel today that those are the most important things in my life. And to develop, to have the interest, and never to be too tired to do anything. I don't get tired of anything. And I find because of the discipline and the respect I have never yet really just worked without being involved in it. If I do something I do it 100 percent. I'm in it, and I demand that others do it, too.

In New York for the first time this year we had two big snowstorms.

But imagine these two big snowstorms without cleaning up at all. Where we lived in Europe, everything was frozen, you see. I would say ten to fifteen feet was the layer. During the whole winter. And then to walk, I mean it was pretty and it was terrible. Very cold. And to sleep, or to go to a lesson. You would have frozen fingers. You couldn't play. I was already 11 years old and I would play with the gloves cut open at the tip, because it was so cold.

I belong to a health club. I go, if I can, every second day at least. You know that's very important physically. I feel much better. I must say I think that all people should really perspire. It's very good to have it. I don't perspire when I practice scales. But when you go, it takes all the dirt out of your body, and you feel much better.

I hope that I can go through without any medicine, without doctors. It is sometimes difficult. I stopped smoking entirely and since I stopped smoking, I feel much better, much younger. It's now twenty-five years since I last smoked. I smoked two or three packages a day, and I was terrible. The blood circulation stopped in my feet and my hands. I had to stop. And I'm glad that I stopped. The doctor who cured me said, "When you want to have a cigarette, take a glass of Bordeaux wine. You'll cure yourself." And I was nicely drunk for a while, you know.

I feel much better really. This I must say. I have problems. You know, I'm 69, so I have arthritis, naturally. It bothers me, sure. And I have problems with my arm, but I hope it will go away. You have to take care of yourself.

Heifetz was born in Vilna, and the violin teacher there was fantastic. He would come, I remember this distinctly, with a half violin—of course, because I was 5½ years old, with a half violin, tuned up naturally—and with one page of scales. I remember the scales were in three or four positions. That was all that he had, and that's how he taught you. And I know one thing. Let's say the violin lesson was worth maybe five rubles at that time. He would charge seven rubles, because Heifetz had played that violin. Naturally, you would pay two rubles more because it was Heifetz, you know. Every father wanted his son to become another Heifetz and thought that the teacher was responsible. He taught Heifetz.

I was 5½ years old. I didn't "start." My father said tomorrow the violin teacher will come, and that's all. That's how I "started." And then came a horrible thing which stayed with me for a long, long time. You see, we had a trio at home. My sister played the piano; my brother, cello; and I played the violin. And we learned one piece of music together, and that was the show-off piece of my father. So he would take us on a Saturday, he would take us to his friends who had another upright to show off his children. And the piece of music had seven bars for the violin before we all played together. In other words, first started the piano, then the cello, and then came the violin. And naturally for seven bars you had to count. And that particular place where my father took us had a clock on top of the upright piano. An old-fashioned clock which made "dom, dom," with the little noise and the movement. And of course, that impressed me tremendously. It was a very beautiful clock, I remember. And when we started playing, I couldn't count the seven bars because I was involved in the clock, you know, and I didn't come in. That happened two times. And that was the worst thing you could do. I got the biggest beating I ever had. Because I didn't come in after seven bars. For years and years it was like a wall in front of me. And when I was 50 years old, my brother arranged specially to get the music, and three of my colleagues played it especially for me.

When we were young, my God, you know, to have a sexual intercourse was something unbelievable. Of course, the desire was exactly the same. We are made of the same blood, same flesh. But the possibilities then were terrible. You were afraid that she would get pregnant. At that time you couldn't have an abortion, definitely not. My grandmother had thirteen children. Can you imagine that? Thirteen children. One woman—she had thirteen children. Can you imagine? It must have been frightening. Well, the pill has helped tremendously. They are not afraid anymore. I imagine that young women are not afraid to make love because they know they won't be pregnant. But what I hear, at least from doctors, is that it's terrible, you know, the sicknesses. The percentage is unbelievable. Much more now, much worse—especially for the young girls.

One thing. Now it's very easy for young people to live together, and they don't have to get married. Wonderful. I think it is absolutely natural. Before you had to lie about it. I remember I had to lie and say that's my fiancée. When are you going to get married? Well, we are planning to get married in a month, so you could rent an apartment and live together. Otherwise, you couldn't. Then, you couldn't have visitors. It was impossible, all those things.

You know, we misuse this word *love*. You know that. Profoundly, strangely, I find it very much in music. Phrases in music which mean love to me, and I would say I wouldn't be the only one, as a musician. It would mean love to many musicians, certain phrase of four bars, eight bars, not exactly a whole movement or a whole work—no, not at all, but there will be something by the composer which really represents love to me. There are many pieces by Mozart, by every composer, every composer has done it. Haydn has. But to explain music in words? I don't think it's only difficult, I think it is impossible. But I feel, for example, there are many pieces, this sounds stupid and funny, when I say, I wish there would be a woman as beautiful as this phrase is. Because this is for me the most beautiful thing which I could know. If a woman could present that to me, it would be wonderful.

I don't see a way to make marriage work, unfortunately. What is it about the institution? Well, you can make it go. You know, it's always possible to arrange anything. If you have discipline. But you see, if two people really, really love each other, it's like two atoms coming together. It explodes—really the thing that's extraordinary is when you make love. This is the height. But living together and really, really having something all the time to give is very difficult. Because you are mostly alone. Without any doubt, I think even in the best marriages there are very few that really live together, because otherwise, you know, it's compromises and all this nonsense. And there is no reason to be married because you have children. That's worse for the children because they feel it in you. The most lasting thing is not intellectual. It's the physical. And then comes the times when this stops. And then there is an emptiness, if there is nothing human, nothing to give to each other. Very difficult.

When people say to me, "Look, we have been together ten or fifteen years," I don't believe it. I really don't believe it. The big exceptions are really something. Is it physical or is it a relation between two people who can fill out the emptiness, which is very difficult. They have to be not only intelligent. They have to have something to give to each other.

. . .

I'm not religious, but I'm very much involved as a Jew. I must tell you something which is absolutely true, something which happened the first time I went to Israel with the Budapest Quartet. I was already in America. It was twenty years ago, and coming through the gate the Israeli there said to me, "Welcome Mr. Schneider—welcome home, Mr. Schneider. Welcome home." Nobody said that to me before. I felt there a feeling of, you know, really being at home somehow. And this has nothing to do with being Jewish, because the Catholics have it. The Arabs have it. Everybody who comes there has this feeling, without any doubt.

I remember I told it at the White House. I told it to Johnson, and Mrs. Johnson, and Humphrey, as a matter of fact. They were at the same table. I said to them, You know, never when I come here to my country, would they say, "Welcome home, Mr. Schneider." You are afraid they may not let you in. And since then something must have happened, because they very often say it now. "Did you have a good time? Welcome home." They do say it now. Which I think is wonderful. Maybe that helped—that one sitting in the White House, telling them that.

I've been afraid, afraid of being not prepared to play something on stage. And I had to play because I'm a professional. I have never canceled a concert in all my life. Not once. That's really rare. Never canceled a concert, even if I was sick and fever and everything. I still played. But I must say there were a few times, once or twice, terrible. Usually you don't remember your dreams, you know. But at times you wake and you remember the dream: that you went out on stage and you didn't know anything. It happens. It happens when you are really tired. It happened to me on a Bach, once. Terrible. But then somehow it continues, you know. I continued. I stopped—I got absolutely lost— and then I continued. Those few seconds are like centuries. Horrors. On the other hand, I've had awful things happen on planes. Horrible. You know, driving a car. Absolutely impossible things, deadly things. They didn't bother me at all.

I did so many stupid things. Which I regret, you know. But you can't take that back. Offending my friends, offending people without any reason.

I had a period when I would write the most terrible letters or tele- grams. For example, when somebody played something really badly and I knew him. Or he behaved badly in music. I would explode and I would go backstage and I would raise hell. The terrible things I used to do. And then with strangers too, whom I didn't know. I would do this, and I regretted it terribly much.

There was a time when all the critics—actually now they are still younger than I—were really like my students. One of them was a very good critic. Good musician, too. And he would always write good things about me. I played miserably, he would write good. So I told him, "Listen, for God's sake, stop this. I played yesterday miserably, why did you write that I played good? That's stupid." So from then on he wrote all the time that I played bad. A few times, I would say something or write to the critics, saying, Have lunch with me, I want to talk to you. Why do you write so stupidly about this and this? First of all, a great artist doesn't need you. He's a great artist. You can write anything you want about him, and he doesn't give a damn. And your personal opinion is not going to upset the public or anybody, it will only upset you yourself. So why don't you, instead of doing that, help young people? I find a critic has a responsibility, not only to help young people. He has a responsibility to the community where he is writing. In other words, the critics of New York have to help the community to build a higher level musically. But really to have a right musical opinion you have to be really a genius, you have to be a great personality and great man. Yes, that's a different story. Let's say, when Stravinsky would criticize some other work or part of it.

I'm more and more involved in Haydn, who is the most extraordinary for me. He is something special. Naturally, Bach is in the top category, you know. And Mozart, a genius, fantastic. And Schubert, always Schubert. But the one who really impresses me every time, more and more, is Haydn. There is something so pure, and such fantasy. What this man has, I don't find in any other composer. The simple material, you know, will never get sentimental. Never. He has sentiment, but he doesn't get sentimental.

I'm happy in my work because I'm involved with music. It happens with music, with me. Well, what do I tell them when I conduct an orchestra? All orchestras aren't happy. They are getting their salaries, but they are not a part of music making. You see, this is a big problem. I tell them I try to make them open up and let them play. Let them enjoy making music, and help them to open up. They are bored, of course. And I tell them that it is up to them to make music. I can't do anything if they don't want to. And they feel better. You live longer when you make music, definitely. Otherwise you die. Absolutely. You have to have the feeling that you are the luckiest person in the whole world, that there is nobody who has it better, nobody. But there is no profession, I find, like music. None of them. I don't think that the painter has the feeling of satisfaction that we have.

What really represents America for me is the extraordinary mixture of people from all over the world. And the biggest concentration of that is right here in New York. Because you have all the nationalities. They don't even speak English, but they are Americans. And they are good Americans, all of them. This is fantastic. And they are all building something which is unbelievable.

Now, you go out, you know, to Boston, and it's an entirely different world. You go to Philadelphia, it's a different world. You go to New Jersey. You are in a different world. You go to Washington. It's a different America. You go to Detroit, it's different. You go to Chicago, it's different. Cleveland's different. San Francisco is entirely different. Los Angeles is different. Absolutely different.

I have a house in France. And I know the village people like my brothers and sisters. But I don't feel at home there. Never. Nowhere do I feel really at home like I feel here with these people. That's why I complain that the people don't realize how good they have it here, and that they should do something to help each other. That's what I miss here. That they only help themselves, you see. And this is horrible tragedy, I find. Europe is degenerated without any doubt. Absolutely. Sadly, I must say. It's beautiful. Very nice to go there for a while. But I can't anymore. To live there, never, I can't live there. I couldn't live in Paris for anything in the world. London is not bad to live in. It has certain freedoms, you know, of expression. But here, it's fantastic.

Let people work so long as they can, so long as they're not senile. What I find out being in orchestras is very interesting. They try to get young ones. So now the older ones who are not yet 65 are starting to work, because they don't want to retire. Which is very good, because they know what to do better. They really have to practice, otherwise they will have to get out. And I think in every profession that's so.

Young musicians today play better technically, you know. But they don't have the musical education. Maybe it's our good luck that we were surrounded with giants, that our whole education was so different, on a much higher level. I don't find it today. From the young ones. They're tremendous talents, extraordinary, but there are a few of them who will be great, definitely. They all have ambition. Oh, yes, there are quite a lot of them. But they make a mistake, you know. By trying to become commercialized. The whole approach to music is from the soul only. Really, to be honest. We talk about being honest with yourself. They forget entirely that you have to be really honest with yourself in your soul to do it. Otherwise it has absolutely no meaning. Like playing a phrase. You can play a very beautiful phrase, and it won't mean anything at all. It may sound beautiful, but if you are not involved with your soul, it doesn't mean anything.

When a friend dies, whatever he gave you, try to augment it in thousands and thousands of ways, and give it to others—that's the only possible way. With Casals, for example, you know? He meant a lot to me, but I don't want to talk about him. Something just comes out of me. That's the only thing I can do for everyone—for my mother, for my father. The best thing I can think of is to make a better world, in other words. To give it to anybody you possibly can. That's the only thing you can do. Zero Mostel died suddenly. We would practice every day together. I mean, I lost something very, very important. The only thing you can do is to try to do better and better whatever he gave you, something. To continue giving that.

As for myself, I hope I can continue, because if I can't work a day, if I can't do something, I feel bored. I'm not the kind of a person to take a rest. When I had the flu for three and a half days, I really couldn't do anything. That was the worst. For me, awful. Because you really can't do anything. I hate that.

# Martha Belknap

*If you take Highway 126 after heading east from Eugene, Oregon, you are quickly into some of the most spectacular scenery in North America. Mountains loom in the distance; forests line the slopes. And soon, through it all, flows the McKenzie River. It is clear and cool, and those who live beside it find a special kind of tranquillity.*

*Martha Belknap is such a person. The family she married into first came to the area as homesteaders in the 1860s. The Belknap name is still found on a bridge, a hot springs, and a crater, but Martha is the last Belknap along the McKenzie. She lives in a fine old white house on the banks of the river; it is reached on a narrow rough road, from the town of Blue River.*

*Martha was born on July 29, 1895, and first came to the area in 1914, to teach country school. Her father had been a farmer and a carpenter; the family had moved around—from Arkansas, where she was born, to Michigan to California and then, in 1909, to Oregon. She attended the University of Oregon, in Eugene.*

*In 1921 she married Clarence Belknap, who owned a sawmill and a farm. The next year they built the house that she still lives in. Martha did some teaching, then settled down to enjoy the pace of life along the McKenzie.*

*Her husband died in 1968; their only son has died, too. Since her husband's death Martha has lived alone, with only her yellow Labrador, Duke, for continual company. Guests come and go: servicemen she knew during World War II returning for a chat, other friends from far-off locations. She keeps several guest rooms for that purpose. She has been involved in the local school system, doing her best to help it achieve excellence. She reads avidly; her walls are lined with books. She goes to parties, to square dances. She gets around in an immaculate Chrysler. She has seen "the neighborhood," as she calls it, change over the years, but the river still glides by her house and she is perpetually inspired by its beauty and its power. She accepts change gracefully. A kind, gentle, witty woman, she has not retreated into her wilderness;*

*rather, she keeps in close touch with the world and holds opinions to match her perception. She is a small woman, with soft white hair, and only a limp from an old accident gives away her age.*

When I first came to this part of Oregon, I liked it. Of course, I wasn't very old, only 18. And I boarded with a ranger and rode a horse two and a half miles to teach at the school. It was a little eight-grade school with about fifteen children. The people were so friendly and so kind. We had so many good times because the new teacher was here. I was the new teacher. There was a man at the dinner here last night who went to that school when I taught there, when he was a kid. It's a wonderful neighborhood. There are a great many very good people. Maybe not wealthy or too well educated, but wonderfully kind. There's a few of the other kind, but you get used to them.

When I came here, we had the hot springs, Belknap Springs, and there's another one called Foley Springs. Only five miles to Foley, so we used to walk up there and go swimming in the wooden swimming pool. Some people named Halfinger had it. Mr. Halfinger was a little Swiss man. And he taught me to play cribbage. When I win, it's scientifically. When you win, it's luck. But it's one of the things that have helped me always. There's a man from Scotland who came here and bought the place, and still comes every summer. And we play cribbage—three games every day.

So that was a nice thing. And then I could tell you about the little woman—wish that you could've met her—who ran the Log Cabin Hotel, the last stop. It had been built way back in the 1880s. She and Uncle George Purcell came up here. And she'd been married when she was 14, and she had four sons by the time she was 20. And left her husband because he was not a good man, and married Uncle George and they came up here. He was a funny little fellow from Vermont. I think she was one of the most wonderful people I'd ever known. Little bit of a woman. She was quite deaf and lame when I knew her. She lived to be 89. She put the first clothes on a lot of the people around here. She had the post office for forty-two years at McKenzie Bridge. And she read a great deal and she never grew old. I can hardly speak of them without tears. It's been over fifty years since she died.

Today, there's a multitude of people here. And so many of these longhairs have come up here. It's kind of a problem. Not bad people, many of them. But they've kind of divided the community. Because a lot of them don't like them. When they go to the drinking spots, it's the loggers and the longhairs. Don't like each other.

When my husband, Clarence, was running the mill, there were three other mills up here. I expect two hundred people were working in them. And there were beauty shops and eating places. But we just don't have those now. We had the big farm over here, 320 acres, two home-steads. Beautiful view down the land. And now it's a golf course. Of course, a great deal of this is Forest Service land. And it's only the deeded property, that were homesteads in this immediate area, that can change hands. So it rather reduces the number of people. But it has changed a great deal. We had four small schools in McKenzie Bridge, at Blue River, at Minrod, and Vida. And now we've combined them and it's one big school. It's white. It's made of wood, they built it in '42. And there's less than five hundred children in all the twelve grades in the neighborhood. Some of them are bused twenty-five miles. But we did have a very good school and it's fallen into disarray a bit.

Time brings change. We have no leisure anymore. Time to sit down and talk. Time to exchange not just pleasantries but ideas, and to come to a person with your troubles, and just talk to them. And they have time to listen to you for two or three hours. Maybe you can't tell them a thing, because the older you grow, the less sure you are of anything in this world.

My mother was a very wonderful person. She wasn't afraid. She was raised in New York State, central New York. And she was raised a Unitarian. But when we came to Eugene, there was no Unitarian church. We went to the Baptist Sunday school and the Methodist Sunday school and they were all friends. And then they established a Unitarian church. And we went there.

Well, she was a small woman, but she had lots of personality. And she loved to talk—at home we talked about everything. She went to take her nap one afternoon and didn't wake up—she was 93. But she said, You know, I don't know what the future is. We were talking about religion. She said, You know, I'm extremely curious to know what happens.

My father was a very genial, friendly man. And restless, very restless. He liked to buy a farm and fix it all up and sell it and go on. Well, you know, his people had settled in the East, they had settled up in Maine. They got pretty tired of that country, I think. It was a hard country. And then they began to move west. They moved first into Iowa, in the very early days, and ran cattle. And he liked to farm. We had a very happy sort of a home. I can't remember any dissension. I suppose I'm not a very rebellious person.

I recall when I was about 6 years old, we weren't wealthy people at all, and one of the things Mother gave me for my birthday was a little white parasol. I was so delighted. And I broke the handle on mine. Tragedy. Real tragedy struck.

I think we had a strong Puritan family. You did your job and you did it well. You didn't start anything unless you finished it and you did it well. It was expected of you. If you were assigned a lesson, you did the whole lesson. We went to high school for four years, never missed a day. Got wonderful grades, we always studied together. It was easy.

About morality, well, I've kind of wondered sometimes, because they didn't lecture us, particularly. But when I went away at 18 on a horse stage to come way up here, I never felt my mother worried about me. She knew that we'd be all right. We wrote back and forth very frequently. She'd give advice if you asked for it. But she expected the best of you. And you knew that and you wanted to live up to it. And, after all, you're far happier if you do.

I've worked awfully hard. I always kept a great big garden and the house. But we could take pack horses and go back and pick huckleberries for three days up on Indian Ridge. We had time to go down to the coast in the old Model T when the roads went around. And dig clams and pine crabs. Pick your own bedding and get these little houses and live in them. I think that's gone. And I think that's one reason our young people aren't happy. They have no opportunities to make their own pleasure. And they don't have to do anything. I can't get a boy to come and cut lawns and things. For sure. They say, "I worked an hour and I want my money because I want to go up to Phil's to get some

Coca-Cola because you don't keep it here." Do you know that's a sad thing we've done to them.

Also, I think that people have lost a sense of pride in their families. We always sat down and ate our meals together and discussed everything under the sun, any problem. I find for myself, the thing I need the most is someone to talk over every little plan that I make. We always talked about things so much. I mean politics and religion—discussed them at home. We didn't have TV. I can remember the first time I heard anything coming over the radio. It was a band in Pennsylvania. My brother taught at the university for many years and he was a chemist. But he made his first radio. Little set with headphones, and we heard the band in Pennsylvania. He loved good music. He never married. He and my mother lived together. Well, I've never forgotten that radio. And thinking of it now—we didn't look ahead to what there was going to be. And I think that TV is—well, that's another story. There's so much good that they could put on. And I listen to the news and that's practically the only thing. The whole weekend, the only thing I could listen to was the news and "Meet the Press."

A woman today can take the pill. Well, I think she's destroying herself in a certain way. I don't think it's the physical part of sex, so much as what it does to you mentally. I think they lose a sense of value. Old-fashioned phrase, maybe, damaged goods. And I think it's part of the evolution, our attitude—the amoebas discovered it, maybe. It's nothing new. And I think most of us who were raised on farms, we understood what it was all about. It wasn't a matter of pleasure. It's a matter of propagating the race. And there's so many other things that are so much more important. I think that people think that that's the important thing in life. It's a necessary part and it's a part of marriage, but it's not the important thing.

Love is important. I think it's a matter of personality. Someone that you find that you communicate with without having to talk too much. That you feel secure with. I always felt that way with my husband. And my sister and her husband have been very happy together. And I think that it has an attraction, a sexual attraction, of course. But it's such an unimportant part of it, that soon dies. But sex isn't what makes you love people.

Well, there's always rough spots in a marriage. But you have made a contract not only with God but with your government, and you have this feeling that you must make the thing work. You've got to keep your side of the contract. And I don't think it's a matter of one ruling the other. It's going together. I was expected to take care of the house and garden and things. If he couldn't get home to milk the cow, I could milk the cow. But you feel no feeling of resentment about it.

I love my sister, too. There's that kind of love. When I go to see my sister, we're not demonstrative people. But just to be in the room with her and she with me, and to say little things, is marvelous.

I met my husband at a dance in Waterville. They used to have little dances where the neighborhood came together. We didn't have to have the police then. Nobody did any drinking. We danced square dances. But I knew him seven years before we were married. He had only had part of high school education, and he was away at war for two years in France. So many things came along. Finally, I had some friends who were English, and Mr. Knox, who knew us, looked at me, and he said, "Why don't you get married and go start living, instead of going to school so much?" You know, it seemed like a good idea. My sister was always a bit more dominant, and I thought I was going back to Columbia Teacher's College with her. And then I just decided I'd get married, and I'm very glad I did. He asked me. In those days, he had to ask me.

We had our son. I think that experience makes you feel more sympathetic, more understanding of other people. If you go through any experience, I think it makes you understand people going through that experience more. I think there is something special about it. We were very good friends. But he was in the Second World War. He was in the Air Corps. Went in when he was 17½. Volunteered. General Hap Arnold was a friend of a friend of ours, and he had been up here and stayed with us. I have three nice guest rooms over the garage. And he'd stay there when he needed a rest. And he talked to Roy about going into the cadets. He did very well. Very happy, but it was '43. And he didn't become a pilot because they didn't need any more pilots. And I think he was terribly disappointed. And then he went into the army of occupation over there for three years. In Japan. And it seemed to me when he came back, he was an entirely different individual. I never could get close to him again.

Oh God, I'm opposed to war. I had another experience during the war. Down by Corvallis Camp there was a big hospital, and I worked with the Red Cross for years up there. And they asked me if I would take some boys from there who weren't getting well. This was in the summer of '44. They would send them two at a time on a two-week leave. They didn't pay us anything, but we had a big garden, a milk cow, and killed our own meat and everything. So they started. These were from the division that went into Guadalcanal. They were the boys who were sick and couldn't go home yet on their home leave. So we said, Okay, there's plenty of room, plenty to eat. And it was a marvelous experience, because in '45 the navy took over, after the war moved into the Pacific, and read the records, and the doctor called me and asked me if we'd take sailors and marines as well. Because, he said, many of these boys were marked 1,000 percent better when they got back after two weeks and sometimes a month. And over two summers we had fifty boys who stayed here. And there wasn't one that ever let us down.

Those boys sure hated General MacArthur. If I got a little bossy, they'd say, "Now don't act like MacArthur." They became a very real part of our life—I hear from quite a number of them. And occasionally one comes by. And it's just like one of the family. My husband was a very gay, happy person. And if they were able to do anything—some of the marines were waiting for more surgery—he'd have them dig postholes and he paid them. And the haying time came, and they'd work in the hay field if they could. And he'd pay them the regular wages. And all they needed was a chance to just get away from it. Because after all, young people are very sensitive. They didn't hate the Japanese. We were trying to force them to hate. They talked about the terrible things that went on. They didn't want to kill people. And when you go into a cave full of Japanese with a flamethrower and kill them all, it does something to you. The only thing you can do is to listen. If they went through it, you ought to be able to listen to it.

I go to my doctor. But I think it's largely a matter of what your state of mind is. I have a bad knee. I slipped on the ice and twisted it and didn't go to the doctor. I had it operated on, and it still doesn't operate very good. But you kind of have to forget it and not expect people to love you for your looks.

I think I've been pretty mean sometimes. I don't like certain things. Well, there used to be a big barn down there, and I'd just take a walk down to it. One day, there were two unclothed young people having a tumble in the hay. Well, my dog Duke barked, so they jumped up. And amazed to see somebody, and they had a boat there and they went down to it, and they were trying to talk to me. And I said, "This is private land, and I think you'd better go on." And she said, "I hope we didn't shock you." And I said, "No, I was raised on a farm. I'm used to it." Maybe that was mean.

I'm not afraid. Not of people. But I woke up one night and there was a light and then a flash and I leaped out of bed. I was petrified. I really thought the house was on fire. So I went to look. I'd left the light on in the bathroom and there was heat lightning all around. It was lighting up the room. Watched it for a while and I was all right. Well, we heard something downstairs. Didn't we, Duke? And we looked all around, but couldn't find anything. Duke was awfully excited. And we went back to bed and pretty soon we heard it again. We have a fire and police station up here and Corporal Ivy had said to me— they're very kind—"If anything ever bothers you, call me." And I kept hearing this bumping and I wasn't feeling very brave, so I didn't go outside. But I was pretty sure it wasn't a person. So Corporal Ivy came over—it was two in the morning. And then we knew what it was, a bear, because we went outside and there were droppings out there. So then he went home and then the bear came back about four and got in the pantry and just knocked all the jars and everything around, terrible hell broke loose. I saw him running away. It was just a little bear and he was hungry. Men and dogs went after him, but they never did catch him. We cleaned up the mess. I didn't want to kill any bear.

I've been to the East to see my sister. We used to go up into Canada occasionally and down into Mexico. I went to England two years ago. I'm a good traveler. I like to travel. And I went to England with a friend that I'm very fond of. She's lived up here—she's a neighbor and she used to teach. And we had a wonderful time. We wrote postcards when we were there. And then we didn't take a picture nor write a postcard for three whole weeks. We got these passes on the railroad train. Just go down to the station and get on a train and go anyplace. We had a wonderful time. And people are so friendly. All you have to do is smile. They know you're an American the minute you open your mouth. Especially up in Scotland. Just as friendly as they could be. Which was a thing that surprised me, because of the tales you hear.

*Kristin Lavransdatter.* By Sigrid Undset. It's the best book I ever read, I think. It takes people through their whole lives. It takes place in Norway in the fourteenth century. But she is a marvelous writer, because they're people. You feel they are friends. It's well worth the time it takes to read it, I think. That's my opinion.

I love to reread Dickens. I'm extremely fond of Thomas Hardy's books. They're so easy to read, and the people are so real. And then you meet somebody who seems just like them. People change so little in the world.

Virginia Woolf. I don't care for her diaries, just the great people that she had lunch with. I think she must have been quite a snob.

I'm not political, except that I have taken a deep interest in the schools and worked hard for them. Mainly to get a good school for the children here. And we need a good school. I feel the first three grades in our school have kind of gone bad. And I think we have very poor teachers, as well as poor parents. In the first three grades they learn their attitudes. All a teacher can ever do is to make a child curious. You can't learn a thing for them. But if you can make them want to learn, you've done something important.

Watergate was the best play I've ever seen. I stayed home from one play in Ashland to watch Watergate. I was very proud that the Constitution stood up so well. I'm a Democrat. I was raised Republican. And it seemed to me it was a terrible thing, the worst thing that ever happened to us. But we did it to ourselves. People will not think. But the Constitution did prevail. Democracy is slow. It's not like a tyranny. In Iran they had that. You just disappear.

Women have always run the world, and I think they're kind of slipping. I think they're demanding, instead of earning it. Oh, I think they should have equal pay and things like that. But this matter of taking over things. Yes, I'd vote for ERA. But I'm still so old-fashioned. You know, the nasty dirty words that people use. I like it if a man opens the car door, and I think we aren't the same physically or mentally. Well, I mean I think maybe it's the result of evolution. The fact that we have always been the helpmate instead of taking charge. But the one that's boss of things often isn't the one who runs it.

I'm very much in favor of civil rights for all people. I think the Indians and the black people have had it terrible, and it's a very guilty thing for Indian tribes to have to walk and beg. What's the matter with us?

Our pride in our work has deteriorated. It's because we've been willing to accept poor things, been willing to buy automobiles that were extinct in a few years. And not even expecting them to run well. But we go on buying them. We buy stoves that will last a few years and then you have to buy a new one. My old kitchen stove has been there— bought it when we were first married—for fifty-seven years. Still works good.

I think that's one of the foundations of a great deal of our difficulties—that people hate their work and don't do it proudly. My husband loved the sawmill business. He was a logger and a lumberman and timber and things meant so much to him. When we were going places, he'd like to stop and look at little mills. He liked it. It made him a happy man.

I believe I am patriotic. That's why I say young people should travel if they can and see that there are many nice things here. They hate the establishment. But who is it? It's them. It's us. And we have the power —it's a slow process, but we have the power—to make it what we want. You don't do it by standing on a soapbox and yelling. So the American Dream isn't in our grasp. It's a terrible thing when you reach your dream. There's nothing to go on to. Hitch your wagon to a star, not an automobile.

I don't think people should be forced to retire. I think it takes something away from them. Now, my husband never retired. My sister's husband was at Princeton all his life. He was an economist. He was one of the three men who devised Social Security. Went to Europe and worked it all out. That's his big baby. And then he was made dean of the faculty there for twenty-four years. He's written several books on Social Security and administration. And then he had to retire when he reached 75. They made him. But his mind was so very clear. He has written four books since. But all of a sudden you're out of the main-stream. Well, they've gone around the world. They've traveled a great deal more than we ever did. But now he's not well, and I just feel that his illness is so much just feeling out of things. His mind is still so clear and that's a terrible waste.

Cruelty makes me mad. To anyone. To an animal, to a person. It affects me more than anything else, and that's one reason I think I hate war so. When I witness cruelty, I'm very apt to raise my voice.

I think life is a process of gradual growth. I think the people who are willing to adapt as change comes do best, and change has been going on for a couple of trillion years. You can adapt to what comes along, say not ride a horse forever instead of getting an automobile. You can even adapt to food. These young people that rush around living off the land, they eat the most dreadful stuff. I think it's all in their minds. My mother used to put our food on the table, and she'd say, "Eat what's on your plate and enjoy it." So I can eat anything. I have an awful feel-ing that these children that are growing up are going to be terribly conservative. Well, they've had so much freedom that it's kind of piled up on them, I think. There is no one more conservative than a young person. Their hair has to be long. They conform. And they wear their very unpleasant uniform. I see so many of them. We drove up to Cougar Dam that's up here, a beautiful place. It's only a couple of miles. And there's a little hot springs on one of the creeks that had been way back in the woods for many years. And we drove past there, and there were vans and old wrecks and the clothes of the young peo-ple. They went up there and dug this thing out, and bathe and they're spoiling the ecology and the Forest Service doesn't know what to do. We drove by and there was a young woman standing with a baby in her arms. She turned and looked at us and she could've been 100 years old. She looked so haggard and unhappy. And here I've read the command-ments all the time and I see somebody who can walk, and go where they want to whenever they want to. They have everything. Why waste it? And they're not happy. There's probably an awful lot of them who are very responsible and doing things. But we don't hear about them.

Well, death comes to all of us and it has happened since the beginning of time. There have been millions of women who've lost their husbands and sons. Why should I think I'm any more abused than anyone else? And nobody wants to listen to your troubles. We've learned that from childhood. I don't like to talk about it too much, because I think it gets you in a bad frame of mind. I'm not a Christian Scientist, but there's nothing you can do about it. And I think many of our death rites are very barbaric. I believe strongly in cremation. And I don't think we need wailing walls. And I'm not at all sure we need so many of these old religions. Two Jehovah's Witnesses came by, met me as I was bringing Duke up from swimming the other day. Standing there. "Have you read the Bible?" And I said, "Yes, I've read the Bible. Have you read Shakespeare?" And then they come and say, "Are you saved?" And I don't know what they mean. I literally don't know what they mean. I say, "What do you mean?" "Have you been washed in the blood of the lamb?" And I said, "How messy."

I don't think there's any reason to believe in our immortality. It's an idea that we humans have had. And propagated in the churches. I think each one of us must decide what we are going to think about it. That's why I live from day to day. There was a Scotsman I knew from Eugene who was a Unitarian, and he said the only true immortality is in the hearts of your friends.

# Milton Rettenberg

$M$ilton Rettenberg spends every morning in his small office on Manhattan's busy West Fifty-seventh Street. On the walls are a photo of George Gershwin, a sketch of Mozart, a framed law degree, a letter from Hendrik Willem van Loon. Rettenberg, at 79, is a strong, stocky man who plants each foot firmly as he strides. His gray hair has become a fringe, and his fading eyesight has made glasses imperative, but he dresses with care and taste. He wore gray slacks, a navy blue blazer, a blue shirt, and a white tie on the day we met.

Rettenberg is a confirmed New Yorker. He was born in Manhattan on January 27, 1899, at 114th Street and Fifth Avenue—there was a farm across the street from his house, he remembers. He has stayed in the city ever since. He attended City College and got his law degree from Columbia in 1922. But he is not simply a lawyer. He has been playing the piano since 1915. As a teen-ager, he played at concerts, dances, and recitals, exploring both the classical repertoire and pop music. When he served in the navy during World War I—it was aboard a ship docked on the Hudson—he entertained his fellow seamen with his playing. Rettenberg had gone to primary school in Manhattan with Yip Harburg, the songwriter, and Ira Gershwin, George's lyricist brother. Those friendships led to others over the years. He played piano with Paul Whiteman's orchestra. He replaced George Gershwin as piano soloist on tour—performing "Rhapsody in Blue." From 1927 to 1951 he was the pianist on more than fifteen thousand radio shows. He has recorded prolifically from age 17, when he did some Virginia reels, until 1961, when he stopped. He continues to practice every day at home.

His first marriage, in 1928, ended in divorce in 1951; it produced his only child, a son who is a political affairs career officer with the State Department and who gave Rettenberg his two grandchildren, a boy and a girl. He married again in 1968. He presently spends only half-days in the office because of his wish to spend the rest of his time with his wife, who has been ill.

Rettenberg is an expert on music copyright, a rare and complex specialty. Ad agencies pay him to screen commercials for possible copy-

*right infringement (is that simple jingle really a chunk of someone else's tune?). He attempts to mediate in conflicts between music publishers, and he defends the rights of composers who seek his aid. He is a consultant to BMI (Broadcast Music Inc.), the music licensing organization. He once had a desk at BMI in New York—prior to that he always worked at home, and for two years now, he has had his own office. His desk is a mound of papers, envelopes, tapes. Yet he does not practice law; he estimates that he has done that, literally, for a little more than a year in his life. For the most part, he has done what he wanted to do.*

New York early in this century? The pace was moderate. The crime rate, outside of apartment looting and con men who came to doors, was minimal. The cops were friendly. The streets were safe to walk on. There was a personal relationship, as I saw it from the time I was 11 or 12, between teachers in elementary schools—between teacher, parent, and child. There was an almost family relationship. Teachers used to write letters to parents. Unbidden. They'd write a letter to a parent: "Dear Mrs. Jones, I'm so happy to be able to tell you that Bill passed the examination for entrance into 3A with such success that we are instituting what is called a skip. He is going over 3A and is being placed in 3B at the conclusion of the school semester." This type of thing went on.

On 114th Street, between Fifth and Lenox, we lived in a two-family house; the owner was a friend of my father's. He rented out a four-room apartment to the Rettenbergs, and he lived upstairs. Across the street from us, I can remember as if it were yesterday, was a two-story frame house—looked like the kind of farmhouse you would've seen in the Catskills. The same thing: There was livestock in the backyard. A couple of sheep and a goat.

The houses were either two- or three-story flats or—west of Fifth Avenue and all the way over to Eighth—all brownstone houses. There weren't any high-rise apartments, except on Seventh Avenue, where there was—in 1906—Graham Court, on 116th Street, and there were four other high-rise apartments between 112th and 114th on either side of the street. Those were eight- and nine-story apartment houses, which isn't exactly high rise. The Graham Court was about a ten- or eleven-story—which still stands, and that was part of the Astor estate, as was the Apthorp at 79th and Broadway, which covers an entire block, and which also is still standing.

Except in cases of family emergencies, you didn't move at the end of every two-year lease. We did because of deaths and marriages in the family. But people stayed put for eight or ten years in one apartment. We explored the city mainly by way of the Madison Avenue streetcar. My grandfather lived way out in East New York near what is now the East New York station of the Long Island Railroad. This was open territory. My grandfather had a three-story frame house there, beautiful gardens, grape arbors, a picture of one of them we still have at home. This is now the worst type of ghetto. At that time it was open fields. In other words, the train station was the equivalent of four or five city blocks away. There was no building between the rear garden and the train station in East New York.

Almost everything has changed, of course. One of the things that I feel is the need of more newspapers today. You see, the Sunday papers —there was the *World*, there was the *American*, there was the *Tribune*, there was the *Herald*. For five cents apiece. Evening papers with the exception of the *Press* and the *Sun*, sold at a penny. The *Sun* was two cents, the *Press* was three cents. And the old *New York Post* also sold for three cents.

More important: We have lost a sense of ease in living—even poor people had a certain amount of ease. My father married on seventeen dollars a week in 1897, but we managed to get a summer vacation every year. Now, people are money hungry. We developed a state where it's really a dog-eat-dog state. There's no question about it. I don't have to tell you. You're not as old as I am, but you know that the guy next door—I don't care how good a friend he is—you don't trust these days in anything. Or your wife or your sisters don't trust every woman they meet. When I was a kid, my folks had friends with whom they courted or double-dated back in the early '90s or late '80s, in the nineteenth century. And we kids, on all sides of the family, referred to these as aunts and uncles, because they were so closely a part of our family. I don't think this exists anywhere in the United States, or for that matter, in the world today.

On the other hand, I still don't know how I lived going to a movie show in mid-August in 1916 in a closed theater. So air conditioning has done a greal deal for that. I do remember attending a performance of *The Gingham Girl* at the old Earl Carroll Theater with Jack Donahue and Helen Ford in September 1922. We had seats in the first row mezzanine, which was choice for a musical. And the outside temperature was about ninety-three. There was no air conditioning. And perspiration was running down my arm and off my fingertips. My arms were over the balustrade so the drops were falling on people sitting in the orchestra. That's one thing that's better.

Another: We don't have so much food spoilage. We have a great many additives in our food. The actual value of them we don't know, but we do know that the average person today runs from three and a half inches taller than the average person twenty-five years ago. So maybe they're building up physique. Maybe they're building up preventives against diseases.

New York then? I loved it when the east side of Fifth Avenue from Sixtieth to Eighty-sixth was nothing but gorgeous private homes. And I could've told you who lived in every one of them. I don't like those apartments facing the park today. Even though they were all stone mansions, the combination of the trees and the low three- and four-story houses gave you a feeling of quiet suburbia, which doesn't exist anymore, and which I think a lot of people would love to enjoy provided they could afford to pay the exorbitant commutation fees.

My mother was an adoring mother. They both—she modernly, my father not too modernly—were great taskmasters as far as my work in school was concerned. My father was a demon on etymology. He wasn't born in New York. He was born in Birmingham, England, and he was very careful in his speech. And at the dinner table, if I pronounced as everybody does today, *route* as *rowt* instead of the normal *root*, which was correct, I would have been hit on the fingers with a ruler by both my father and my English teacher in school, who didn't permit anybody to say *rowt*. My father taught me to respect language. For example, you will not find the word *lyricist* in any dictionary published before 1951. It did not get into Webster's until 1953. I have a 1949 International—the large, the expensive big one with everything in it. There is no word *lyricist* in the book.

Getting back to the family. Three of us were alone. We ate dinner together every night. We talked over the table. My father taught me to read before I even entered kindergarten. I was only 5 years old during the Russo-Japanese War and I could already read all of the headlines and a great deal of the smaller print.

My earliest memories go back to several incidents, all occurring before my fourth birthday. Once on Thanksgiving 1902, in the days when kids ran around dressed as ragamuffins and wore false faces, an aunt of mine who was only six years older than I was, and who by the way is still alive, walked into the house with a false face on. And I screamed. I was so horribly frightened. On another occasion I can remember dipping a biscuit into a cup of tea and the biscuit broke off in its softness and landed on a brand-new Windsor tie I was wearing. Number three, this is a commercial for Rogers Peet. My mother, when I was not quite 4, had bought me a beautiful blue serge reefer with brass buttons. And the first Sunday afternoon I wore it I fell in a puddle on Lenox Avenue and 115th Street and ruined it. A reefer was a small pea jacket, popular with the kids in those days. And the other one, actually, was before my third birthday. A cart drew up one night in mid-October across the street from our little apartment in front of the frame house. Horse-drawn cart, which probably was a vegetable cart during the day, on which there was a load of red flares lighted and a man was making an election speech, for whom I don't remember. But I remember seeing the glare from the bedroom window and getting out of bed and leaning over without falling out of the window, and seeing and hearing this man make a political address from the rear of the truck. We had no radio, TV in those days.

I learned from my parents. One thing I learned from my mother and father both, and that was watching the dollar. My father went into business in 1907, in the summer, with an ex-employer. And they built themselves up a nice trade. He was president of the printers association. But the first thing that failed in the October crash of 1907 was the bank in which the firm had all its money. And my father started to draw out of the business, after he had earned anywhere from $75 to $150 a week. In the early part of the century, that was a hell of a salary. He drew $30 a week out of his savings to run the house, which was not what you would earn then, and my mother was such a good manager that on that $30 I still got four weeks summer vacation at a resort. That's how I learned how to watch dollars. That was a hell of a good experience.

I love walking, probably because my father loved walking. And he had two or three cronies with whom he played cards on Saturdays, and on Sunday mornings we all met during the early fall and we walked as far as from, say, mid-Harlem to Park Hill in Yonkers. With me along. My father was an avid baseball fan, so when the weather was right, we used to go out with this group and we'd play pick-up baseball with the older men. I was the only child. But I played along with them. Later, I was a registered AAU soccer player for seven years. And I also played water polo in college. A sport which interestingly enough, when my father saw it for the first time, he saw it during a period in which he had told me he'd take me out of school if I didn't stop playing that horrible sport, soccer, in which you are so susceptible to physical injury. But frankly after he saw the first half of a water polo game that we played with the University of Pennsylvania, he decided that water polo was the thing I had to give up. He didn't give a damn if I kept playing soccer. Even though by this time both of my shins were corrugated from taking kicks. I was sports-oriented, and I read a great deal about sports. I could probably give you a list of any one of a number of intercollegiate champions as far back as 1904, and the batting averages and positions played by baseball players who operated in the National League prior to 1912.

It may interest you to know that there was another person who could do the same thing, and it's rather an anomaly. That person was Ethel Barrymore. The damnedest baseball fan you ever met in your life. She knew McGraw personally and she could tell you that Sy Seymour in 1905 hit .377 and led the National League, beating out Mike Donlan and Honus Wagner for the batting title.

In recent years, I've tried to reach an understanding of my own values. You see, you get fears. I'm getting older. What is going to happen to me? I won't have capital or income on which to live. Besides which, I have been paying alimony to my first wife, which I still do, because she lives nicely. Paying alimony, sending the check which goes to her lawyer, had to become a reflex, or it would trouble me. I write it out as though I was writing out a tab for a shoe shine.

I had to realize a complete understanding of the fact that I have a talent that people are willing to buy. I do not market it as such. I do not advertise it. But apparently I serve an important segment of the radio and TV industry, which doesn't want to see me retire, and two of them within the last year have given me substantial increases when I threatened to retire. But I wouldn't threaten to retire anymore, because I have discovered that the entire mental makeup disintegrates with retirement.

It may interest you to know that it has nothing to do with me at all. I know two women whose husbands retired at 65, well able to take care of themselves. Millionaires, who hung around the house. And whose wives had to get psychiatric help because they couldn't stand having husbands around the house. One of them said, "You know, I married Henry for better or for worse. But not for lunch."

I think in the growing-up period there was a certain sense of security in the family relationship which does not exist today. And I have so many examples of young folks today to whom the family is just a name. It's something you define. Whether you enjoy the fruits of family life is negligent. And what the young folks do these days, God knows I'm no prude. Because I haven't lived a prude's life, especially when I was doing one-night stands, if you know what I mean. But when I see, as has happened in the last couple of years, the granddaughter or the grandson of a university dean openly live on the campus with another student and marry on commencement day. But everybody in the institution knew that they had been living together for four years. And the grandparents—they took it. The kids are happy. I would've thought this was something that was almost sheer blasphemy. Thirty or forty years ago. But I've taken a freer position on it, probably because a couple of the most blatant cases are very nice kids from very nice families, who see the order of things as governed by a set of rules which wasn't recognized sixty years ago.

Do you subscribe to *The American Scholar?* I wish to heaven I could show you an article in it on sex and the college campus written by the dean of an important California university. His article was full of four-letter words which I was not allowed to use when I was a kid 10 years old. And it was in the *Phi Beta Kappa Quarterly*, which isn't *Hustler*. Frankly, from one point of view, I don't think it's all bad. Our society is open, and I think strangely enough it is opened a great deal more since shows like *Oh! Calcutta!* and *Hair* have made successes. The human body is nothing to be ashamed of. At one time sex was promiscuity. And love was blessed of the Lord. I can tell you that well over fifty years ago I used to date a very fine girl from an eminent Jewish family—if I mentioned the names of the relatives, which I won't, you would realize the type of family it was—and she finally told me at dinner one night that she would never marry a man that she hadn't tried out in the first place, because among her parents' friends there were too many divorces completely based on sexual incompatibility. This was well over fifty years ago. It isn't new. I want to tell you something else. Mugging isn't new. In February 1916 at the entrance to Central Park, a quarter to nine P.M., a thoroughly lighted street, Lenox Avenue and 110th Street, I was held up by three adolescent youngsters at the point of a gun. That is now more than sixty years ago. So that isn't new.

Marriage isn't new either. Mutual respect isn't new. Let's forget the word *love*. I think we take that for granted, unless some gigolo marries a woman who has a fortune and just wants someone to take her around so she isn't alone. We have a lot of promiscuity. The reason I say this is that in my own personal experience if my wife and I at this moment were to sit down to write an invitation list to a cocktail party we might want to give, before we had the name of one married couple, we have twelve to fifteen, not divorced females, but alone females whose husbands have passed away. Many of them still probably miss their mates and don't want to enter into a promiscuous relationship with any old Tom, Dick, or Harry, look around for some nice guy who will take them out to dinner, and if, by God, the thing develops to a point not of marriage but of satisfying each other's sexual wants, it goes on all the time. And nobody knows better than I do, because I was single from '51 to '68. Besides which I played the piano very well and still do. I was a desirable guest. I had enough money to take a woman out to dinner. I had relations with a lot of women during that period. As I look back, there were probably eight or ten more that would've been easy prey if I felt so inclined.

And then there's marriage. First time I met my first wife was a very strange thing. It was at a party given for a girl who was to be married the next week, a girl who I had dated for six years. But well, interestingly enough, she had a friend—she didn't come from New York, but she had a friend from the old hometown who knew that she sang and who knew I played a hell of a piano, and he said, I think you ought to meet Milton Rettenberg. So I was introduced to her—she was a friend of the bride-to-be—I was introduced to her and we had a date within three days. Three and a half months later we were married.

We had our son. When he was growing up, he was pretty well under the domination of his mother. He went to nursery school, where I never saw him. When he went to prep school, he went to Horace Mann —where fortunately the relationship grew because I used to conduct assemblies and give recitals. Or I would give a talk on the life of a famous musician whose birthday took place that week. This sort of thing. So I became close to the kid. But it's much better now than it was immediately after the divorce. Immediately after the divorce it was a very poor one, and that's not due to any failing on my part, but due to the fact that his mother had no one else to cling to, and he became a sort of a protective genie. She rubbed the lamp and her son was there to help her out. But he learned. Eventually he came to my office, apologized, wanted bygones to be bygones, wrote me a letter when he announced his engagement. It was very friendly. I kept it because it's a kind of memento. The wheel has turned full circle.

I believe in an inner spirit. I do not believe there's a guy up in the clouds with a big beard. I think God is inside every person, but the person has to recognize him. That belief has helped to give me a belief in myself. The joke of the whole thing is that belief has been utilized to the extent that in the last two years, as my income tax statements will show, I've made more money than I've made in any two individual years in my entire existence. I'm a retired man who is, you know, working a half-day five days a week.

Of course, I've taken care of myself. I use a great deal of preventative medicine. Well, in the first place, I've been a sucker for pharmacology, thanks to my closest personal friend, who happens to be a great internist and lives twelve hundred miles away but with whom I communicate by letter a great deal of the time. I was a guinea pig for many drugs. I learned a great deal about the properties of drugs. I knew what to take, and I knew what not to throw money away on. If the people that buy the expensive proprietary drugs had sense enough to read the labels, 90 percent of them would buy three hundred aspirins in a cut-rate drugstore.

My wife had an uncle who was a distinguished practitioner in the Middle West, and he told me one day—he said, "Look, you know, I go to some old patient, I give her a complete physical. I take all the information. Heart, lung . . . I come to a definite conclusion that all she needs is a couple of aspirin three or four times a day. But I cannot give her aspirin because if I do, she'll tell me she can go to the corner drugstore and get that. She doesn't need me to prescribe it. So I give her a six-dollar drug which doesn't do her any more good than the aspirin, and then she's satisfied."

Travel has been useful to me because it led me to the point where I decided that living in New York offers a lot more than any other town in the world. I've never been to Berlin. I've never been to Moscow. But I've been all through the British Isles, all the Scandinavian countries. I've been in Spain, Portugal, Madeira, Rome, Florence. I've been in Greece. I've been in Turkey. I've been in North and South America. With the exception of Aruba, I've been in every island of the Caribbean. I've also traveled through the hills of Guatemala. I've seen a great deal of civilization. I started going to London when I was 24 years old. And I have often said to my wife, If I were to get out of the country, you know, for the purposes of retirement, I believe I could live in a style to which I am accustomed in two towns in Europe. More easily than any other towns in the world. One is London, the other is Copenhagen.

Theater has mattered to me, too. In the twenties, before I was married, I saw practically every important play that was produced on Broadway. In one season—1921–22—my book showed that I attended ninety-four Broadway shows. Frankly, I think of the theater mainly for entertainment, and when I know that one, two, or three members of the cast are going to give me the satisfaction of their own performance, I will enjoy a show even if it's a lousy show. For example, how many people remember a play by Noël Coward called *The Vortex*, which was produced in 1924? It was a flop. But Noël Coward in that show gave me the ultimate satisfaction of one performer.

I knew Paul Robeson. I first met him when he entered Columbia Law School back in 1919. And I was very friendly with him up until the time of his speech in Madison Square Garden in 1951. And I didn't break off. He was afraid to call me on the phone because his phones were tapped. In fact, FBI men came to my office, and this soured me. I was a very close friend of Paul Robeson for over thirty years, and he was in and out of my house as often as three nights a week.

I once went along when he played in a basketball game. I recall he played against a team organized by the National Sugar Refining Company in Yonkers, a factory team. There were about seven or eight whites who played on their team, and I don't think any of them could sign his name straight. And when we came up to play the game, they could find a place for the white players to dress and undress. But the black boy who was this marvelous character, who was a Phi Beta, made All-America for two years, best scholastic record in college, best singer in college, best actor in college. He had to dress in the men's john. They couldn't find a place for him to dress. That was my first experience with Paul. In my own building I had to instruct the doorman. I said if a black man comes here at such and such an hour, please don't send him to the service elevator.

Sure, it's gotten better, but I believe it should have a long time ago. I can tell you of instances before he entered law school, when he was an All-American at Rutgers and they played an Ivy League team. After he was down by the rules, guys piled up and walked on his body and no white referee ever called a penalty.

I was very much in favor of the civil rights movement. Look what Charlayne Hunter is doing today. She's doing a beautiful public relations and editorial job. We had a son of a bitch of a governor who didn't want to let her get into the college.

I can admire this country. For instance, I saw a marvelous program on public TV last night on the grain-elevator situation. I found out something that I'd never known. I thought I knew something. That grain dust is six times as volatile as coal dust. Also that the care taken is negligible because we don't have the manpower. We have tens of thousands of grain elevators operating in this country daily, and we have fourteen hundred inspectors under the aegis of the federal government, who cover six other things as well as the grain elevators. And they run from 2 to 6 percent efficiency because they don't get to them. I learned that. In this country we can criticize.

The thing I regret most was not in my early days asking enough for my services. I didn't realize my value. I accepted much less than my services were worth. And from that point of view, I didn't understand the value of the money that I had within me. Not the money that I had when I went to market to buy food. I could've gotten anywhere from two to five times what I was paid. It was timidity, not paranoia, but a fear that if I asked too much I wouldn't get anything.

One of the things that gets me angry is just reading what goes on with the young folks. I mean, three kids raping and killing an 82-year-old woman. I boil. My wife doesn't even want to hear it on TV. She can't imagine things like these happening. If this ever happened before, it didn't get much publicity. I have a feeling that it did not happen before. The thing that I have been against for a long time is the treatment of criminals. Hardened criminals under the age of 16. I think this is desecration. I think it's the ruination of anything that you want to call a democratic function of society. That kid had seven prior arrests and he killed an 82-year-old woman before his 16th birthday, spent two nights in a refuge, and came home on parole. This has got to be changed. When you get somebody like this, you don't send them to a correctional institute for forty-eight hours. You put them away for life. No parole. And a lot of these kids, daredevils, do what they're doing with the idea—what the hell—forty-eight hours and I'll be back out on the street.

I have another fetish which makes me angry as hell. I think that we learn a complete incorrect English language because of the mispronunciations by anchormen of the three major networks of very common words. This drives me nuts because it happens every night. And so far, I have only found one newscaster or commentator on any of the networks whom I have yet to find guilty of mispronunciation, and he just retired. Eric Sevareid.

This is the list. There is no word *ēffectual*, there is no word *ēfficient*. There is no word *ēffective*. Because Eisenhower didn't know that there was no long *e*, they copied Eisenhower. This is every night of the week. *Affluent, affluence, influence*—all wrong. *Repercussion. Culinary. Cuisine Penalize. Medieval. Saboteur, provocateur*. I don't expect an interview with a football player to be bereft, so to speak, of mispronunciations. But you get your idols, you've got your Chancellors, your Brinkleys, your Cronkites—people listen to these guys, and if they say it, it's got to be good English. And they copy them.

I heard a kid in an elevator the other day: "I woke up like nine thirty this morning." I don't know what you're like when you wake up like nine thirty. But this is destroying the language.

And there's worse. If everything goes the way it's going now, I think that you probably will be taking three pills a day for your average meals. I think we're getting into a computerization of our entire livelihood, including the preparation of foods, which bodes no good, because we will be living a life-style gravely devoid of true human values. I'm talking about everything. You scratch my back and I'll scratch yours. You begin to get false values as to who is and who is not a friend. And the young people. I think they're all groping. Yeah, I think.

I don't think we've seen the end of this third industrial revolution, so to speak. We've got a bunch of kids who are given such freedom of election. In all aspects of life. I think there is actually too much freedom in the nature of electives at the universities. I'm so tied up with university life. I'm a fund raiser for this outfit. I'm on this minority business. I'm tied up a lot with things academic. Maybe I see more of it than the average guy.

Well, let me say this about death. I am not a believer in funerals. In my own family I have attended one funeral in the last ten years, and I assure you more than one of my relatives has passed on. The last funeral I attended was a funeral of an aunt of mine about four years ago. There have been two or three dead since. But I have my own life to live. I believe in being gainfully occupied. If you can't be gainfully occupied, unless you're physically incapacitated, go out and find something to do. As for my own mortality, what comes to my mind is, well, don't buy stocks which may not improve for ten years because you may not be alive in ten years to pay that 25-percent tax. I'm aware of death, but I don't think about it. I don't let that pall come over me.

My father had a better EKG at 70 than I had at 50. At 78 he got out of bed, singing, and he walked to the bathroom singing, and he never came out. He never worried about death.

# Sara Bloom

*T*here is nothing openly extraordinary about Sara Bloom. She is a tiny gray-haired woman who lives in an immaculate Victorian house on a quiet street in Lynn, Massachusetts. From her kitchen window she can see the Atlantic. She is surrounded by strong, old furniture, by books, records (old 78-rpm albums in abundance), family photos, plants. There is a lace tablecloth on her dining-room table; it is a room that seems appealingly frozen in time.

She did not finish high school. "I've always considered myself an unfinished product," she says. She was one of ten children, her parents coming to America from Russia before the turn of the century. The entire family worked hard; most of the children sacrificed their education for work. Sara has worked for most of her life—in a local bank, for a coal company, and, for twenty-six years, as "chief cook and bottle washer" for a trucking company. She has never left Lynn.

She was married in 1929; almost twenty years later, her husband separated from her, and they were divorced in 1953. "He had a roving eye," she says emphatically. They have two children, daughters— Elsa, a writer, wife, and mother of Mrs. Bloom's two grandchildren; and Verna, a respected actress. She has lived in her present house since 1942. In 1949 she sold the upper half of it to her sister.

What gives Sara Bloom her strength, her identity—and the respect of those who know her—is her individuality, her independence. She took swimming lessons at age 77 (she was born in May 1900 in Lynn). She has kept in touch with books, music, theater, and films over the years. She has been intensely loyal to her family—and inspiring to them. "I love myself," she says. "You can't care about others unless you do." She is known and liked by many longtime residents of Lynn. "I'm a friendly person," she asserts, "who treats people as equals."

She pursues her interests actively, without a sign of wear. She walks briskly, her head up, comments emerging in a steady flow. She dodges adversity, or disregards it. Her spirit is a positive one.

"I'm not ready for the rocking chair," she says. "I retired at 75, and if the darned firm hadn't moved out of Lynn, I'd still be working." She no longer goes to a job every day, but she refuses to stagnate.

*To those in her family and beyond it who have been touched by her sense of affirmation, her presence continues to be reassuring.*

Lynn was beautiful when I was growing up. We lived on Blossom Street, near the Commons. We had a nice house right beside Saint Stephen's Church. And they had a tennis court and there were lovely people. We went to the schools around there. There was a little conflict with the Christians calling us "sheeney" and ridiculing us. That's the way they were at the time. And my father, when he came to this country, he wanted to rent a flat. But when he told them how many children he had, they wouldn't rent it to him. The section where we first lived was very, very nice, but like all sections after a period of twenty-five, thirty years was very run down. So he bought this house on Blossom Street.

He had a store, a clothing store where he sold ladies' apparel and furs. He was a tailor by profession, and he was very trustworthy. So they just cleaned out the store, and he lost that. He lost the business. Everything seemed to climb up, and there was illness, too. And that probably disturbed him. When I was young, I couldn't understand all the problems. As I got older, I realized that my mother was overwhelmed with life. She came over to this country with her mother, who couldn't read or write or speak English. But she was very strong, and she did everything. She cared for my mother just like she did in the old country. And then one child after another was born. And it was just very frustrating, and she never prepared meals for us. She couldn't. My grandmother was the mainstay. When I got older, I realized that I never got that special attention from my mother like some children do, making clothes or special love and care. And I just grew up feeling that way. I remember when my little brother Frankie was born. After so many girls my father was so happy he had a son. Well, my sisters Rose and Doris and I came down with whooping cough and he did, too. Complications set in, so he had to go to the hospital. And my mother used to take me to the hospital. And I would just stand there and I would cry because he was sick, and I felt terrible. We had no telephone. And so when he died, a policeman from the hospital had to come and tell us. And they brought him home. And I saw my mother carry him on her shoulders.

We managed all right. We always had enough to eat. We didn't have any of the luxuries. I mean, we had good food, but I remember we never had strawberries and cream. We just had mashed strawberries and water with black bread or a pear and black bread. And we had a lot of cocoa. And we had to get our own breakfast. Life went on just the same.

We had a synagogue there. It wasn't that my father was so religious, but he enjoyed going there. And he had a group of men that were financially better off than he, and they used to play cards. And he enjoyed doing that. He enjoyed those nice things.

The minister of the church, Saint Stephen's Church, he was nice—his family was very nice. And we knew quite a few Jewish neighbors in the area. And we used to visit with them. But we had a large family of aunts and uncles. And they would come down. And we would travel by electric streetcar to Boston, Dorchester, and visit them. But most of them would come down to Lynn.

I remember my father taking us down to Lynn Beach to go swimming. He went swimming. And he went and got a bathing suit, you know, in the bathhouse. And I was annoyed, so I just took my clothes off, and I went in in my petticoat and walked home wet. My other sisters didn't do that. I just wanted to do the things that he did. They never had the spunk that I had.

Her mother took care of my mother. She was used to it. So she just expected that treatment from her children. And my other sister took over. And she took care of her. Well, my mother developed asthma. It was the dust that did it. But they didn't figure it out, so we used to have to get some kind of a powder and burn it and she would inhale it. Because it was hard for her to breathe. And we had to take fans and fan her when it was hard for her to breathe. She was a very lovely woman. The only thing is everything had to be smooth. She couldn't stand any aggravation. She had to have an even keel. But one thing I remember about her particularly was that she got sick and my father got nurses for her and doctors, and she pulled through. And she said that father said as long as they had bread and milk and water, and as long as she was living, that's all he wanted. And, of course, that pleased her. But it didn't please my older sister, because she was very annoyed that my father insisted on his pleasure, you know. And she didn't think he should. Sex. And she didn't understand, and after all it wasn't her business because that's the way they were. And I used to think, well, as I got older, I didn't get a very wholesome outlook on sex, and I rationalized and I said, well, kings and queens had children. If it's all right for them, it must be all right for my parents. Because they never told you about the birds and the bees and those things.

I always liked my father. He used to bring me lovely dresses. And I liked little kid gloves, so I would scrounge around for kid gloves that were damaged. I remember getting a pair for forty-nine cents, and he made a coat for me, double-breasted with a brown velvet collar. It was very tailored. It was lovely. And I enjoyed that.

Then I wanted to take piano lessons, so I hounded him, and I did take piano lessons. But there wasn't anyone to say, Practice. I had ability then, and I just didn't keep up with it. You see, mother had so many children, she couldn't give us the individual attention or the reinforcement, say, Do this or do that. So we'd get our breakfast, our own breakfast, and go off to school. And we'd go into a store and buy four candy stars for a penny, and divided them among the three of us. And then come home at noon, and I can't remember now what we had for lunch. But we had to clear the kitchen table and the dishes. She wouldn't do it. And that went on for a long time. And the one that got up the earliest got the ribbons and got the best clothes to wear.

When I think back on it, I think I learned from my father the art of living—that is, the way he liked to live. It didn't matter whether he paid any bills. He enjoyed life, and he thought he was doing the right thing by his children. I remember when he bought a new car, we lived in our house, and he never kept up the payments too well. I think I must have been between 18 and 19, and I said to him that he had no right to buy the car because he was using the house money for it. So he slapped my face. And when that happened, I said to myself, Well, he was right. He's my father, and I had no right to talk to him that way. That's one thing I learned.

I—being the oldest and with less education and things—I always fought my way. Like the oldest always generally does. I never let my father dominate me the way he did the others.

I weighed ninety-eight pounds when I got married. But I was pretty spry. And I attribute that to the fact that we didn't have a lot of rich food. We had the essentials. My sister Rose says, "You've got strong genes. I don't know who you get them from—your father or your grandmother." And when I got married, I didn't eat too much. I remember going on my honeymoon and my husband insisted I have milk and eat well, not that he wanted to fatten me up. But he was always in shape.

I've always tried to take care of myself. When I went to work as a bookkeeper, I got the bookkeeper spread because you sit a lot. And don't forget I was 35 when I had my first child. And in those days, if you had a child at that age, you were liable to die. Well, I didn't. And I never knew I was pregnant until I tried to bend over. I wasn't too big. And I had no nausea at all. And of course when Elsa was born, I nursed her. She was just like a little chicken. And I nursed her. It was such a joy—she was such a joy and such pleasure.

I went last year to take swimming lessons, after 77 years. I did all right. I learned to float and then put my head underwater, and at the beginning it was rather difficult, but I was really more embarrassed because I should have learned when I was young, but I never had the opportunity. I saw those little kids from the nursery school going swimming, like my children. They went when they were young. And they learned to go horseback riding. And they were just great in everything that they did. And bicycles. I didn't exactly catch up with them, because I'm not as proficient a swimmer. The Channel, I won't swim.

I learned about ethics only from observation, because don't forget what I was subjected to—morality wasn't much. It was all sort of distorted and it wasn't like the prince and princess. And I always said I was waiting for Sir Galahad on the white horse, because I loved the stories of the Round Table. I was quite a romanticist. But I have had a lot of pleasures along with the heartaches.

I learned what was wrong by being hurt. After living with my husband, I knew the type that he was, and I said to him once he had no right to get married because if he had wandering eyes, he should've stayed single.

Thank God when I was growing up, my family was always very close, and we still are. We have our differences, and when we used to visit and the six of us would get together, well, you'd be amazed. But with me, I would give them anything, and I don't expect anything in return.

If sexual freedom is what women want, I say to each his own. If that's the kind of life they want, more power to them. They're not hurting me. They're only hurting themselves. Because nothing good comes of it. When two people live together out of wedlock, if that's what they choose to do, one of them is going to get hurt. Either the male or female. And if that happens, they have to be ready for it, because if they felt closer, they wouldn't be living together. They'd get married. Marriage is very difficult. You have to work at it.

My daughter married a young man. He was a very nice young man. He wasn't Jewish, and he was in the same field that she was. And we were walking one day, and she said, "If I meet a non-Jewish man and fall in love with him," she said, "I'm going to marry him." I said, "Oh, it's hard enough getting along with a Jewish man when you get married, let alone borrowing trouble." Well, she did marry him, and the trouble was that she loved him more than he loved her. He wasn't bad. He was sort of a dreamer. I didn't expect the marriage to last.

When you love someone, you love with your whole being, and you expect the same in return. I want the real thing. The same with my children. I don't want them to love me because I'm their mother and that's what they're supposed to do. I want them to love me as a friend, and respect me, and feel that they can come, you know, and discuss anything with me. So far it's been that way.

Getting back to marriage, you have to consider the person that you marry. He's an individual. You can't change a man, and if you marry a man and try to change him, you're wasting your time. He has a right to his own personality, his own individuality, and his artistic views or whatever. You can't make him do what you want to do. And the same speaks for a man and a woman. And I think the most important thing is respect and consideration, and thoughtfulness.

My own marriage? Well, he lived in Lynn and he went coasting on one of the big hills. He coasted down into a tree, and he got himself a broken leg. He was a young man then. And my brother was an orthopedic surgeon at the Lynn Hospital. So they called him. When he got out of the hospital after my brother took care of him and got him all together again, he went to work for my brother in the tailoring business, delivering, but I had never met him. I happened to go in the store once and he was there, and the blue eyes and the way he talked, kind of dreamy. And I was impressed. And I just walked out. We used to go to a dance hall, on the streetcar. We'd go over there and we'd have a lovely time. So he followed me out there one night, and he had a hat on, kind of stiff-brimmed, and he was an adolescent—you know, his face was breaking out, and he had a double-breasted suit on. And I said to myself, Oh dear, he's all dressed up. And he wanted to dance with me or date me. Then, he got in touch with me, afterward. And I guess I impressed him because he said he used to love to watch me eat because I was so dainty. It was all ridiculous. Well, we started going together. He took me to Provincetown because I'd never been down on the Cape. And then we went to New Hampshire once. Going off with him was bold, but it didn't bother me then.

At least the marriage produced my children. I thank God for that. If you give them joy and love, and raise them, it's just like tending plants. If you give them tender, loving care, you get results. And if you expose them to music and good art and things like that, it's very satisfying. It was just wonderful, going out with them, to the theater, going places. We had such lovely times and they enjoyed it so much.

My sister said, "What do you want Verna to be an actress for?" I said, "She should be whatever she wants to be." If that's what she wants to do, I don't care. It's a tough life, but she chose it. It was hard, very tough for her in the beginning, but that's what she wanted to do. And that perhaps helped make her a better actress.

After my mother passed away, I used to light the candles every Friday night. Of course, when the children were home, we belonged to the temple and participated. You don't have to have a kosher home and be that way just to be good, if you know fundamentally what is expected of you. Today, if a nice educated Christian man wanted to marry me, I wouldn't hesitate. But my marriage was traumatic. I wasn't humiliated. But the way he did it, leaving his responsibilities as a parent. I just told everybody what happened. I didn't hide. I didn't put my head in the sand. I just went on and did what I should have done as a parent. And when people said to me, "Oh, there aren't many mothers that would do that," I said, "Well, that's what they should do. When you have young children and you love them, you're supposed to protect them."

I hadn't been to a doctor for about fifteen years, I think. And I knew this doctor, knew the family, saw his parents get married. So I went to see him and he checked me out, and didn't find anything wrong with me except when he looked in my eyes, he said I had high blood pressure. I said, "Oh dear. I don't want to join the club." My sisters had it. I had that on my mind and he gave me some pills and it brought the pressure down, and that is all right now. I used to see him whenever I felt the need for it. In 1968, I think it was, I had had pains in my stomach. I didn't pay much attention to it. Well, I had X rays taken, and they discovered I had a growth up there. And I needed surgery. And I went to this young doctor. He was handsome and kind and just lovely. He told me what the trouble was, and he said, You can't tell until after you're operated on whether it's benign or malignant. It was my good fortune that it was benign. But I had a basketball, a growth as big as a basketball.

Thank God I don't get frightened. My sister is scared to death of anything. I've been alone so many times. And it just didn't frighten me.

I don't think I ever did anything that was bad except I was angry at my husband. I fished through his pockets, and you know when you're looking for information, you get what you deserve, and it was a letter from his dame, and I was very angry. And so I told him to sit down on the love seat, and he did, and I told him to take his glasses off. And I slapped his face back and forth, and he sat there and took it, and that made me all the more angry. Because he knew he was wrong, and if I had a lead pipe there, he would've had a cracked skull. And after that I had no love for him, and I didn't care what happened. I just wouldn't take him back for anything.

If I want to see a movie, I just take myself into Boston for a movie, have lunch, and see a movie. When I'm at home, I read. I used to read a lot of D. H. Lawrence. There's something about him and his writing. I've seen some of the movies that they have made from his books. I was fascinated with his work. And I liked Thomas Hardy. One book that I read that was so beautiful was *Green Mansions*. I was so taken in with that. It was so beautiful. And all the greenery, the plants and the flowers. I loved it all.

For a long time I didn't know what the hell they were talking about, about Watergate. I didn't know what Watergate was. I didn't know if it was a hotel or the plumbers. When I got deeper into it, I was very disappointed.

Women's rights? You mean liberated women? That to me is for the birds, because I think women have been liberated for years. Those who wanted to be liberated. Years ago, when I was working and I was married, my mother-in-law said, Oh, she wished I didn't have to work. I said, If my husband gave me three hundred dollars a week, I still would want to work because it's the best experience and the best thing. I say a woman can have a career, she can get married, and raise a family and be fulfilled for the rest of her life. She can do that. She can do every-thing. A man, of course, can't do all these things.

I believed in the rights of the blacks, and of course they get a lot of opposition here. I still say that it's important. They had it harder than the Jews, because the Jewish people, at least they were white. When I was working, the neighborhood where the office was, was one part domestic and the other industrial. And there was a black minister who was moving into a house across from the office. One young man said, "They'll all move away from this street." I said, "I don't think so." I said, "I'm surprised. You're supposed to be a good Christian, you're supposed to love your brother. But by the grace of God you're white. You could've been black." Well, he says, "If you had somebody black living next door to you, would you like that?" I said, "I wouldn't mind. He'd have to be able to afford to live there and he'd have to be edu-cated." "Well, how would you like your daughter to marry a black?" I said, "That's stupid. That's the attitude that a lot of people have, and I think it's bad."

I think 90 percent of the people who work hate their work. Why? Be-cause apparently they're not doing what they wanted to do. I'd say to find out what you like to do and do it. Even if it takes you a long time or if you have to do without. There are ever so many people that have given up. You can be a ditch digger and still have your pride. An honest living is hard to make. But if you have something that you can fall back on, like teaching, that's all right. If you have your edu-cation, you can educate yourself.

But if you don't allow yourself to learn a craft, if you just do nothing or do work that you don't like and always feel sorry for yourself, that's no good. What you do with your life and what you do with yourself is up to you.

I retired when I felt it was time for me. Some places tell you to quit. I don't like that. I don't mind being my age, and I don't mind being elderly. But I don't want to be classed with the senior citizens. Because I'm used to going and doing as I like and being my own person. I never belong to bridge clubs because I don't like that feeling that I have to have a group over and play. And I don't like to impose what I like to do on other people. If they like to do what I like to do, I don't mind.

I remember seeing Teddy Roosevelt when he came to Lynn, on the horse and wearing a big hat and tails. Oh, he was quite a man, with his mustache. And I remember him very well. And I liked Franklin Roosevelt very much. He had a lot of charm, and, of course, I was a little disappointed after reading about his life with Eleanor and how he treated her and what he did. But he had a lot of charisma. John Kennedy was a doll. I met him, I think, when he first started out in Congress. I was working and there were factories around there and they took him in. The door happened to be open, so they just walked in and introduced him to me. We shook hands, and, oh, I'm telling you, he had such charm. And that particular night my sister and I went to the Oxford Club in Lynn to hear him speak at the Red Cross. He had so much charisma. I never liked his father, but he was a doll.

I always say I'm a genius because I make things easy. I do everything with a minimum of energy. And I do plenty. And I try to cut corners. I do the important things in the home. I do all my own laundry. And my own cooking, because I feel the meals that you get out are terrible. I read the papers and I get a lot of magazines, and you'd be surprised all the information you get from them. And I listen to radio. I have FM in one room, AM and FM. But I like FM. In my room I have FM. And in the big room I have a radio that my son-in-law gave me, a little one, just AM. I stay in touch. I always say to Verna, I say, "You'll be living in the year 2000. Will you write to me and tell me what's happening?"

You have to be a realist about death. You have to accept it. I wouldn't want to live as a vegetable. I wrote to my daughter, and I said to her, "If I ever get to the stage where I can't take care of myself, put me in a home." She wrote back and said she thought that was beautiful. And she said, "You won't have to worry because we love you."

# Dr. Sidney S. Greenberg

*D*r. Sidney S. Greenberg has spent his 66 years in the city in which he was born, New York (in October 1912). In his modest office on Manhattan's Upper East Side, he sees patients he has treated for years and patients he has never met before, ranging from a famous entertainer to an unemployed welfare patient. He specializes in internal medicine. He has treated Lana Turner, Ava Gardner, Frank Sinatra, and others whose names would evoke instant recognition. He will take care of anyone who walks in, in need, "as long as I can help them." His office is strewn with gifts from the well-known patients; his memory is strewn with the gratitude of those who could not afford to give him anything, even a fee.

Dr. Greenberg went to Columbia University. He continued to medical school at the Downstate Medical Center in Brooklyn and served his residency at Mount Sinai Hospital. In training, he made a point to study psychiatry—then an uncommon passion among doctors other than psychiatrists—pathology, X ray, and lung diseases.

He has been in private practice since 1942; his present office is just a few blocks away from his first one. He was married in 1947 and has two children, a 19-year-old daughter and a son who is a journalist. He remains on staff at Mount Sinai and devotes time, as well, to teaching medical students at Bellevue Hospital and New York University Hospital. He is an adamant anticorruption fighter in the medical field in New York, whether it be graft in the city's addiction treatment system or individual doctors he feels are defrauding their patients. He enjoys talking to patients and does not put arbitrary limitations on the time he spends with them. His sense of ethics colors everything he does, in and out of his field.

We lived in a neighborhood not far from here, a mixture of poor and middle class. And the people were mostly blacks and Jews and Italians and Irish—all on one block, and we lived with a very communal feeling. Everybody knew everybody. And everybody was proud to live on that block. Everybody knew everybody in the tenement, and if somebody got sick, everybody ran to help. If a woman was having a baby, all the women went up and brought the hot water or the food and the milk and all that. Today we don't know anybody. I have thought about it many, many times. I haven't gotten on any soapboxes about it. I think a lot of it is due to what you call progress. First it is due to the technological progress. Buildings are bigger, more elevators, less contact with people. We drive in cars instead of sitting on buses or streetcars. Everybody knew everybody on the streetcar. If you needed something and you didn't have it you had to go to the community bakery for it, or to the community storekeeper who knew you. Today you get everything packaged. You don't even talk to the dealer or to the salesclerk.

And then because of the increased technology and the increased drive to success, and the increased education, because there's not a place all over this world for everybody who has degrees, they all compete. The competition is greater. I'm better than you because I have a degree or went to high school. I'm better than you because I have a job that makes fifty thousand dollars a year driving a truck, and you're a professor and you only make ten thousand dollars. The competition is great. Everybody wants a television set.

I think that technological progress has impaired social progress. The feeling for people. If you wanted to know what's happening with Mrs. Smith or Mrs. Brown, you went to see Mrs. Brown or Mrs. Smith. This way you pick up the telephone. You can always cut him off and you can't study his expression or know how he's feeling. It's very nonpersonal. The same thing in the store. You went in, you saw your butcher or your baker. And you knew him, you bought something. Go in the store today, give me item number three, you buy through the mail, you press a button, out it comes. It's very impersonal.

Another thing, talking about my own work, what's becoming very bad is the impersonal relationship in medicine. I think we've progressed more, we've found new technologies that help people more, but I think we did a lot more help with the personal touch between the doctor and the patient, rather than saying go on in that room and the machine will take the picture and press this button. Call me tomorrow and the report will come back.

Up to recently I made house calls. I think the reason I don't is it's not as important as it used to be. It's very hard to educate the public that you don't need house calls. And secondly, I'm getting older. And thirdly, because of what we call progress in medicine, we have defensive medicine. If I come to your house and you have a cold, and I treat you for a cold and you get better, fine, but if in the course of it, I forget to do a blood test, things that I can't do at home, I'm criticized and subject to suit. So there's a lot of reasons for it. And of course it took a long time. And I think the ones who educated the public first to the lack of making house calls were the pediatricians. You see, families used to call pediatricians right away and the mother would scream and say, "My child has a hundred and three degrees, please come. I can't take him out."

So that I think is a good thing, if you can educate the public. It's better medicine. But at the same time, you lose that personal touch. And that's what I think is the biggest change. That's the thing that I am very annoyed with in medicine. And it's a reflection of life in general. Whether it's because of the increased demands of the increased population which we now have, and the decreased number of doctors available, most doctors practice assembly medicine, which I think is wrong. It's very easy to say, "Take this pill," or "Here go have this test," and this is the result, and good-bye.

I've told this to my students. I tell it to anybody who comes in. If you come with a cut finger or if you come in with a very serious problem, and I never saw you before, I'm going to spend a lot of time trying to find out about you, because I don't believe an individual has a cut finger or a pain in the side or a headache—you've got to know something about it.

And I think spending time is very important. People are lonely. They're separated in their social life. And it's one of the resentments that people have who go to psychiatrists. The psychiatrist, because of his work load, has to limit his time. They all do it because it's the easiest way out. You can be in the middle of the most important thing, and your forty-five minutes are up, you're out until the next visit. By that time your whole attitude changes.

And in my own work, even today, I'm only seeing one patient. And I'll give that patient two or three hours. Because that patient is coming in with a specific problem—I know the problem. If I sat down and talked with the patient for thirty minutes or fifty minutes, I'd leave them hanging. I usually drop the session when we've reached a certain point, and it may be an hour and a half or two hours. And I think it does a lot more good and causes less frustration. It's very tiring and very demanding on the physician, but I think if you're going to do something, whether it's a painter or a doctor or a builder, you do the best —what's best for the patient and for the individual. Otherwise I don't think it's fair.

Maybe my views have something to do with how I grew up. Then, the household held together. People stayed home until they were ready to go someplace. If you were a man, you stayed home until you finished preparing yourself for your career, whatever it was, or you got married. And women always stayed home until they got married.

I remember when I was about 4 or 5, it was always an event that stuck in my mind, like a big snowstorm. I remember the first eclipse when I was about 5 years of age. We looked through the window with smoked glasses. Or a member of the family being taken to a hospital or somebody dying. There weren't too many great tragedies in my family, fortunately. But I do remember little things, always associated with an event.

The family was run—I always like to say that the father ran the house—it's not always true, and I don't think it's always true now. We got to see more—there was only two in my family, my brother and myself. We got to see my mother more than my father because in those days nobody worked from eight to four or five, even though he had his own business. Many times he didn't come home until eleven, twelve at night. And to work on Saturdays and Sundays was not unusual. And so the house was really run by the mother, but there was a tremendous amount of closeness. A tremendous amount of feeling and respect, which you don't have now.

And don't forget, even though I did not come from a religious household, the fear or the interest in religion was much greater than it is now. One of the things that irritates me now is all these parents saying "I go to the PTA" or I do this or that. That's just showing off that they're a parent. And in those days the parents were more concerned that you crossed the street safely and you were dressed warmly, and you were fed, and you came home if you wanted to discuss something. But they were not involved in the school—that was the teacher's job. And that was the community's job, and that was the home. And that's the difference. And your neighbor was concerned about you and your family. It's different.

In my family the example that was set is to be respecting, and that's one thing we don't have much of today. We do, but to a very little degree. The family is a unit. The father, mother should be respected. And it's not just my family. We saw that all over. You always used an example of somebody who was better than you. You had to accomplish something. You should do good. And there was no reason for us to rebel. We were scared, to be honest with you. And don't forget, everybody had to fight for their little thing. And even in the neighborhoods, you were a member of that block. And if you strayed, everybody knew about it. It was a community spirit and a respect, which we don't have today. There's a lot of freedom. A lot of "I'm going, I'll see you later." "I'll call you." There's no such call. "You gotta be home at five o'clock, you gotta be home at five o'clock." You couldn't pick up the phone and say I'll be late.

I think if you're interested in physical activity, you should do it. If you're doing it for the sake of your own personal enjoyment, then you should do it, with limitations. Although people don't know about limitations, unfortunately, because they always want to show they're the best. Competition enters into it a great deal. Unhealthy. You know, the big drive now is for jogging. You do as much jogging as you want, but don't say I did fifty laps or I did it fast, and you're going to fall flat on your face. The biggest problem we're having today is that everybody wants to be a tennis player. They don't realize that it's a competitive sport and it's a vigorous sport, and if they enjoy it, play it like a match. Most people don't.

I'm not athletic, but I'm giving my impressions. I was never encouraged as a child to get involved in athletics. It was a little different than now. Remember, in going back to my childhood, whether you came from one family or another, if you wanted to get involved in athletics or sports, you did it on your own. The team was the block team. There was nothing like you see today. And if you were meant to be a student or you had an illness or so on, the mothers became protective. There was no working mother. There was always somebody home. And they said, "Look, you're too weak." It's better to be careful. Everybody was scared of illness and trauma. More so than now.

So I would say I was much more protected. I happened to have been an ill child, so that added to the protectiveness. And my family was not a family that was interested in sports. Jewish people weren't.

I learned other things. I lived in an area where there was a lot of poverty and I lived through the Depression. I never saw people steal. I never saw anything like that. And if somebody did something wrong, it was always something physical. I came from a block where I think in those days, when they had capital punishment, I think five or six people ended up in the electric chair. I think there were only four of us who ever ended up in college from that block. Two of them are state supreme court judges. We were taught to be friendly and respect people. We didn't take. There was no welfare. There was no begging. If a neighbor needed something, somebody came and was very nice. People were more giving than now and more concerned about each other. And in that way you developed a feeling that this is the right thing. Of course, not that I came from a religious family, but there was much more—more kids went to Sunday school, and the Catholics and Jews. As a matter of fact, I got so interested in those days I almost thought I was going to become a rabbi—not that I was studying it—but I liked it. It was a good feeling. And the competition was not there, and everybody was helpful.

But the most important word I would use that adds to the thing that you call moral attitude is *concern*. People don't have much of that today. And as I grew up, I even disliked people who never hurt me, but did not show up for somebody else. That annoyed me more.

A lot has happened since then. You had wars. Fathers were away. Brothers were away. Mothers took jobs in industry. People needed money, prices went up. Technological things increased, so everybody wanted a radio. I remember when one person got a radio, everybody wanted a radio. Different things. Vacations became popular. In those days a vacation was to sit outside or go up to the roof.

Today, we talk about the destruction of the family. I'm not a religious person per se, but I believe in certain things. I think religion brought people together, and it's gradually bringing some people back today. But there were the wars, the increasing pressures of the time, the increasing population. And don't forget there was a tremendous amount of immigration at that time. And everybody—Oh, you're from so-and-so. Well, I came from . . . so on. The Irish. Russians. Italians.

Today there's no such thing. Everybody wants to travel. The airplane made things closer. And people ran, and by going, you separate.

It's true that there were a lot of things we did not do years ago because we were scared. A lot of people sat in moral seats and pointed fingers at everybody they felt did something wrong. If you did something, everybody in the neighborhood knew it. I think a lot of tensions were built up, a lot of resentments, hostility, and that. If carried through to a reasonable degree, sexual freedom, I think, has released a lot of that. And has been encouraged by the progress of birth control pills. Fear of pregnancy was greater than the fear of disease. And today it's accepted to have a child out of wedlock. In those days you were sent out of the house. I think it's an improvement. However, like every other advance, it goes overboard. And when it goes overboard, it produces a lot of new problems. For example, I'd define love as a warm feeling of relationship and concern and interest in another person. I'm leaving out purposely the physical.

Years ago you were limited. If you had a concern and a feeling and an attitude and a warmth and a feeling of affection for an individual and got close, sex became involved, physical love. Today it is so almost mechanical, and the choice is so wide. You aren't limited. That's why we have so many separations.

I met my wife when she was doing public relations work. It happens to be through Sinatra, as a matter of fact. I don't remember whether he was ill or at a social thing, and she came to do a story on him. I was there and I met her. I was just beginning my practice. Second or third year. She'd just come to New York from California and was busy in her career. And our interests: She was probably interested in me beyond my being as a person, in terms of my work. I was interested in her work.

Don't ask me how we made it work. It depends on many factors. They always say the woman will blame it on the man and the man will blame it on the woman. There's so many outside influences, so many personality differences. See, it's hard to answer.

People misunderstand. They ask how does it work. The only word I can use, and it's a word that I'm very, very, very fond of, and most people don't understand, is *adjusting*. Nobody understands it—and I use that word *nobody* because it fits a very, very high percentage of people. And the reason I use that word is because when I ask people what's the definition of an adult, most people hem and haw and don't know, and give me "older" and "experienced" and all that. That's not the answer. Most of the time if I'm asking it for a specific reason, the thing that I accept is somebody who can "adjust." And that's the difference between a child and an adult. We're not talking about age.

When an individual can adjust to life situations which can become very difficult as you go along, then that's an adult. And that's what's important, in adjusting in any kind of a partnership, whether it's a marriage or a business or an association with somebody.

Well, I happen to be very fortunate, I think, in being a husband and a father. I have kids that I can feel proud of. That's the first thing. They've accomplished a lot of things themselves. They've been very good, very concerned, very devoted. I feel very, very close to my children. And I think they do to me. I enjoy being with them. They're kids that I can get something out of. I enjoy talking to them. I enjoy being with them. It's a personal relationship. They are concerned. For example, when my son Peter was just starting out in California, my wife used to scream, "Oh, the phone bills are so big." I didn't give a shit. I really enjoyed it. I'd rather pay for the phone bills and have him call me so I could see how he is, and have him ask how I am, than to go pay because he's arrested for selling pot or something. To me, talking to my kids has always been the greatest pleasure, and to this day I enjoy it. And I enjoy seeing them. I don't stand on ceremony. "You didn't call me. You neglected your father." I call them and I take them to dinner and we go to the theater together. We have common interests. It so happens, you know, if you have a child that's interested in sports and you're not interested in sports, there's a little hiatus there. But my kids have so many interests that I have that we can participate in.

Going back to my early days, we had an ordinary simple Sunday school —a vacation Hebrew school, things like that. I enjoyed being with those people. I enjoyed listening to the discussions. I don't know if I understood all of it. The type of rabbi or the minister or leader—those were entirely different than today. But it was a place to meet and a place where I had a feeling, and I think my kids have it, too, even though they're not religious, that you could sit there and feel at peace.

During those days, being involved in a community where people were far more religious than I was, there was a certain fear that you had to belong to a certain group. I don't.

But I still believe that there is a certain thing that you have to believe in. It's almost like sitting down and daydreaming or rationalizing, it helps you survive certain situations. I think by knowing or believing that somebody is taking control, looking at everything, gives you a certain amount of security. It gives me peace.

And it keeps me from doing—if I was the sort of person that wanted to do something bad—it keeps me from doing that. Not that I'm afraid of being punished, but I think this is the right way to live.

The body needs care, too. Now I'm going through a lot of personal and physical things that are not that serious but are enough to annoy me. I become very angry and hostile. And it keeps me at times from doing what I want to do. I just repress the anger, and in doing so I'm guilty of making myself depressed. It's a human trait. Especially if you have a great desire to do certain things, and I happen to be an individual who never feels I've finished anything. My hobby happens to be painting, and when I paint, I never feel I have finished any painting. You know.

So I have a lot of things I'd like to do, and I give the impression I'm easygoing and I'm taking things easy. Which I do. I have my own pace, like everybody else does. When I don't feel well, and as I get older, I get those things, I feel I'm becoming a burden. Thank God I'm not a burden financially to my kids, but they're worried. If they need me for something, I want to be around. As far as patients go, I think being an internist is the most difficult job—the most difficult job. I don't know if doctors realize it, and I'm not talking about laymen. But to this day, the most difficult thing to me is death. And I'm not talking personally. Because in my profession when I see somebody die, it not only is disturbing because it involves so many people who are disturbed by it, but it represents a failure in my field. And not that I want to save everybody, but I figure maybe I didn't do this or didn't do that.

When a friend or a relative dies, it depresses me. Even though many times somebody's died from an illness that was very disturbing. It's a loss, whether you saw them once a year or once every day. Somebody that you felt close to—it's an emotional feeling. Nobody likes to lose anything. Like if you have an old toy as a kid and you don't like to lose it. You're attached. But that is very hard.

And internal medicine, you know, you refer people to surgeons and this and that. The other ones will walk away when the thing is behind. The internist has to handle it and has to talk to the family. And it's a very difficult approach, and I think I have managed it fairly well over the years. But people don't realize what a toll it takes on the doctor, at least with me.

You have to deal with disappointment. You make a wrong judgment. Or you trust people. I'm a very trusting person. I think I can sense people pretty well. I'm still looking for the first time how to avoid trusting the wrong person. Once I've made a mistake, I don't think it's ever repeated. It's cut out of my life. But how to avoid that first time. I've had many disappointments. A lot of people have. Various things. We've all had pain and illness, things like that. Social things, breaking up of emotional relationships with people. Disappointments in your judgment when you thought if you invested money in something because you thought it would make money. Not that I'm a gambler. And if it didn't turn out, that wouldn't bother me.

Years ago when there was no place in this city to put a person who has an emotional problem from drugs or alcohol, I went ahead and tried to build a whole hospital. I didn't have the money. People had faith in me. I put together one of the biggest and most important and stimulating staffs, who had respect for me and came along with me. But in order to get the money, you have to be involved with business-people who have the money. And when I found that my judgment was bad, I got out after four months. It took me five years to build the hospital. The hospital's still there, but it's not a hospital today. And they all turned out to be dishonest and I felt they didn't have the feeling I had for it. That was a great disappointment.

A lot of people will say I'm a person who's always afraid of everything. I'm not. I think I'm just very cautious. I wouldn't walk into certain areas late at night alone. A lot of people say, "Oh, you're afraid." Well, that's being cautious. I don't think that's being afraid. I've been in situations where I was scared stiff. One was when my son was little and we were riding in a subway train, and we saw people pull out knives. I wanted to get off. My son said, "No, let's stay and be quiet." I had fear. He had, too. He handled it a little bit better than I did.

The main fear I have, which I think happens to everybody, is a fear of physical inadequacy and physical pain. But I don't have fear of starvation. I have no fear of loss of money. I sit in my chair here very content. The people I feel sorry for are the very rich. If you put a gun to my back and asked me if I knew of any rich person that I wanted to change places with, I would say no. I'm talking about the average very rich, and right now at least five or ten people that I know, who sit there in complete fear, come to mind. They have millions—I'm talking about millions. They have nothing else in life but the money, and their biggest fear is to lose it. And if they lose it, they have nothing else. They can't adjust.

I'm thinking of a few people right now: There was a guy here only a few days ago who stood and cried, "What happens if I lose my paintings and my Rolls-Royce car?" I don't give a shit. If they threw me out of my apartment, I'd sleep in a sleeping bag. You don't have to eat in "21." I'm not impressed by that. I've been with people in restaurants, and they walk out if it's not the fanciest place or the prices are not big enough. I tell the famous story about my coat. My father really was in the woolen business and I knew a little about wool. My brother and I helped out a little bit, but we both became doctors. If I wanted to stay in woolens, I would've been a millionaire. And a few years ago I wanted a certain coat and Saks Fifth Avenue had it. And I went to Saks and it was two hundred dollars—in those days it was very high-priced for a spring coat. But they didn't have my size.

So I walked out of the store and I ran into some old cohort of my father's who remembered me as a kid, you know, and he's still in the woolen business. He says, "What are you doing around here?" "Oh, I went to get a coat and they didn't have it." I described the coat to him. And he says, "Oh, I know that coat very well. The manufacturer was stuck with a few of them, he couldn't sell them at the high price. They're being sold in Klein's. So you go down to Klein's, you might find that coat in your size." And I went down to Klein's, they had four coats, and one was my size. And I still have the coat. It was a gorgeous coat and people rave about it, and it only cost me sixty dollars.

So when people met me and they said, "Gee, what a gorgeous coat. Where'd you get it?" I used to say Klein's. Now I say I bought it in Saks—it makes them feel better. You know, there's a whole business of people selling labels to put into garments.

The minute I leave my office, my mind is at ease. I'm a very curious guy. I like to see different people, different places. I enjoy music and art. I read biography or fiction, I go to see a comedy or drama . . . everything has a feeling for me. When I went to college, I had no spending money to go to the theater. Even though movies were fifteen cents or a quarter, I don't know how much the theater was in those days, maybe one dollar or two dollars. So I worked on weekends and Saturdays and evenings, checking coats and selling candy, and that's how I got to see the show. I used to pick the shows that I wanted to see. That's where I'd work. You know, I didn't have a steady job. I'd say, "You need an extra candy boy?" To this day I still collect all the theater programs.

Women's rights I was always in favor of, except you're dealing then with emotions. And when you're dealing with emotions, women go overboard, and they don't know their limitations. You can see some of it now. Women have become far more aggressive, not that I'm against them being aggressive. I don't like to see women just being meek and wishy-washy—that's wrong. But they don't know their limitations to the point where there's a great deal to be said about the emasculization that's occurred. They don't know when to stop. I think you're dealing then with emotions and power. It's the same thing as, you know, talk to the average guy. He always brags about how successful he is sexually, but it's not him, it's the woman who arranges it. And once the woman gets into the position to handle the sexual situation, her greatest pleasure is the power. It's not the sex itself. And it's the same thing with women's rights. Fine, give them voting and give them equal pay and all that. And go to work and all that—fine. But then it gets to the point they don't want to stay home. They don't want to take care of the kids. That's another thing that's happened to the family.

People aren't happy in their work. I've seen it. I think there's more to it. See, people go into certain jobs with false expectations. If I went into medicine with the idea that I was going to become a millionaire, then I'd be unhappy with my job. Say I wanted to be the chief of a hospital. Now I have spent hours and hours over the years with many cohorts of mine who were disappointed because they weren't promoted or they didn't become chief. And I remember I walked with a guy along the beach. He was going to throw himself in the ocean because somebody became chief and he didn't.

Not everybody can be President and not everybody should be President. You know. On the tombstone it's just old Joe Schmoe, and you're dead. But it depends on the value. If you go ahead and want to be a plasterer and you're building a building and you're plastering away, and it looks good and you're getting pleasure, you're going to enjoy the job. If you're going with the idea so that you can become the builder and make a fortune, you're going to be miserable. It depends upon your goals.

Whether a guy ends up with three dollars a year pension or he has a wealth that's twenty million dollars, I would not permit him to retire. I have never seen anybody who retired who was able to maintain themself physically and psychologically. I just went through recently where a close friend of mine who's worth millions was having problems adjusting to the changes in his business and wanted to retire. And he was reaching retirement age. I said, You want to retire, don't come to me, because I know what's going to happen. You haven't got too many outside interests, so develop interests now. Otherwise you're going to end up drinking. You're going to end up moping and doing things that will make you depressed—and you're a depressed individual now and most people get depressed as they reach that age. And it's going to get worse.

So he got interested as a result of my pushing and when he was here only a week ago, he was telling me that he's so busy now—more than he ever was busy. On the board of this museum and that. You have to have some interests in life. You can't just sit home and twiddle your thumbs. That makes me mad.

What gets me mad too is man's inhumanity to man. That's the worst. Because I think people essentially are very self-centered. I always say this world is made up of givers and takers, and the percentage of givers is about 10 percent, and the percentage of takers would be about 90 percent. I'm sure I'm exaggerating because I have such deep feelings about it. But the people who take—and I don't do things always expecting to get something back—should be concerned and considerate and fair. Dishonesty is one of my biggest pet peeves. And I'm not upset when people are weak. I'm not upset when people can't handle situations. I think that's human. But I do not think we should accept people who are cruel, people who lie, and people who cheat or take advantage of people for their own advantage. This goes on much too much. And that involves everything, whether it's business or politics or personal life.

Will the next generation do things any better than we're doing them? I think so. I think there will be periods where they will do better. Because we go in cycles. The sixties were bad. The seventies were better. Although I think they're suffering more because they don't know where they're going, because the world didn't move as fast as they did, and the world didn't adjust to them. But I'm not concerned. I admire youth. I think they've done very well. I think they're very misunderstood by the older people because they have to give up more to understand. I don't think they move as fast as the young people, you see. In the sixties, when the kids were rebelling, whether it was against the Vietnam War or it was against society in general, whether they were rebelling by taking drugs and all that, I think they had a right to rebel. Nobody said that they did it the right way, but we were unprepared to accept their rebellion because we were stubborn—"we" meaning the older group. And we didn't bend with them. Then when they began to realize that they ought to go a different way, we're still not doing what they are looking for. But I think that there will be changes. And of course, youth changes. I never look down upon them when they rebel. I never looked down upon them when they took drugs. If you understand the reasons why it went on. I think the failure was in the adults, not in the youth.

Death is a subject that has to be handled in many different ways. First of all, it's only in the last fifteen, twenty years that people were able to express their fear of death. And it was only in the last ten years possibly, maybe a little longer, where interested parties began to see it was a subject that you had to face and discuss.

Up to then, the only thing that they had was a religious consolation. A minister or the rabbi or priest would pray. And in prayer there's a higher body that's going to take care of you, so it gave somebody some hope.

I think the approach today is a lot different. There's a decided movement. The average person is still fearful of talking about it. Once you sense that they have that fear or once they express that fear, you have to just handle it at the appropriate emotional level. Because most people who have that fear get depressed. There are a certain number of them who become manic and don't know what to do. So you have to handle those symptoms. To reassure them—and we're not talking just about drug treatment or antidepressants or various things like that, or tranquilizers that people call upon—because the average person who has that fear needs more.

I think you have to say, first of all, it's not the end. We don't know. I mean, I like to believe that. I don't know if it's true. I haven't got any look into the future, but I like to believe that. And then the other thing is to point out all the good things they've had, and all the good things they still have. That's the only way.

# Earl J. Bitzenburg

*H*e appears to be in his fifties. His hair is blond, with just a touch of gray around the edges. His blue eyes are clear. He is almost six feet tall and weighs 185 pounds, some of that centered in a paunch he would like to eliminate. His idea of the perfect evening would be to pick up a woman, take her dancing, and have a great deal to drink. He is, some of the time, a farmer in Carrollton, Missouri, the town in which he was born on February 11, 1902. On his forty-four acres he farms corn and soybeans and lives in a small house he calls his "shack." Earl Bitzenburg is a man who can lie about his age and be believed. He is particularly proud of the fact that his teeth are his own.

Bitzenburg attended local schools in Carrollton; he went to high school for two years and then took a commercial business course. His father had been a farmer and construction worker. Bitzenburg has followed a similar career.

He left home at age 15 to work in a factory in Racine, Wisconsin. In 1919, at age 17, he began earning a living on pipelines in Oklahoma and Texas, living in tents. He has since worked on many pipeline projects—in Canada, Venezuela, Mexico, and most of the United States. He was an inspector foreman on the Alaska pipeline for two years (thirty-five thousand dollars of the money he earned—all his expenses were paid—is getting 7 percent interest at a bank in Alaska). Usually, he would return to the farm in Carrollton between pipeline jobs, but occasionally he would simply abandon it, taking his family with him on pipeline locations. He has owned the farm since 1942.

To define his family takes some dexterity. He has been married, legally, seven times—and divorced seven times. He has at least seven children. One son, in his early thirties, lives on the farm with Bitzenburg; his mother was a Mexican woman Bitzenburg met in Monterey. Five other children—four women and one man—are scattered not far from the farm. For the record, they all had one mother. However, Bitzenburg remembers another daughter, the product of a collaboration with his ex-wife's mother, before he married that wife. There are grandchildren in evidence as well. Bitzenburg claims that his favorite ex-wife is the one he was married to during the Depression; he hasn't seen her *in thirty-two years. He does see the mother of most of his children; she has remarried, lives nearby, and is "friendly." During his stint in Alaska Bitzenburg almost married a woman he met up there; he decided to back out at the last moment.*

*When he isn't at work on a pipeline, he stays at home on the Carrollton farm. A wise man with money, he knows that an eighty-acre tract he owns near the farm is worth at least fifty-six thousand dollars. He isn't eager to sell it unless his children need money. He is very attentive to their needs. He saves his money for them, not for himself; he has no wish to leave a vast estate. He sends his children to school with the money he has earned, and otherwise he holds it until they need it, for any worthy objective.*

*Bitzenburg is an unpretentious man, not a man of many words. He is not one to fret or worry. He solves his problems as they arise. He cares for his loved ones. His values are, for the most part, traditional. His father moved to Missouri from Maryland when he was 11, and his life was one of hard work; Bitzenburg learned from him about the importance of work. In his simple, dedicated, and occasionally wry way, Bitzenburg is keeping that ideal alive.*

Carrollton was a farmer's town, the county seat. No work, only farm work. Looked then 'bout like it does now. Well, we have two factories here now. We have a cookie factory and we have a Banquet Foods; I think it's owned by General Foods. Make these Banquet lunches and send them all over the United States. But Carrollton is about the same size, nearly five thousand. Just under five thousand.

In one way, things are getting better. But maybe it was the snowball got so big and something happened to it. Inflation or something is going to eat us up. We're gonna have to do something. Something's gonna have to change. Can't go on the way it's going.

Well, when I was a kid, we skated and our sports were different. We didn't have automobiles. We didn't have television. We didn't have radio. We went by foot, we walked and we skated on the pond. Things were just different than from what they are now. Slower. Nobody was in a hurry. Buggies and horses and wagons. No roads. The roads wasn't worth a damn. Old mud roads. Now our country looks so much better, but I don't know how long it's going to last. I don't worry about it. No. Nothing worries me anymore. Hell, let it go. I've lived my life— 76 years. It can't hurt me anymore. My kids, they'll have to learn just like I did.

My parents was very good to me. They was awful good to me. Well, they'd let me go to town at night. I would go to the show, or I could go where I wanted to. They didn't discipline me. Come here when I get ready. Get up in the morning and go to work. Everybody got up early and went to work. Daylight come, you were out milking the cows, feeding the chickens. I have two sisters and one brother— two boys and two girls in the family. They used to live here. Now they're all scattered. I'm the only one in Carrollton. I have a sister in Marceline, a sister in Kansas City, a brother up here at Henrietta, Missouri, and I live here.

My father was a small fellow, very small. But active, worked hard, worked awful hard. And lived to be 91 years and 9 months. Hard worker. He used to be a molder, too. He was a farmer and a molder. He worked here. We had a molding factory here. It moved to Ottumwa, Iowa, when I was about 6 or 7 years old, and then he went up there and worked quite a while. And he came back to the farm.

My dad used to take me to church some. I've been baptized in the Baptist church here.

My mother was a wonderful woman. She was a tall dark woman, Irish. Got along with Dad well, and had no fights. He might have been from Germany way back, but I don't know how far back.

Well, I started school when I was 5 years old. I was 5. We walked to school. School was right straight down the road—this house over here where I was born, was right straight east, it's the Root School. School is still there. Oh, the building's changed. I think the building fell down and they put a new one up. But it's still the Root School, where I went.

You had to work and be careful. That's what my parents taught me. That's right. Everything you do be careful and work. Don't take too many chances with life. But I took a lot of chances anyway. A lot of them. But they were careful people. Yes. Dad didn't even want to ride in the car with you. I bought a car about 1919, a Model T. He said, "I'll just walk." So he'd walk right on into town and back, all the time. He walked. Finally, sometimes he would get in the car. I'd take him to Texas with me. I'd be keeping time in the twenties with the Humble Pipeline Company, which is Exxon now. I kept time for them for about four years in them camps. I'd take him down there with me. I'd get him something to do. I got work for everybody. My brother and half of this town. I took half of this town. I'd take them out of jail. I'd take them and get them out of here, put them to work. I had a pickup truck, and I had a homemade bench on the back of it. They'd load them all in there. I'd say take them, get them to work. Sheriff would tell me, "Get them out of here, I don't want to fool with them."

I didn't behave too well when I was young. No. That bothered my folks. Well, they'd just tell me to be more careful. I'd do the same thing if I was coming up again. If I had this life to live over, I'd keep active all the time. Oh, yeah, very active.

I was a leader when I was a boy. Yeah, when I was 11, 12, 13 years old, we used to hoe this corn, hoe it out with a hoe. Well, I was the boss. They'd make the boss out of me and they'd send about eight or nine or ten kids out there with me. They said, "You keep up with this man here, you're working for him, this boy here." They said, "If you don't work to suit him, you're going out. No more money for you." A bunch of them followed me from here to Racine. We was all in school. They said we want to go up there with you. Most of them have passed on by now.

My family, we're all doing all right. Everybody's living. I help them all, even today. When they need help, they come to Dad. Sure, I give it. Dish out that money to them. They need it—hell, I'm not gonna take it with me when I die. I want to help them now, not after I'm gone. They're close by. They come by, do my washing. Clean my house up. Oh, yeah.

Kids today know a whole lot more, they're a lot smarter. Know a whole lot more and got a reason to. They've got television, telephone, all this stuff. News—we didn't get no news. We'd get a paper maybe once or twice a week or something like that. We didn't have the environment that they have now.

Sex didn't make me nervous. Get them pregnant, it was all right. Now, young women have that stuff to use. Time brought it on. Times change.

Love? Well, I'd say that's doing better by other people than they do by me. I want to do more for them than they'll do for me. I know they can't do the same for me. I go out of my way to help everybody, but I don't expect them to do that for me. Yes, that's love. Give more for your fellow man than he will do for you.

Do I remember the first time I ever met my wife? Which wife? I've had about seven. First one? Oh, well, that was in 1922—that was a shotgun wedding. Yeah, I had to marry this girl. She was working in the telephone office, and I had an old Model T Ford. I divorced all seven women. I left and they'd get the divorces. I never got any of them. Marriage. I don't know. I never took it too serious. No. Didn't worry about it. My mother and dad lived happily. I think it's harder now than it used to be. Because you've got so much activity. You meet so many people. Many different routes. When I went someplace to work and I met a woman, I wasn't thinking about "before." I was thinking about the minute then. I've lived with maybe a couple of women at the same time. One somewhere and one someplace else. I'm glad I got the kids. Sure. I just love all of them. I like being with them. When they were little, we played ball and everything together.

I believe in God, but I don't attend church like I should. I'm a Mason. I went into the Masons in Covington, Kentucky, in 1938.

Sometimes I drink too much beer, which I shouldn't do. I went twenty-eight years without touching alcohol one time. I quit in 1939, and I didn't go back to drinking until '67. I just wanted to make some money and be good to my family, so I didn't touch it. Alcohol or tobacco either. I don't use tobacco yet.

I've done some bad things, I guess. Well, in Cisco, Texas, in '27 I was in a fight with a Mexican. Broke my hand. Uh-huh. Ruined that hand. I just forgot about it with drinking. I've never been scared. Not that I can remember. In '31, '32, '33, they'd shoot at us. The railroad boys would shoot at us. I don't know whether they was trying to hit us or scare us or what. We asked for a place to sleep, in a jail or somewhere, to keep out of the cold.

I've been to a lot of places. I like Virginia, around Richmond. It was historical. We laid a pipeline across where the war was ended. At the Appomattox Court House. We laid a pipeline right across that crater where they drew them up. That's where Lee gave up to Grant.

Right in the Appomattox Court House. I worked there a year or two, down in Richmond, Virginia. And I liked that country.

I used to go to movies. Not anymore. If I do, I go to a drive-in or something maybe. Well, old Liz Taylor was pretty good in that *Cat on a Hot Tin Roof*. Pretty good, yeah.

I been in politics. I run for office here twice. I run for sheriff and I run for some office in the courthouse. Didn't come close at all. They even burnt the ballots up the next morning. Oh, yes. This was a Republican county and I was a Democrat. Never had a chance. I don't know why I ran. Just for the fun of it. Watergate? Well, I think that's just one of the things that's come out. I think there's a lot more that could come out that may be just as bad. Yes. I don't think Nixon was the only thief in politics. Couldn't make me believe that. I believe there's a lot more of them haven't been exposed.

Women should have equal rights if they want it. If they want to go out and fight and do the same things we do. If they want it that way, I'm not agin it. I worked with women on pipelines. I did. All over Alaska we did. Sure did. All the girls.

Civil rights is all right, but I won't mix my color. My children didn't either. I wouldn't want my children bringing in a big black buck for a son-in-law and they didn't. I'll help them all I can because they lived the way I wanted them to live.

I couldn't stop working. Never. Oh, I enjoy meeting everybody, working with them. All kinds. All walks of life, all countries. They come from everyplace. Philippine boys and Vietnamese boys. They all wanted to go with me. Said, We want to go with Earl. We like to go with him. They liked me. Everybody on the line liked me and they liked to work with me. And the money's always good. One job lasted two years and four months. It was going on before that. I could've got on quicker, but I didn't know about it. Didn't take after it. There's money there. Depends on where you're at. You could make forty to fifty thousand dollars in a year. Most of them good jobs are foreign. And they send you and keep you.

I've been in several other countries. America is the best one I was ever in or ever hope to be in. I've been in other countries, and I think it's the best place in the world to live. I'd come back here to die, a half a mile from where I was born. You can have anything you want. It depends on how hard you work for it and want it, how bad you want it. If you want something bad enough and you worked at it hard enough, you could almost always get it, I think. Harry Truman did. I belonged to the lodge with him up here in Kansas City. We used to shake hands with the fellow. He told us about how he figured out where to drop the shot on Hiroshima and them places over there in Japan to keep from killing most people. Wanted to kill the least, but he wanted to end the war and save our lives. He was a fine old man. He was rough, but he was a fine old man, I thought. Roosevelt was pretty good, too. We were hungry and he gave us clothes and food. After the Hoover boom. The bums call it the Hoover boom.

I'm 76 years old, and I want to work and I think they ought to hire me regardless of my age. But they wouldn't. Insurance companies wouldn't insure you. You'd have to lie to go to work. I had to lie when I was a kid when I was 15. I told them I was 16, I think. I was supposed to be 16. I still do it.

Our work, our construction work has changed a lot. Got better equipment. When I started, we didn't have much to work with—didn't even have equipment. Did it by hand. Kids today'll do it better. Got newer stuff to work with. They know more. They're smarter mechanically and all that. When I was young, I'd done well to fix a wheelbarrow, an old cultivator, or an old wagon or something. Now everything's mechanized. Any kids know how to do it.

When one of my relatives dies or an old friend, I handle it. I come back from Chicago or wherever I'm working and bury him, and then go right back to work.

I live day to day. I'll try to keep out of that truck's way if I can. A lady once ran me right off the road. She was coming down and I saw her coming. That was coming out of Boston. I bought a new Pontiac over there. Just bought the thing. She didn't even slow down. So I had to get off that big highway and go through a filling station to keep from getting hit or hitting her. That's just what I did.

# Lillian Oppenheimer

*L*illian Vorhaus Kruskal Oppenheimer *is a tiny woman whose ener-getic style gives the impression of a much larger person. As she bustles around her Greenwich Village brownstone apartment, she seems tire-less. Her apartment is filled with examples of origami, the art of Japanese paper folding: paper birds, trees, flowers. The books she has written on origami line the walls; few scholars of the art are unfamil-iar with her work. She teaches as well, increasing the legions of origami devotees. She puts on her own puppet shows. All of this activity gives her a kind of robust glow, a perking sense of action, and that—coupled with her admiration for words—keeps her in motion. One of her friends wrote to her not long ago: "You are like the flowers, lovelier now than in your distant spring." Were she not modest, she would agree, because that distant spring was not as happy and productive as the lively present.*

*She was born in October 1898 in New York City, her mother's birthplace as well; her father came to America at the age of 6, from Poland. She attended public schools, and attended Ethical Culture and Fieldston high schools. She never went to college. In 1914 her father moved the family to a farm in New Jersey; he had studied law, but when that didn't pay off, he took a course at Columbia University in raising chickens and bought the farm. Her mother lasted one cold winter on the farm, and the family fled back to New York City.*

*She was married at 19, had five children (out of ten pregnancies), lived in Westchester, divorced and remarried the same man. He died in 1949. That signaled the beginning of a new life for Lillian. She started a florist shop in Manhattan, The Green Thumb (which is still in business), and in 1954 she married Harry Oppenheimer and spent "eight happy years" with him before he died. Since then, she has been productive—in origami, in being a puppeteer, and in appreciat-ing the successes of her children and the varied lives of her twenty-seven grandchildren. Her apartment contains a piano, hundreds of books, a scattering of mementos, several oriental rugs, and comfortable furniture that has withstood the test of time. Yet she thinks about moving into a loft, where she would have more room to expand her activities, to get things in order. Her friends wonder why, at her age, such thoughts cross her mind. She doesn't wonder at all.*

I came into a family where I was the low man on the totem pole. There were three older brothers, a mother and a father, and a grandmother and grandfather all living together in a big brownstone on the East Side. I think it was 109th Street. The school that I went to I remember exactly, along with my mother saying, "How are you going to act when you go to kindergarten?" They were training me to be co-operative, you know. And I dashed to the little armchair that was mine, and I sat there and I folded my hands. See, good girl, good girl. I was already brainwashed to be a good girl, which I have tried to be the rest of my life. And everybody was naturally looking at me and insisting and shaping, and being sure that I would be a good girl, which I tried very honestly to be until I learned that I was being brainwashed and that it's much more fun not to be a good girl.

What I remember best about our neighborhood is when the subway was finished, it went as far as 145th Street, and my father, who had this large family to take care of, took a subway ride to the end and then walked and found a home in a row of many between Broadway and Amsterdam on 149th Street. And we rented that house so that we could all live together, and there was a school at 145th Street.

There was a lot of open space. In fact we were very far up when we went to 149th Street. And then my father's parents followed and took an apartment nearby. Families tended to stay together, and that was your whole world. I only knew my family and that was my world. Later on, when I had Freudian analysis, I learned that I had thought that what my world was, was *it*—was going to be everywhere, you know, in the rest of my life. It was very constricted, very confined, and we needed each other very badly. But it was good.

I saw so many changes, you know. I saw everything being electrified. My father said to me that he has seen the greatest and most wonderful growth in any generation. He doubts that anybody will ever have the advances experienced that he did, because he came here and saw the horse cart change and the lamplighter change, and the telephone came in at the time. He took me to my first movie. He just was amazed at all the things that were happening, and he hadn't any idea how far we'd go. So I never make the mistake of telling my children that you'll never see my advances. It's going to be terrific in the future, I know.

I feel that we're all human beings—there's always going to be corruption, and that's what I think we're suffering from. We have a wonderful country here, and we have more than any other country. I've traveled a great deal. But human nature is human nature, and it was that way before. How are we going to change it? There are good people who think for the good of all of us, but there are those who are pulling us down all the time.

I don't think it was better to live then, not in my life. Because I think you accommodate as you grow. You can take in other things, and sure, it's complicated, but we are more capable of doing complicated things. I think it's a natural growth. I think it's exciting, and I never have said, "the good old times." Because I feel that there were just as many bad things as there are now.

When I grew up, I just didn't have a thought. I was completely hypnotized and brainwashed, I assure you. With three boys, three brothers, hammering on me, and every time they went out and saw a girl who did something that was naughty, they'd come back and make sure that I knew about it so that I wouldn't do it. And my mother would not allow me—my mother or my father would not allow me to go out with anybody, any young men, in high school. "When you're eighteen," my mother said, "then you'll go out." And I listened very docilely and took her advice, and did everything I was supposed to do, and I guess I was pushing it all down. But when my eighteenth birthday arrived and now I was allowed to go out, there was nobody to take me out because I hadn't made any friends. And that was my first disillusionment—my mother had lied to me. And it wasn't really a lie; it was her wish to keep me pure, and she didn't know what to do. She was a wonderful woman, but bringing up three boys was tough, and she didn't want them to be diseased. And she worried about it a lot because she used to say to my family—this is what was dinned into us all the time—you have healthy good blood, all the way back, parents, grandparents, as far as we know. You have wonderful hearts, good digestive systems. Keep it that way. You know, that was the way she told us. She made us feel very proud of our physical assets.

She had a mother who was more dominant. The matriarch. The

grandmother who really ruled and brought us up. And I remember my grandmother more than I do my mother. She was in residence. She was a wonderful woman, wonderful. And you know, a curious thing, she was born in another country. And I would ask her questions—What was it like and where did you go to school? And she didn't—they didn't have school in those days. And I have thought as a grandmother now my children don't come and—my grandchildren don't ask me any questions. They never say, What was it like? Maybe because they think they know because it's the same city. But I was always asking my grandmother, and the stories she told me were the ones that made a great impression on me. But the funny part of it is that one day I heard my brother, who was a doctor and the one really responsible for my upbringing and my thoughts. He was my nearest and dearest in age and in every other way. And I heard him tell a story about his grandmother, and I said that isn't what she told me. My story was entirely different. Children grow up and they have different stories about the same thing. Well, for one thing, she didn't know how to read or write. And so when I was—oh, I don't know—8, 9, 10, whatever, I wanted to teach her, because I was learning myself. And she always said, I'm too old. Well, I figured out that she was probably then only about 60. She lived to be 96. She would've had many years, but she didn't know it, of course. Her first language—our first language—was German. But a particularly bad patois, as I learned later when I went to German class. They frowned upon the way I spoke. But that was my first language, and I can talk for hours in German, very badly, but I get across.

But I remember she told me her story, as I recall it, and probably I've embroidered it. She was one of very many children. Her father was a farm owner, a land owner, so he had some status. And the mother and all of these children, and she was one of the younger ones. Her father was killed on a runaway horse. His horse ran away as he was going around his land one day. And from what my grandmother said, the relatives swooped down and completely cleaned out the mother of any assets or anything. And she was so poor that she had nothing to do but give the children to various relatives to take care of. Which my grandmother resented very much because she was one given away, whereas her mother kept the baby. As you look at it now, that would've been the natural thing, but the child resented it terribly. And Grandmother said that she—although that child was her favorite sister—she still resented the fact. She was shipped around and wherever she went, she was like a maid, I guess. She had to do the work. And when she was 16, she was in a doctor's house in Budapest, I think is where she came from. And I asked her, Did you go to school? There was no school. In those days if you were wealthy, you had a tutor, but otherwise there was nothing—so she never learned to read or write.

And she said that the children were taught, for instance, sewing. And at night she'd sneak upstairs with a candle and get the work that they had been taught and repeat it. And that's how she learned to sew, which helped her a great deal when she came to this country. And she was 16 with beautiful blonde curls, she told me. You know, they didn't have a tutor, but every day a woman came and dressed all the women's hair. Isn't that odd? That was in the 1800s, in Budapest. Every house, even if they weren't too wealthy, the hairdresser came, so she had her beautiful curls, and one day the doorbell rang. And a young man was standing there, my grandfather. And he had come with letters of introduction from Hungary to the doctor, but of course when he saw her, he fell in love with her, and soon afterwards they were married.

They had a child and he wanted to come to America. I don't know why. So they got on a boat, came to America, and the boat foundered and was shipwrecked. And they were picked up by a sailing vessel going around the Cape of Good Hope. So they went a very long way out of their way, and in the meantime she lost the baby because there wasn't enough food and the stress and strain. And when they arrived in Boston, the city was all bedecked in black because Abraham Lincoln had just been shot. So we can pinpoint the time of their arrival in America. And she used to always say to us, Golden land, America. Golden land because they treated her so well here. She had nothing to eat. They were poor—of course they came without knowing the language or anything. And Thanksgiving Day she opened the door and there was a basket of food on the doorstep, left by good ladies who anonymously went around and left baskets of food. And so she always gave credit to America as being a golden land of opportunity, which of course it is.

And because she didn't know how to read or write, she made up her mind that her children would, and that they would become educated, which they did. She had eleven children and only raised three. The others died in children's diseases and accidents, as was common in those days. And her two sons became outstanding lawyers of their time. Today, everybody is dead. It's terrible to live and see everybody dying out. You're like Rip Van Winkle. Anyway, she lived to see that her sons were well educated, and her daughter married. So she was the cook of the family. She did all the cooking. And we lived in a brownstone where the basement had the kitchen and the garden. You know, going right out to the garden from the kitchen. And I remember my grandfather always sitting in an armchair, rocking chair, with a little cover over his knees. He was invalided as long as I knew him. He went to the fair in Chicago in the late 1800s and got a sunstroke. And after that he was no good for anything. She had a lot of contempt for him, you know, and she was a matriarch. From where she came from, you addressed your husband by his last name, not his first. It was Grossman. Grossman, come here, and Grossman, do this. A kind of contempt, I suppose.

Anyway, she'd do all the cooking at the big stove. I remember there was always a pot on the stove, and it was warm and smelled good. It was a place that children liked to be in. And she pushed me out. Go upstairs and read. Be a lady. If you don't know how to cook, nobody will ask you to do it.

So all my life I have been led by that rejection, and it's funny how it's come out again and again until I reached the age of 70-odd that I could first begin to have my own kitchen and do my own cooking. So you can imagine what joy went into it. It's not a drudgery for me like it is for other people.

I guess my earliest memory is of a photograph I saw of four little children sitting together on the steps of the brownstone with their nurse. I was one of them. You know, you see a picture and you imagine yourself as that. Oh, I remember being frightened by my naughty brothers all the time—there was a bend in the apartment, and every time I went around the corner somebody would say "boo" and jump out. Or they'd pull me into a closet and light a match and draw in the air with it—that scared me no end. I don't know why. You know the matches that make faces? I was always being teased by older brothers. And yet my mother tells me that I was treated like a princess because she wanted a girl so badly and had one boy after another. But I still remember the bad things, I'm sorry to say. Nevertheless, my brothers were wonderful to me.

In my childhood I learned to be good and obedient, and do what you're told to do. It was just as simple as that. I don't know why I was so complacent. But as a psychiatrist explained to me later, it's much better if a child is bad when they're young. Because if you have a divorce like I did and upset my whole family, and the repercussions were as bad as they could possibly be, much better to do something naughty like stealing an apple or not picking up your clothes or whatever.

Well, my parents had a loving—a love marriage. And I know that my mother as a young girl loved him—we'd lean out the window watching for my father to come home from the elevated train. He had to walk a block, just to Central Park West, where we lived, and we had a side window. And I remember, many times, she'd always look for him to come home, and as he walked, she'd say, "Isn't he handsome? Isn't he—look at that carriage. Look what a wonderful man!" So I know there was love there. And so it was good to grow up in a house like that. I particularly think that having grandparents is wonderful. I remember particularly that my grandmother was always there to back us up. For instance, the boys used to play—I think they call it cat something. They'd take a little piece of wood, and with an ordinary stick they'd hit it like a ball. Cat something. See, we didn't have toys. Our playground was in the middle of the street at 149th Street, and there were gangs. That whole block had its own gang of kids, and every other block did, too. And occasionally the other gangs would come in and invade our block. And then there'd be real fights with the boys. Well, if the boys were in trouble, they'd run down to the basement because that was where my grandmother was always to be found, in the kitchen. And she'd come up with a rolling pin. And boy, she was the best protector any of us had. She was wonderful.

And so I remember that. Also we had a streetlamp right in front of our house. And our house was the only one on the block with one —you see, the block goes up a little bit, there's a slight hill. And our house had a stone seat, and it was the only one. You see, these things make such a difference. You have one little thing better than all the other boys and girls on the block. It gives you something for your ego. So we had this lamp—the reason I remember it is that I got terribly punished one day because of it. When my father came home at night, that's when all the troubles were told, and he dished out the discipline. And I had climbed the lamppost. I saw the boys do it, so I did it. And I was given a lecture that it wasn't ladylike. And I was a little girl. I didn't know what was a lady and what was not. And I remember feeling the injustice of it, that I was being punished for something that boys did. Why couldn't I? And so that lamp stands for something.

Growing up on that block, I know the boys had wonderful times. I remember my brother, the doctor, finding out by reading in the dictionary what a gentleman does to a lady and he taught me how you must take your arm and go across the street. He came home one day from school terribly excited at lunchtime. He had something to tell me. He learned the remarkable fact that two plus two makes four. And *A* plus *B* equals *C*. He taught me. All the things that he learned, at that time, he shared with me. And also the positions of guns. He gave me my grandfather's cane and I had to stand there and—as he booted out the orders, I had to go to the shoulders and wherever. So he really was very close to me and used to wheel my carriage around. My mother said he was so proud of me in the neighborhood.

My mother never turned from anything either. She used to come home when we were there at lunch, she'd tell us how she helped the neighbor who had a new baby, and how she changed the diapers, and you know, it was helping one another. A neighborhood.

In those days you had a chance to care about your neighbors. Here, today, where do you have a chance? I'm sure people would react that way if they had the chance. Like in the blackout look how wonderful everybody was to everybody. I think intuitively we're good if we're just given a chance. But our lives are so swift. If you have the time and the wherewithal, anybody would willingly do it.

We had a tennis court. When we bought our farm, we built a house, and my father and mother in their naïveté just drew a box and divided it into four so we could have a kitchen and a dining room and a parlor and a drawing room. And then upstairs, a straight stairs, and then the two bedrooms on either side, and the two bathrooms. And they took it to a builder and he said he'd have to have blueprints. They didn't know that. They thought that he could just build it. So they built this ugly little box on a knoll, and then we had clay pits at the end of the twenty-six acres that we owned. And they pulled up the clay and brought it and made a lovely tennis court. And that's where there were always lots of young people. Every weekend—company, simple but company.

Living on a chicken farm. We had chicken every weekend. I can't look at a piece of chicken to this day. But it was there to be had. And my folks loved having lots of young people around.

My father bought a little Ford. The first little Ford in 19—let's see, it was 1914, because I was 16 and I had to learn to drive. I had to drive —there were no buses, no means of getting miles out of town from the farm into Westfield, so they could go to New York on the ferry and do whatever they had to do—business and whatnot. So I had to drive. So I had to get a license. And I had to get a special license, being 16. My brother planned the whole thing. I wore my mother's skirt. When you were young, you wore short skirts, and when you were older you wore long ones. Pinned my long hair up. When you were older, you wore your hair up. And I went and took this special writing exam and driving exam. And all the time that my brother taught me, he really was a marvelous teacher, and he played all kinds of tricks on me. He'd pull a wire on the floor that choked the engine for you. And he would pull it surreptitiously without me noticing it. And the car would stop, and he would say, "What did you do now?" And he would scold me. And he taught me very well. He taught me to listen to the vibrations and hear the noise. No windshield wipers in those days. So I can drive anything. He made a very good driver out of me. I'm known today at the place where you rent a car as that little old lady that can drive anything, you know? Anyway, I need it because I'm a puppeteer, and you know the amount of stuff a puppeteer hauls around.

I always knew the difference between right and wrong from my up-bringing. That was very rigid, right and wrong. You knew what was right and wrong. I mean, it was laid out for you.

If you disobeyed your parents, that was wrong. In fact, my mother was so severe about that that she never would let me sleep over at anyone's house. I don't know what she was afraid I'd find. But girls used to sleep over at other people's houses. I never was allowed— that's why I wasn't allowed to go to college. I might learn something. I had the experience of a few months in a public high school, and it was horrendous. You were in a jail. I mean, you ran up these iron steps with the iron railings, and the hordes of kids coming.

But then, when I went to Ethical Culture, the first day I went to this new school, two girls came over to me and said, "Will you walk?" —there was a time when you walked up and down the hall at recess time—put their arms around my waist and the three of us walked—I felt immediately taken in. I'll never forget that feeling, because it was the first time that I felt a cohesive feeling of amity among people who were strangers to me.

That school made me question what I took for granted. I never thought of thinking out anything, because the rules were laid down for me. But here they said, Is it right that a man does this and that? What would you do in a case? But I was not very analytical and I was not very bright. And I didn't do very well in school. I was not ready for it. I was so hemmed in—I see it now because I have very brilliant children. My three sons are all Ph.D.'s and great in their own fields. Well, I guess it didn't all come from my husband, who was a self-made man, who had no education. But I just never was ready for it.

My husband said to me when my oldest son was 16, "I want him to come into my business because I want a son to take over the business." My son was a brilliant boy who went flying through with honors, a natural student. I was horrified. I said, "You can't have him. He's got to go to college. He's a natural for it." So I fought like a steer. He got his master's and his Ph.D. and he went ahead. He did go to the business for two years, to oblige his father. Two more miserable years he never had. But he said, "Mother, at least I gave it a try."

The family unit really hasn't vanished, because the kids today get together and live together. They've got to have family. They have communes. There are six or eight or ten, and they need each other. That's the only form of life they look for. The reason is they didn't have it before, evidently.

If you don't have a family, you make one. I have twenty-seven grandchildren, so I have plenty of observation, and I find that they don't go and live alone as their rebellion against society. They go and join up with other boys and girls. And it just shows that we need to have one another, don't we? I have found it in my own life: I need so badly to have people around me.

I don't think the sexual revolution is good or bad. It's a natural growth. You see, I was brought up where everything was a secret. And I don't think that's good at all. My mother told me that when she menstruated, her mother hadn't warned her about it. When she came home from school, she said she noticed that there was blood and she was terribly frightened, because she was 11 or 12. And she ran to her mother. Now her mother, my grandmother, was cooking at the stove and feeding the men who worked for my grandfather. It evidently was just like a little sidewalk business. And my mother didn't realize where she was—she was so frightened, like if you'd cut your finger suddenly. And she ran to my grandmother and said, Look. And my grandmother was furious with her, because she was embarrassed with the men there, and she sent her up the hill to the widow woman to tell her what happened. She couldn't face her daughter and tell her. Now, my mother could tell me about menstruation, but she couldn't tell me about marriage. I was really forced to marry the man I married. He was fourteen years older than I and there was no love. And that I think is horrible. Today, let them have their choice. Let them do what they want. Let there be love, because that's beautiful.

Love is commitment, total commitment. I mean, if you find somebody special, something happens to you inside and it doesn't happen too often in life. And you just go like a magnet. And if it's returned, it's beautiful. And then of course, you have to work out all the other things that happen afterward. If you're talking about living together and loving together over a length of time, I can tell you about that because I often wondered about it. There is something that grows—I mean, after all, you love and you do and you have together. But after a while, anything, no matter how blissful, becomes ordinary. Doesn't it? If we do it often enough. But I think with love there is something that grows deeper within. For instance, I'm thinking of my brother who had a child—got married and had a child and was having another one, and he came to my husband and he said, "How is it with the second? Can you love the second? I love my first child so much, I'm worried." You see, that's practically the same thing. You find room somehow to love your second child, don't you? Maybe the love for the first was a special, but there's sure love for the second and the third and the tenth, right? And where does it come from? It's just like a woman who's going to have a baby and doesn't want it. But something happens, biologically, spiritually—I don't know what. But when that baby comes in the ordinary course of events, a love develops, an acceptance for what's coming. And that I think we're born with.

I made marriage work the second time. I didn't make it work the first. I was a different person. I was mature. I was a grandmother. My second husband and I had raised children in the same era. We knew the times around us. We never had the problems that I had with my first. I mean, people who get married have terrible problems to overcome. Sometimes it's financial. Your love can fly out the window when you're battling against hunger and all the other things. Secondly, you're raising children. My husband objected to the way I raised them, and I objected to his way. We were at opposite ends of the pole. I wanted my children to have a happy childhood. That's all I cared about. And I was a child with them. And he wanted them to be taught and to be disciplined. And all right, maybe that's good, but we fought that way. And we had so many things to fight about, to have arguments or quiet little differences. And he would punish me by not talking to me for three weeks on end, and that was the most miserable punishment. Because if you're living with someone and you're verbal as I am, and have nobody to talk to but a blank wall, that's real punishment.

In the second marriage there were no problems. We both had children all raised. There was no financial problem. I had my income; he had his. The children were well off. Everything was beautiful. We only had to go ahead hand in hand and share each other's interests.

Another thing I found out is that when the woman gets married and has the children and a home, everybody is pulling at you. All of a sudden it stops and you evolve. And what are you going to do with your life for the rest of your life?

My first husband was a friend of my father's and grandfather's. I was 7 years old. And he saw me grow up. He watched me. I didn't know it. I wasn't aware of it. And as you know, I didn't go out until I was 18 and then there was nobody to go out with. And he used to say, I want to marry a Jewish girl from a nice Jewish family and have a son to carry on the business. But I never dreamed I was the girl that he was watching.

The marriage was planned. He saved my father's name. See, we had another depression and my father couldn't pay what he owed. And my husband took care of the debts. And I was the obligation. Now, here's a man who never communicated with me. He was charming with other people, but we never had anything—if company went out of the door, the door was closed, he never spoke to me again. And he was a self-made man. At 21 he had his own business. But I had nothing—I mean, I was just beginning. And when he took me out—I remember the first time—the reason I was thrilled to go out with him was that he had a racing car. And I was mad about cars.

Well, he took me out to dinner somewhere out of town, in Westchester, at a nice place. And we walked around the grounds, and we came home. I was so bored that I was fast asleep when he woke me and said, You're home. So it was a very sterile sort of thing, and he took me out. He took me in a whirlwind. We were in front seats at every show. The best restaurants. He knew how to do it. And I was swept off my feet. I didn't love him. But then one day he said to me, "What would you do if I kissed you?" And I was shocked because, you know, a good girl never kissed. And he kissed me and then I had to marry him because I thought I was going to have a baby. That's how little I knew about life. Oh, yes. Sure. And I went and told my folks. I said, "He kissed me, I have to marry him." Of course, he asked me to marry him. But what would you think of a man who is engaged to a girl and never lays a hand on her? I who had never gone out with anybody and didn't know any different, I was beginning to wonder. This was the man I was going to marry, why didn't he kiss me or love me or hug me, or whatever? Things were talking inside of me. And we used to go around the park and park in the car in this wonderful car, you know. And maybe he put his arm around me, but that was as far as it went. Until two or three nights before the wedding, he said to me, I think he asked me if I knew what a man had, you know. And I said no. Now, I was raised with three brothers and a father and I never saw a penis. Would you believe it? I mean, when I think back, I wonder how could it happen. I didn't know what a man had and I didn't know what I had. And I knew I wanted children, so I asked my mother, Well, where does the baby come from? Because I couldn't notice any holes around me, you know. And you know, my mother retreated. She said there are some things a man, a husband, has to tell a wife. Now, that's all right, but she should've told him. Because he didn't know what he was marrying—he'd never had a virgin. He didn't know what to do. It's horrible not to be in the know. I used to sit in a trolley car and see a woman pregnant. You know what it's all about, I used to think, you know what it is.

I had five children. That was my life. You see yourself reproduced. For one thing, they gave me companionship, which I didn't have with my husband. And I began to grow while they were growing. I was like another child.

Today, we're the best of friends. I pushed them out of the nest very early. I wanted to. I don't know whether it was because I wanted to start something of my own; I have no idea. But they're very good friends, and doing marvelous things in their own communities.

When they were growing up, we did a lot of music. All my children played instruments, and we used to play together.

I never considered myself anything but a child within. Not a wife within. So we've had a lot of music in our house. And we had an orchestra, and one child learned to conduct. Went to Oberlin, graduated. She was 14 when she played with the New York Philharmonic. She played clarinet, which was very unusual. And my son was at Juilliard. He was a flutist. Chamber music was always in our house.

My father's father—my grandfather—was a very religious man. And my father tells the story of when he was a youngster in the streets, playing, that his father would call to him. It was Friday night, time for prayers. And he resented so being called away from the games that he was thrilled with, that he told me—he made up his mind that if he ever had children, they would never have that happen to them. So we had no religion. I tried very hard when I was first married. I threw myself into the temple and tried to communicate with the rabbi and get some questions answered. It didn't happen.

I believe in self-hypnosis. I went through a harrowing experience having my first baby. I was several days in labor. The bag had burst before and I had a dry birth. And I was pulling—they tied a sheet to the post to pull, and I pulled. So I just said to myself, It's not going to hurt. It's not going to hurt. Every time I thought of it: It's not going to hurt. Do you know, it didn't hurt. I can't tell you whether I really convinced myself, and I didn't know that it was self-hypnosis until many, many years later, when I tried to find out whether I had really done it to myself. My brother was at all my births, because he was a doctor, holding my hand and encouraging me and helping me. And I remember that night he said, "Doesn't it hurt?" He had his watch and he was counting the time. And I said no. Finally he said, "You're not hiding something from me, sister?" I said, "No, I would tell you." "Because," he said, "this is the time that they all scream." He said, "Look, feel." And he took my hand and put it on my belly. And I could feel something contract and get very hard, and then it get soft again. And I didn't feel the slightest thing. So he says, "You're not fooling me, are you?" I said, "No, I wouldn't have any reason to." But I didn't tell him that for nine months I'd been saying that. And I wanted a natural birth, because I didn't like the idea of waking up and finding a baby presented to me. It could've been anybody's baby. So I made them promise that if everything was all right, he'd let me have it naturally. So I had it and they lifted her up and showed her to me, and so I saw.

Do you know the thing that bothers me about old age and deterioration? I go every year to the same doctor, of course, for my yearly examination, and he always says, "How are you?" And I say fine. Then he goes down the list. Do you have dizziness—do you have—I don't have to tell you. And no, no, I don't have anything. And I feel wonderful when I'm in his office. I wondered if it's one's attitude, because I say to myself, What have I got to look forward to in my eightieth year? And I sure don't want to be inundated by pain. The death I don't care. Let it come. But pain—who wants it? So I must get above that pain. If I'm going to live with it, I'm not going to take drugs. I'm not that kind—I never take a pill or anything. If I tell myself it's not going to hurt, it doesn't. And I think that's the greatest trick I've learned.

I went through Freudian analysis, and I said to the doctor, "When I'm through, what am I going to do?" And he said, "Well, you have friends." And I find that that is the greatest help. And I have been a shoulder for many a person in a lifetime. I'm very free to admit everything that I feel. It comes very easily.

I didn't think I could handle a granddaughter—the favorite granddaughter of all—coming here with a boyfriend. How was I going to handle the sleeping situation? I knew what was going on, of course, because I'd been living with it. But here's my favorite, named after me. How? You know, with my upbringing? And when the eveningtime came, and all I had was the couch and my bedroom. And when she came in and said to me, "What are the sleeping arrangements, Grandma?" I found myself saying, "What would you like?" And I was able to live here for two nights, seeing my granddaughter sleep in my bed with a young man. And you know, she just loves my attitude and my liberality.

The worst thing I ever did was the divorce. No question about it because I was brought up to believe that what I did was the worst thing in the world. The worst thing I did was to have sex without my husband. That was the way I was brought up. I don't think he knew.

I hope not. It ended in divorce, but I hope he didn't know it. He suspected that it was his daughter that the man was having sex with. My daughter. We both loved the same man. This happens very often, I understand. Having had sex with somebody other than my husband was about the biggest crime I could've committed. I paid for it, once, in fear. My lover and me, and he's drunk. And we're all alone in a loft locked up in a room for the night, and I can't get out. And he takes a bottle of wine and he spills it over me. My hair is all wet and drenched and he won't let me out to clean up. No bathroom or anything. And he was so drunk that he took out a knife and put it to me. Right to my breast. It was the end. There was nobody around. I had to die, had to. And at that moment such a surge of strength came through me. I don't know why, because I'm a timid person. But I just stood there and said, "Go ahead. Go ahead." I can see it to this day, whatever made me do it. And, of course, he dropped the knife.

When I was about 7, I guess, I saw *Peter Pan* with—now who's the actress? You see, in old age I get forgetful of certain things, but it'll come to mind. The famous one, of another generation. Anyway, way, way back we were asked if we believed in the fairy, you know, to wave our handkerchiefs, and in those days every little girl had a hand-kerchief tied to her belt or in her pocket. Today you only have Kleenex. But I remember taking out the handkerchief and I was bound to the theater and have been a devotee of it ever since. Well, social plays, of course. When you get to be my age, and you have seen every plot repeated over and over again, you can't help but be blasé. I try hard not to, loving the theater as I do. I love the theater.

I'm terribly sympathetic to feminism. I see it in the younger generation, with my grandchildren. And when this young whippersnapper of 25 who is now an attorney—my granddaughter—and has all the ideals and is horrified to think that a woman, because she's a woman, can't get a credit card in her own name or can't get various other things that are denied her—and who says, "I don't want to get married." Of course, she says, "If I want a child, I might consider it. But right now I don't want to get married." And has lived with two that I know of, and has loved them. Has been monogamous and loyal, and wouldn't even look at another one. You know, I feel about her so she could do anything and she couldn't be wrong. Do you know what I mean?

You have a love for someone if you see yourself reproduced. But she thinks she's like me and I think she is.

Everybody has to do something. You couldn't live your life with your hands folded and get any joy out of it. Everybody's different, and what pleases you wouldn't please me and vice versa. And the hard thing is to find out when you're growing up, what you want.

I wasn't very actively involved before I found origami. I introduced the word. Paper folding has been known to people all over the world. You've always made airplanes, haven't you? That's origami. People have done it and didn't know. I didn't like the word *paper folding* because people misinterpreted it. They'd come and say, "Oh, I saw somebody do paper folding," and it was sculpture or it was cutting. And we don't use a scissors. So when I heard the Japanese word, it sounded good to me.

It isn't that it's given me pleasure. It isn't pleasure. It has been great for the ego because I am a completely different human being. Whether it was the Freudian analysis, I don't know, whether it gave me the courage. But from an intimidated frightened child who was told the only thing in life is to marry a man, put your head under his foot, and let him stomp on it, I changed. My mother told me: Never say no. And there were many times in my life when I wanted to say no, but I was brought up to say yes. I finally learned. It's pride. Pride is caring. If you drive a nail in or whatever you do, if you don't care, that's when working is horrible, when you do something that you hate or that you're not interested in. I can't imagine a worse fate. If you're clever enough to find out what will bring you an income and it happens to be something you like, you're set.

Well, all my life I said, What do I want out of life? If I knew I wanted to be a doctor, I could get the courses. If I knew I wanted to be a lawyer—but nothing spoke to me. You're lucky if when you're a young man or a young woman and something speaks to you and says do this and do that. Even if you change afterwards, that doesn't matter. Change is wonderful. Not like the Russian countries and the countries, say in Japan, once you're in the bank, that's your life, whether you like it or not. I had a young man come over who did the illustrations for my book, and he was telling me what it was like. He had to leave Japan—he was with a bank there, and he couldn't do anything else but be a bank teller or whatever it was. So he came over here, and he's an artist. He's a free-lance artist, and a marvelous artist. And he had to literally lose all his identity with his past, leave his family, and—I understand now from having brought up children and all, that what you think you want sometimes isn't what you want. Because you don't know. My brother became a doctor because his uncle was a doctor. Well, suppose after a few years he found out he couldn't stand the sight of blood or whatnot? Of course, it didn't happen, but it could have. If what you started with is what you're going to die with, that's not being very clever or knowing human nature. I get a new profession all the time. I've just recently become a professional puppeteer. I believe in it. Because I had a friend who took up the cello at 50, and I thought, Gee, that's marvelous. So, that was my incentive.

I have regrets. Oh, how can you live and not? Of course. Mostly all the wasted youth. Sit in school and turn yourself off because you're bored with what's happening, and you lose all those vital moments. I met a doctor once at a dinner party. This doctor was fabulous, and he said wherever he's been in a group he's always tried this. It makes for wonderful conversation, incidentally. Everybody goes round the table and tells about the teacher who made the most impression in his life. And usually the people cannot only tell you about the teacher and what subject he taught, but can give you his name and sometimes even his address. And the other teachers mean nothing. But that one teacher—it was a turning point in a life. It was true. Everybody around the table could bring up one teacher, showing that education can be an ecstasy—my grandson once sent me that book—*Learning Can Be an Ecstasy*. Well, there aren't enough talented people to inspire everybody, unfortunately, but when you find a person and you can be inspired—you surge ahead, no question about it.

I guess I appear as an aggressive old lady. But it's such a change from the characteristics that I had at first. Now I have no qualms. I can say anything I want and that freedom has given me such joy. With the protection of age, I can tell people things that I wouldn't have had the nerve to have said, and feel perfectly calm about it.

I try to be fair and square. My grandmother used to say that to her dying day: "I'm fair and square." I find myself saying it. I have five children. Fair and square I want to leave them their father's money, fairly and squarely. Here's the will. Does it suit you? Tell me if it doesn't. We'll arrange it so that the money is yours. I'm just living on the interest of it now. Fair and square. Treat them all the same. And have some fun for myself.

You're 50 years old, you're 60 years old. You might have a few years left. What's going to be fun? Fun is what I never had in the beginning. And I lost myself in my babies. Every time I was pregnant, and I was pregnant ten times, I had my own world and I didn't care that I wasn't this or that.

I learned. I made terrible mistakes. But the one thing that analysis did is to show me that I'm not alone. It's just like with masturbation. You think you're so guilty. When you find out that everybody does it— oh, that cloak disappears and you say, Well, you're not the one that has been selected by God to be the sinner. The minute I learned that other people make mistakes, then that is the way you grow. If you never make a mistake in your life, you don't grow. What a relief that was, to learn that.

You inure yourself to death. You know you're going to have those problems the longer you live. I went through a terrible thing just now. Two of our outstanding people in origami died. I don't want to be hurt. I don't want to be hurt. I had to make my peace with myself. I went around asking everybody, just like I always say, share your problems. Maybe somebody'll help you. I say to my friends or to my children, I say you know, when it comes, and I've already had a grace of ten years, a bonus that I'm not entitled to, don't be sad and upset and worried, because I've had whatever kind of life it was. Just know that I did whatever I wanted to do at the end. I didn't do it at the beginning. But I've done what I wanted to do. I've had a great life. You know, if it ends, good-bye. Please God it happens like that. The only thing I really fear is to be a vegetable and be a problem to my children. All my friends know it: Pull out those pipes, those tubes. Don't let me be kept alive one hour as a vegetable. Let me go.

You know, my grandmother used to say—she had a wonderful philosophy—at 96 she said, "The good Lord takes the good." I must have been a very bad girl. He hasn't taken me yet.

# Sam Strinel

$S$am Strinel looks healthy, his gray hair and mustache are neatly trimmed; his tan is deep and impressive; his forearms are muscular; he does not have a prominent paunch. His apartment, on Chicago's far North Side along Lake Michigan, is neat, organized, and filled with books, paintings, carvings, and comfortable furniture. He has lived in that apartment for twenty-seven years; he is happy in it, as he is in the hotel in San Miguel de Allende in Mexico, where he spends nine months each year. He is not a wealthy man, but he is pleased with his fate.

It was not always so. Strinel, who was born on September 15, 1904, came to America from Russia with his mother when he was 3. His father had come over two years earlier, to earn the money for their passage. In Russia Strinel's father had been a shoemaker; in America, he sold ice in summer, coal in winter, and peddled junk year round. They lived in poverty in the Williamsburg section of Brooklyn. By the time he was 12, Strinel's mother decided he had had enough of learning how to steal and how to become a truant. She brought Sam and his sister to Chicago (the father came along later) for a more satisfying existence.

Years later Strinel recalled that many of his Brooklyn compatriots wound up in prison. He did not. At his mother's urging he studied and finished high school, then attended some evening classes in college. An interest in the military led him to work in a military-equipment store. Eventually he joined a company that sold military uniforms and equipment. He retired, at age 65, after thirty-eight years with the firm, in 1969.

He had married the director of a nursery school in 1942; they had two children, one of whom died at age 12 in an auto accident. When his wife died, in 1970, his life seemed to stop; theirs had been a happy marriage.

For a year he did very little; he still serviced several military-equipment accounts on his own, to compensate for the lack of a pension. In 1971 he went to Mexico, stayed for a month, and liked it. He went back the next year, then decided to rent an apartment in a hotel in San

Miguel de Allende, covering the cost by renting his Chicago apartment to Northwestern University students. In Mexico he could spend time riding horses, a pleasure that dated back to the first time he had seen horses pulling a fire wagon shortly after he had come to Chicago. He made friends in San Miguel de Allende with both Mexicans and resident Americans. He went to concerts, to art openings, to films—and he began to explore Mexico.

Today, when he is in Chicago, he brings the tan with him. He has given his car to his son and gets around on a bicycle. He shops, visits old friends, listens to music, and reads. He has a large library of records and books; they all appear to have been used. "Classical music is as important to me as food," he says.

He is a man who changed his attitudes as he grew older. Once macho, he is now for women's rights; once an admirer of the military, he is now vigorously antiwar. He seeks new experiences and new insights.

We lived in Williamsburg, which was wall-to-wall concrete. I never saw a tree or grass unless I went to the park. We played in the streets. And the houses in Brooklyn are cheek by jowl, one next to another. You can run a whole block on top of the roofs. And we made our own pleasures. Sneak on the el and go to Coney Island. Playing handball against buildings. Playing games. I don't know what they were called, but we used to whittle a broomstick, both ends, and then take the stick and hit with it. I think we called it stick-at-a-boo. We had our own names for things.

The neighborhood was all Jewish. Jewish neighborhood. And we lived in buildings that were four stories high. Walking up, in these old tenements, with outside toilets in the hall. They were railroad flats: kitchen, bedroom, bedroom, living room. And no windows except the skylight in the bedroom, which didn't give much light. Whatever light you had was in the kitchen and the living room. I remember the kitchen. We had two washtubs, where you washed clothes and where you took a bath. And you'd heat water and put it in an oval tub and that's where you took a bath. We had a kitchen stove. I can't remember any other stove except in the kitchen. It was very cold in the winter. And I remember being very sickly. I had all kinds of sicknesses. I had all sorts of diseases. Names I can't remember, but I think one was diphtheria. And mumps and measles and whatnot. The area was certainly not conducive to good health. We didn't know we lived in a slum until we went out of the area and saw the way other people lived. We lived in that neighborhood until we moved to Chicago, in 1917.

Since my mother, my parents, came here by ship, we thought the only way to come to Chicago was by ship, too. We knew nothing of the geography. And so we took a boat. In those days they had people who brought people over to America. They'd send tickets. And they went to this person and he told them you have to take the ship to Chicago. So we took a ship and I think we landed in Lake Erie, as I remember. I think it was Cleveland. Must have been. I don't even know if it was Lake Erie. But I imagine it was. And then we took a train to Chicago. And when we came to Chicago we took a street-car, and my uncle lived on Artesian Avenue near Division Street. We got off the streetcar at Division Street and there was a street with trees. Tree-lined streets, with a plot of grass in front of each house. And I thought my uncle must be a millionaire to be living in a place where there were trees and grass, because I'd never seen grass or trees unless we went to Prospect Park. And they had a yard in the back and a porch. A porch in back so you could get out. We had no porches in New York. You just looked out of the glass. So it was fantastic. It was unbelievable to be able to walk on grass and to have trees and hear birds. You never heard birds in New York, no natural sounds. Only artificial noises.

I made friends. I made some friends who I still know today. My oldest friend, a fellow that I met when I first came here—Pete Simon. I think I met him two or three weeks after I arrived in Chicago. And we've been friends since. He just died, last year. And we were close. I was closer to him than most brothers are.

Of course, my whole life-style changed. I learned about books. I learned about music. Because we associated with some of my friends' brothers or sisters or parents who were interested in books or read books. I never read a book. I don't remember ever reading a book in Brooklyn. And we had no books in the house. There was a library on North Avenue in Chicago, and we went to the library and I read a book. A fairy-tale book.

In those days, my first books were fairy tales. And then I read adventure stories. Buffalo Bill and Jesse James and all these dime novels, and westerns. I always wanted to be a cowboy and to ride a horse. So I read very many western stories. I enjoyed them. I enjoyed reading, and I've enjoyed reading ever since. I read constantly.

I don't know about Brooklyn today. I went back to the neighborhood, and it's all terrible. Well, if it was a slum when we were there, at least it was a clean slum. I was back there about twelve years ago and it's just awful. It looks like a war had taken place there. I look back nostalgically to my childhood in Chicago, not in New York. Because there I belonged. We joined the Boy Scouts and we went on overnight hikes and camped. And that's something I never had done before. And associated with other kids whose parents I met, and their parents spoke English and they were Americanized. My parents were from the old country and spoke English with a broken accent. It was a turning point in my whole life, coming to Chicago. I don't know what would've happened to me if I'd stayed in New York.

I think our childhood was much happier than the kids today. I think more innocently happier. We didn't worry about atomic bombs. We didn't worry about conscription in the army. We never heard of a soldier and never saw one. Except me, because I went to places where they were because I was interested in them. I remember once going on a vacation, and just going to visit army camps. Imagine that? Of course, my thinking has changed completely 180 degrees. I now resent any money being spent on the military establishment.

You know, life has changed so much, so many things have happened in the past sixty years. There were no airplanes. There was no such thing as even a sports shirt. We wore the same clothes, winter and summer. Long sleeves. There was no plastic. There were no radios, television, telephone. All these things came along since we were grown up. Certain things I am grateful for. I would just as soon think we could do without nuclear power. I don't like to see the country going through the state in which it is today, where we're supposed to be the world's number-one policeman. And where the military is the dominant power in the country and influences foreign policy. In my day it wasn't. There was no military-industrial complex. And life was more carefree. Yes, I worked—my parents were very poor, so every vacationtime I had all kinds of jobs. I wanted a bicycle, and in order to get a bicycle I had to work. And I worked for a firm that made briefcases and they sold in Marshall Field and all the fine stores. It was very heavy. Remember the old days, the ones with the straps around them. And I delivered those things to different stores. We put them on a stick and went on the streetcar. And they were very heavy. I was 14, 15, then.

My mother was a very kindly and lovely person. She spoiled me in a way. I was a very difficult child, I presume, now that I look back. I wouldn't eat any of the food that the family ate. I wouldn't eat any Jewish food. I wouldn't eat gefilte fish on Friday night. Every Friday night we had gefilte fish and chicken and that sort of thing, matzoh balls. And she cooked separately for me. Because there were only two of us, and she overdid it. I think she was too good to me. I didn't have too much discipline. I didn't take advantage of it, except in my eating habits.

My mother apparently was wise enough to know that Brooklyn was no place for me. I would wind up like most of my friends did when Prohibition came in. Most of them became bootleggers and they wound up in prison, and doing worse things as well. She was wise enough to know that this was no place to bring up a child. And so we came to Chicago, and as I told you, this changed my entire life.

She was a typical Jewish mother, from the old country. And her ways were of the old country. She carried on not only the tradition but the life-style, as far as she could do it in this environment. You know, she dressed very simply and she never had a car or used anything but the streetcar. Transportation was by streetcar. Laundry was her norm. She washed and cooked and she scrubbed and she cleaned. And, of course, she worked hard all her life. But she was so good and kind and generous, and I don't think she ever raised her voice to me. My father, too—I don't think he ever raised his voice to me.

I remember when I was leaving New York and my friends were runing away from home, because they were beat up. Most Jewish fathers physically beat their children. And I wanted to be the same as my peers. And I used to provoke my father so he would strike me, give me a reason for leaving home. But he never would raise his hand. He was like my mother. His life was as it was in the old country. He worked very, very hard. In Chicago he peddled. He got a horse and wagon and he peddled fruits, vegetables. He didn't make enough money at that, so he'd peddle junk in the alleys. And so from that he made a living, and when I started to work, I would turn my money into the family.

And I was given spending money, fifty cents a week or something like that.

They taught me patience, understanding of other people. I didn't always practice it with my mother and father because I wasn't aware at the time, until I got older, what type of people they were. When I was young, they were just my mother and father, who fed you and you had a place to go to to sleep at night. We didn't have too much communication because we lived in two different worlds. I was brought here so early I have no recollection of the old country. The only recollection I have is being on the ship. I remember being in the hold of the ship, in the bottom, where people were sick, seasick apparently. And I remember I raised so much hell, I screamed and carried on that I remember one of the crew, whoever he was, steward or something, told me he'd throw me overboard if I didn't shut up. He frightened me into being quiet. And that somehow sticks in my memory. And I remember coming to Castle Garden. That was where the immigrants came in, like Ellis Island. This was another place. And I remember my father. I didn't remember him, but my mother pointed him out to me. My father was standing behind this fence. And he was standing behind there and it was the first time I'd seen my father. I remember that.

Whatever I do, I do because I enjoy it. I love horses and I can't remember the time when I didn't love horses. I used to hang around the fire engines in the days when they had horses, waiting for the fire to come, so the horses would come out of their stalls and get into the harness and the harness was dropped on and they'd go to the fire. How I admired that man, usually an Irishman, driving that team of horses. He was my hero. And that's why I was enamored of the military, because I associated military with horses, cavalry. I ride a bike a lot now. Even now, when I ride a bike, I do it for necessity. I have no car, so I use it for transportation.

There are many influences that work against family life today. I think the most important thing is the automobile. There's no reason to stay home like we used to do. You get into a car and you have mobility. We didn't have mobility. Children didn't leave home until they were married, particularly girls. Your life revolved around the house, around your home. You came back and you went to your home. Your parents didn't know about vacations or going anywhere. Everything was the house and the street. Now you have the broadened vision of radio and television, which show you how people live. We didn't know. We were so insulated from it. Going to California was like going to Europe. I don't think it's a bad thing. But then, I'm an implacable enemy of the automobile. Because the automobile, instead of being a servant of man, has become man's superior. Everything revolves around your automobile. And what it has done to this country. I resent the automobile for cementing over the world. Wherever you go every year, more billions of acres of grass and natural land is being taken over by concrete. And it doesn't help any because the more roads they build, the more cars there are. So it's always a parking lot.

I remember when I was a kid, I looked forward to owning my car. And I did when I was 18. My friend bought a Model T Ford for sixty dollars and we traveled to California. And in those days—this was in the twenties—there weren't any roads. It was quite an adventure to go to California by car. We had a lot of experiences. But getting back to the automobile, I guess I long for the more simple life. As I live it in Mexico, where cars are unnecessary. You walk everywhere. And if it's a hilly town, if it's uphill a mile or so, you take a cab for fifty cents.

When we were growing up, particularly in New York, where you had separate schools for boys and girls, I never came in contact with girls. The only girl I knew was my sister. We had no contact with women or girls. And when we came to Chicago my contemporaries, while we had coeducational schools, wouldn't dare go out with a girl. I remember I fell in love with a girl in my class in the fifth grade, and I would have loved to have walked her home and carried her books, but I wouldn't dare because my peers would hound me, you know. So we didn't go out with girls like today. When they have their first dates when they're 12 or 13 years old. I had my first date, I think, when I was 15 or 16. When we got into long pants. In those days we wore short pants until we were 15 or 16 years old. And I think in some ways it's better today, because you should feel as natural with women as you do with men. And we didn't. I was very clumsy, you know, I didn't know what the hell I was doing.

I'm for birth control. Absolutely. And particularly in Latin countries where it's so prevalent. Where millions of children are born. Well, the Church is against birth control. And it's a way of life, too. This macho business. Shack up with a woman, and if you don't produce a child, you're impotent. You can't boast to your friends that you shacked up.

I would define love as an understanding between two people, a man and a woman. An understanding and tolerance of another point of view. My wife and I had a very fine life together. Because we were so compatible. Other than riding, we had everything in common. She was a great lover of books. She read a book a day for years. And we loved the same things. We loved music. We loved travel. I was very, very fortunate. I married late in life, and I was very fortunate to find a woman who was compatible with myself, who liked the same things I did. I think our marriage worked because we understood each other. We tried to make it a point, if we had an argument, never to go to bed angry. We would make up. I usually did the making up because she was very stubborn in that respect. And so I would say okay. No point in carrying this on. I apologize, I'm sorry I did this, and so on. If I thought it was my fault. But we always did. And we did everything together. I never went on a vacation alone. I never was unfaithful, which is unusual because most of my friends were. I did a lot of traveling in some of my life, and opportunities were there with a lot of women. But I had a code of ethics that I thought that if you love somebody, you couldn't very well sleep with another woman. And besides, I did that when I was young. Since I married later, I had already gone out with many, many women. From the time I was 16 or 17 until I was married, in my thirties. So that was all behind me and it wasn't necessary to prove to myself that I'm still a ladies' man.

I think some marriages fail because they marry too young. They don't know what life is about. They think life is all sex. And sex is important, but you can't live on sex alone. You have to have some intelligent conversation. And interest in life.

I could tell you exactly what she wore the day I met her. I was very drunk when I met her. A lot of us fellows would go up to a resort in Wisconsin, in Baraboo, Wisconsin. And they have horses up there. I went there to ride. And a half-dozen of my friends, we'd go up there on weekends or spend our vacations there. And one day, they had dancing at night. And an orchestra. And we used to drink—I drank quite a bit in those days. And I was feeling pretty high, and I was sitting down at the table and I saw this beautiful blonde woman sitting there wearing a green shirt and yellow slacks. And I went up to her. Her room key was on the table. I went up and took the key, put it in my pocket and then I asked her for a dance. Because I thought she wouldn't dance with me because I was drunk. But we danced, and I started talking to her. And give her a song and dance, give her a snow job about coming to Chicago. She was from Milwaukee. And told her she should come down to Chicago and pay me a visit so we could go to the theater. I don't remember whether I even recognized her when she did visit because I was so drunk that night. But anyhow, we started off a romance and she came to Chicago, much to my surprise. She came to visit me in Chicago. She worked for a bookstore in Milwaukee. She came out here mostly because all the action was in Chicago. Wasn't very much in Milwaukee in those days. And so she came here and the first thing we did was go to a play. I remember the play. *Accent on Youth*, with Luther Adler and Sylvia Sydney. I still have the program. I save programs, theater programs. I have eight volumes from 1930 on. She had them bound for me as a Christmas present one year, a few years ago, before she passed away.

The courtship lasted about nine months, nine or ten months. Then we got married and had children.

I had a peculiar notion about marriage and children. Since I had this military influence on me, I couldn't see a man—I guess I was macho—carrying a child or pushing a baby buggy. That was women's work, you know. But when I had a child, I took to it very well. I did most of the diapering, you know. And I thought I did it better than she did. I was much better with my hands. And pushing a baby buggy was a joy. My first son was a very bright child. We used to call him the walking encyclopedia. He had a remarkable memory. And what stands out for me is the nights I used to talk to him and try to get him interested in horses and riding. And in those days I had—I still do—a lot of statues of horses, plaques. And I remember sitting and pointing out the different parts of a horse and the technique of riding and so on.

I'm against religion. I think it closes men's minds and it has a tendency to separate people. You know, it's the old story. And I've been an atheist most of my life, after reading Tom Payne's *The Age of Reason.* It had a great influence on my thinking about religion. Sometimes I envy the religious, like when I lost my son. We had a rabbi downstairs in the same building. And he officiated at the funeral, and he came up here and talked to us. And the rabbi finally talked me into going to synagogue. And I tried it. I went there two or three times, but it didn't do any good. I couldn't find any justification. If there was a God, why would he take away a 12-year-old child? I haven't been to a synagogue since then.

I don't have any serious health problems. Hereditary, I guess. Because I abused myself when I was young, during Prohibition. We did a lot of drinking. And I am surprised that I still have a good stomach, because some of the stuff we drank was terrible, cheap booze. But I watch myself. I'm a faddist on foods. I don't eat certain food. I don't eat onions, cucumbers, radishes, cauliflower. I think I'd rather starve than eat a radish. And my eating habits now, since I cook for myself . . . I don't know how to cook. I'm not a cook. So I broil whatever I make—fish, chicken, hamburger. That sort of thing. And when I go with my sister, I go down there and every once in a while she'll do a little shopping for me and make chicken, brisket, or something. Or she'll fill me up with homemade borscht and that sort of thing, which I wouldn't eat when I was a kid. And now I'd give my right arm to eat homemade gefilte fish and matzoh balls.

I remember the first time I came to England, I felt like most Jews going to Israel. I have a feeling for England, British history. And all the things I'd read about all my life, all the great writers like Shakespeare, Browning, Milton—when I came to England, I felt as if I was coming home to my motherland. And I got such a thrill going to the British museums and seeing the beautiful library. And all the manuscripts in the glass cases. Manuscripts, the original, by all these famous authors, writers and poets and playwrights.

Some of the plays of Lillian Hellman—*The Children's Hour, Watch on the Rhine*—had great effect upon me. And Arthur Miller. *View from the Bridge* and *Death of a Salesman.* Later on, I identified with Willy Loman. When I left my firm after being there for almost forty years. And the firm had changed. My original boss had retired and a nephew took over. And I retired and I didn't even get a watch, let alone a pension. I just left as if I had worked for the house only a month or a year or something. And then Willy Loman came to mind. I had put all these years into that firm. You see, this nephew of his who I'd known when he was a child in the business, and like in the Miller play, the new owner of the business, says, "What have you done for me lately?" He didn't know the contributions I'd made to the firm, which I felt was a great deal. I felt I was responsible for making the firm what it was, being the largest of its kind in the United States at the time. And we weren't when I came with them forty years earlier. So I made a great many contributions. I was on the road for ten, eleven years. And I took an interest in my work.

I felt outraged by Watergate. Betrayed and outraged. Of course, I hated Nixon with a passion. Followed Nixon's career since he first entered politics. When he painted his enemies with a pink brush. He portrayed all the evil in not only politics, but in human beings as well. I just hated that man with a passion. I think I could've killed him with my own hands, I hated him so much. I met a fellow once in California who went to law school with Nixon, and he told me he would walk over his own mother to make money, to make a dollar, or to enhance his political career.

I feel very strongly for women's rights. I certainly would like to see the ERA passed, and I think it's high time women got the same privileges and equality as men do.

My wife and I both were very involved in civil rights—especially she, she was more active than I was. She went many times to Washington to march. She was in that march in the 1960s with Martin Luther King. And we marched in town here against the war and during the civil rights movement. Vietnam. Oh, my God. I resented the United States' foreign policy. With every President since Roosevelt. Roosevelt's the last President that I had any enthusiasm for. I hadn't had any since, except when McGovern ran for President. I worked for him. I don't know whether I did it because I liked McGovern so much. I really believed in him. I thought he was a very honest and capable man. But I wanted Nixon defeated badly. So that was the incentive for me. It's the first time in my life I ever rang doorbells. I dislike ringing doorbells. But I worked,

I rang doorbells and I worked in the downtown office taking care of mail, answering mail and so on. I thought we had no business being in Vietnam, ten thousand miles away from home, killing people who had done nothing to us. Most people in this country never heard of Vietnam before this thing happened. And what we were doing there, killing the people, using all our sophisticated weapons on a boxcart economy, on a people who lived in a different world from us. Here we were, the first power in the world, more sophisticated, with all of the deadly weapons, invading a country in which we had no right to be, and killing thousands and thousands of people. For what reason? I was incapable of giving it any thought.

Most people have no choice about the work they do. During the Depression—because I'm a child of the Depression—the point was to get a job, not to get the work that you liked. And I think most people who do physical work, if it's not a profession, work because they have to make a living. Take people who work in the automobile plants. The monotony of work, that work, must be deafening. It must be killing. I don't see how they can avoid it. It pays well, the unions being what they are today. So I guess most people do it because of the money. They have families and responsibilities and they're strapped. And since jobs are not easy to come by today, they are forced to stay there.

I'm not very happy with America in the twentieth century, since World War II. I think we've been arrogant and I think we've tried to make other countries in our own image, because of our power. We've abused it. We're responsible for killing thousands and thousands of people. We're responsible for many of the dictators throughout the world, who we support with our money and our power. And I resent the hypocrisy with which we use our power.

I didn't give it a thought when I was 15, whether America was the land of hope. My parents chose to come here because my father deserted from the Russian army. So he had to come here. He had no knowledge—he couldn't read English or speak it. So he had no knowledge of foreign policy or the country as a whole. All he knew was he had to make enough money to feed his family. His scope was very, very limited.

Oh, I know there are many things good about America. Its physical beauty is beyond belief. And I like its openness. The opportunities are much greater than they are in most countries of Europe. And the chances of bettering yourself are greater here than anywhere else. I think that if we had a good, compassionate, understanding government who actually represented the people, I think this could be a paragon—this country.

Well, I think I've matured. I think it was my own broader outlook, when I started to get interested in things around me, the world around me and foreign policy and politics. I could see what was happening. And if you have a feeling for people and for the injustices in this world, you either change or you go along and you rationalize it. And you say, Well, that's the way it is, that's the way it should be and it's for my own benefit and to hell with the next guy. When I was enamored with the military, the military was not an important factor in this country. We had an army of 250,000 before the war, 12,000 officers. And it was an insulated little way of life. They lived on military posts and nobody ever saw a soldier. If you did, it was a novelty. But after the war, I changed, especially after they instituted conscription for the purpose of changing other people's governments, because we were untouched by the war, we made money on the war. We became rich and powerful. And other European countries were devastated by the war. And we became Mr. Number One.

I think I have an inner resource. I am a very emotional person. And I show my emotions. And I cry. I weep when tragedy strikes me. And I think that somehow relieves the pressure inside. If I didn't, I think I'd probably go batty. Everybody has to die sometime or another, but when you die of a sickness and not of old age, it's a tragedy. And having lost a son and then a wife, who I loved very much, and then my old friend Pete. I wasn't here when he died. I was in Russia when he died. And I wanted to cancel the trip, but he wouldn't have it. I was gone for three weeks and I came back and he was dead. I felt a terrible pang of remorse that I wasn't at his funeral. Being his oldest friend, I would have liked to have said a few words. You know, he had a lot of his friends come up and I was his oldest friend. I would've liked to have paid my respects to him.

I'm getting to the point in life where I see death amongst my friends.

You get to this stage in life, people pass away. I lost a number of my friends, and I think it'll have to come to me, too. And I just hope that I don't have to suffer like my wife did and some of my friends who just went did. One chap I knew sat down in his chair and was reading a paper and he died. His heart stopped beating and that was the end of it. That's a wonderful way to go.

# Horace Marden Albright

$T$he young campers who make their way through Yellowstone Park today probably have never heard of Horace M. Albright. It is quite possible, too, that many of Albright's neighbors in the modern condominium building in Sherman Oaks, California, in which he and his wife live, have not heard of him either. Especially if their minds are on urban matters.

Several years ago, when the American Scenic and Historic Preservation Society chose to create a medal to honor those who respect and protect the American landscape, it named it the Horace M. Albright medal. In his biography of Albright, Wilderness Defender, Donald C. Swain referred to Albright as one of the prime movers in the cause of conservation during the first half of the twentieth century. He honored the man and his philosophy: Preserve the wilderness but guarantee the public access to it.

The Albrights' apartment is cluttered with the evidence of a life spent in defense of the environment. There are carved animals, landscape paintings, photographs, and books—most of them related to Albright's own career.

Albright was born on January 6, 1890, in a small mining town in Nevada; the birth was registered in Bishop, California, because that was where the nearest doctor lived. Albright's father was a Canadian who came to Nevada in search of silver. He didn't find it, but he became a dedicated and skilled woodworker who helped construct mine shafts, among other tasks. His mother's father came to the West from Maine via Nicaragua; her mother came from Arkansas. She was born in a California mining camp. She had four children.

In 1908 Albright went to the University of California, at Berkeley. He was graduated in 1912, and when a former professor was named to the Interior Department in Washington, Albright went along. He finished his work on a law degree at Georgetown and in 1917 became acting director of the National Park Service, an organization he had helped create as an Interior Department attorney. From 1919 until 1929 he was the superintendent of Yellowstone National Park, returning to Washington to direct the Park Service for four years.

*He moved to New York after that, to help direct a large mining company from its corporate headquarters. It became the United Potash Company, and he worked for it until retirement in 1956; he stayed on as an advisor for another five years, then moved back to California.*

*He and his wife have lived in their apartment for seven years; they were college classmates and were married in 1915.. They have a daughter (their only son died), four grandchildren, and six great-grandchildren, with two more expected.*

*Although slowed down by arthritis and fading eyesight, Albright is a man allied to the cause of nature. He keeps in touch with national and state park affairs, wildlife activities, and conservation groups, including the Sierra Club. He also finds time to write on conservation issues. He continues to drive the family car (as does his wife), although he wonders if the state of California will renew his license; when it expires, he will be past 90. His concern for America remains constant. Though he is a conservative in political viewpoint, Albright does not want to return to the ways of his childhood; nevertheless, he does feel that people today may be able to learn from the virtues of that age.*

As a small boy I lived in a mining camp. Mining camp isn't much of anything. It's just a place where men get up in the morning and go to work and come back at night and go to saloons if they're unmarried. And if they've got a family, they'll probably go home.

There isn't much of anything to do. In those days we had no automobiles. Whatever you did, you did on horseback or foot. And it was a good life. I have no recollections of ever having any bad times.

We had to make our own games and our own play. And whatever we did, we had to do ourselves. We had to make it up, of course. We only had one school, elementary school. Same with high school. We had the only high school in the county, and our county was as big as the state of Massachusetts.

In the summertime, you got took up to the mountains if you had a camping outfit, or you'd work. Most of the time you'd work. Work in the hay fields or farming country. When I was a boy, about 4 years old, that was all farming country. There were mines around there, back in the mountains. But they were not important.

My father had a mill in town. Well, he best described his old business by recalling his letterhead. He had a letterhead and it said, GEORGE L. ALBRIGHT in the middle. And underneath it, it said, CONTRACTOR AND BUILDER. Which he was. On the left-hand side he had, PLANING AND FEED MILLS. On the other side, he had, UNDERTAKING AND ALL ITS BRANCHES. When I got big enough, I remember asking him why he had UNDERTAKING AND ALL ITS BRANCHES, because all he could do was make a coffin. Get the body and put it in it and bury it. Because there was no undertaking. You couldn't be a mortician, in other words. The only thing was to get the body as soon as you could and bury it. But he was the kind of a fellow that got along nicely with people. He was an ideal person to be around when there was death and grief and sorrow. And he treated everybody alike, wherever they were from, whatever they had, including the Indians. Of course, a number of people never paid him. You don't get paid for everything.

We had two flour mills in the county, but they couldn't make cornmeal. They could only make flour. The grinding material, the grinding apparatus was just for flour. So my father ground the cornmeal. So we had cornmeal hot cakes, cornmeal mush, cornmeal bread, cornmeal brown bread, anything you could make out of corn. And I still like it. He had enough to keep him going and he traded it in the stores for other things. So cornmeal was quite a thing in our town. Also, we'd gone to salt. The salt was right out on the ground in a nearby valley. You just scoop it up. You blow the dust off it. Just dust, there isn't any dirt because it's all salt. And then they'd haul that up to Bishop, which would be about eighty miles with mule teams or horses. Take it to the mill and my father would grind it. I suppose in the same machine he ground the corn. And after that, the salt went all the way up on the railroad, clear up to Reno. And as those communities grew and the mining camps grew and they discovered gold, they bought the produce and they bought everything we made over there. So they thought, Well, we ought to develop this salt business. They organized a company to really exploit that salt. They built a tram. My father supervised that tram, building it. Others bought the materials and he had it built. I don't know how long it took him. But that was just as I went to college, because I remember very well that all he could spare for my freshman year was twenty-five dollars a month for my room. Everything else I had to earn myself. Everything, my books and my clothes—everything. And when he built that big project, he never took any money for it. He took stock. It was the only way he could buy stock. He was sure it was going to be a bonanza, you see. But of course, they weren't in a position to know or didn't try to find out the situation of the big companies like Lesley's Salt and Morton Salt. They just flooded them out. They came in by train as soon as it got to be worth doing. And killed his market completely. I don't know that they ever used the tram.

We didn't think we were poor. We didn't know we were poor. But we certainly were. We wouldn't go anywhere or do anything. Of course, we had no automobiles, we had no power, we had no lights, we had no sewers, we had no water systems. There was no such thing as air conditioning or electric lighting. Still we got along all right and didn't miss it because we didn't know anything about it. I don't know that we longed for anything in those days. I suppose women longed for hot and cold water and everybody longed for a fresh toilet. They weren't anywhere. But I don't remember anybody complaining about not having anything.

My father was a Canadian. He was the youngest of quite a big family. He wasn't quite as big as I am. He was a little shorter. I was six feet until recently. I've been sinking a little bit. I would say he was about five foot ten. Sandy complected. Very quiet fellow. Very gentle —very, very friendly fellow. He had a mustache, but he was fairly bald otherwise. Awful hardworking fellow. I got along with him. We never had any trouble. He never disciplined me. Our mother did the disciplining. He was an awfully hard worker. He had this shop and this mill, which he ran himself. He had a horizontal engine, steam engine which he ran, and he'd start up the engine and then he'd go to his various machinery to plane the lumber. He'd put the lumber through the planer. If he was making cornmeal, he'd run that machine. Making feed. Anybody who had grains—barley and oats and so forth—he churned it up for feed. He didn't do it all by himself, sometimes he had help.

My mother was something different. She was a very fine woman and a very highly intelligent person. But I think because my father was a gentle, kindly Canadian, I think she had to be a little more positive than otherwise. I think to have three boys in tow, she taught us early to help her. She didn't have any help. She didn't have any daughters. She had a sister who had two daughters. She said, "Why couldn't I have had one of her daughters?" I heard her say that. But she taught us to wash windows and scrub the floors and beat the carpets and wash dishes. Getting the wood, building fires, and all that. She had us working. And we put in a little garden. We had an orchard on this place. We had a lot of fruit. She'd put it up. We'd pick it. But she was real bent on education. She was very strong for birds. And she taught us not to hunt. Her father and mother had nine children. The three older ones were born in the mining camp. The older one, James, died of typhoid fever when he was about 7 years old. Next one, Ezra, joined the army in the Civil War, and the very first day in battle he got shot through the shoulder, so he never could use that arm again. He just had one day in the army. But he went back to Maine. That's where he lived the rest of his life. Then my mother, she was the third, and the others, they moved over to Nevada and they had five, six after that. There was a girl came next and then came four more. And then diphtheria struck. And in February 1878, just one hundred years ago, it took four of their children in ten days. It took Frank, who was 8; Daily, who was 6; Richard, who was 4; and Pearl, who was 2. There was a monument up in the mining camp up here, a cemetery. It's a very interesting cemetery.

So there were four gone and five alive. And then, the next year after the four died, the boy was out hunting, 18 years old, and climbed through a fence with his gun cocked and it went off and killed him. Guns were taboo with my mother. That was only about ten years before I was born. She didn't want any guns around the house. But she was very much interested in wildlife, conservation, very proud of the mountains, those mountains right there.

She had a phenomenal memory, but so did my father. My father's memory was fantastic. One of the things they did in this mining community—everybody belonged to lodges, you know. The oldest one, I think, was the Odd Fellows. And then they had the Rebeccas. That's the women's side of it. My mother was a member of that for more than sixty years. And my father also belonged to the Masons and the Woodmen of the World, and the Ancient Order of United Workmen, which sounds like a union, but it wasn't. It was a lodge. And Knights of Pythias. Gave him something to do. Well, they had parties and they had dances, and what philanthropy there was, and they also had insurance. It was an assessment proposition and as you paid so much, then when deaths occurred in the course of the year, they portioned a certain amount of it. But that went out with two things, the incoming insurance companies and the fact that there were too many deaths for them to handle. I remember my father just kept up until we were ready to go to high school. But the thing about him that I remember more than anything else was that he had such a fantastic memory that he could remember the secret word—these were all secret societies. You had to learn an awful lot of stuff. You couldn't get in and then you couldn't get out of it, without the secret words. And he could do that. He was constantly coaching novices. He could remember the word of all these men, and I don't know of anybody else who could. But it did take him away from home a good deal. My mother used to say to him, "You belong to so many lodges you never lodge at home."

I learned an awful lot from them. My mother, for instance, she was so proud of her memory and my father's memory, and my grandfather's, her father. So she was bound we were to have good memories. And she used to train us. We were standing around the stove waiting to have breakfast, she was making us recite poetry. I still have my old poetry books. We learned an awful lot of poetry.

She was religious. She helped to build the Presbyterian church there. She was the secretary of it. We only had a Methodist church before that.

I think my interest in conservation had a lot to do with them. I was a boy when Theodore Roosevelt was doing things. They were building the Forest Service. It was being discussed because it affected the cattle industry. The cattle industry was important. They'd been grazing the cattle wherever they wanted to, and the sheep the same way. And they ruined a lot of public domain. And they used to say of Senator Warren of Wyoming, who was a very wealthy sheep man, they used to call him the greatest shepherd since Abraham, because he had his sheep all over Wyoming. He was a millionaire. But then the Forest Service came in, in support of Roosevelt, to put some regulations on that. My grandfather, who quit the mining business the year I was born, in 1890, went up to Shasta County and went in the logging business. But he didn't own a mill. He didn't own anything except a logging outfit. He could cut timber and put the logs on the cars to go to the mills, that sort of thing. And he was in that business while I was growing up. But on the other hand, he was a conservationist. He thought that it was a shame that the price of lumber was so low that if you cut down the trees, you couldn't dispose of the limbs. Then, the next year they'd start a fire and burn—not only burn up all that stuff, but burn up a lot more timber. So I learned lots of principles of conservation. Of course, mining was in the blood of both of my parents. There wasn't anything I could do about that. If my father spoke at all about what we should do, he'd have liked to see me go to the school of mines, which was just set up in Reno. But my mother didn't see that. First of all, I think my mother had had enough of mining camps. She grew up in one. Born in one and grew up in one. She wasn't anxious for her sons to be in the mining business. But she didn't fuss about it much. She just didn't think I was mining material.

Well, in 1903 she had something wrong with her. I don't remember what it was and I don't know much about it. Of course, she lived a long time after that. But they were worried about her, and we had no surgeons up there. We just had a couple of general practitioners. They said that she ought to go to San Francisco to get some treatment. Well, that was a terrible blow to the family because we didn't really have any money to do that. And then, we were in high altitude and the doctors advised against it. They said that if she did go to San Francisco, she should go by train by day. And someone should go with her, carrying some spirits of ammonia and so forth in case she should faint or anything. So it was scheduled that I should go. Of course, I'd never been out of there, never been anyplace. And I was 13. I was to go. I was a grown boy then. I was to go, and I was going to go with her to Sacramento, and she was to go on to San Francisco, and I was to go on north to my grandfather, and he'd look after me, give me things to do around the logging camp. And then she'd come up there, after she got well. She'd come up there, and we'd go back together.

So just before we were ready to go, there was a girl who had been up there all the time, a girl by the name of Cobb who belonged to the mining town over on the other side of the mountain. She had to go around by Reno and Sacramento to get there. And in those days girls didn't go anywhere unless they were chaperoned. And, of course, she couldn't get home unless somebody would take her home. She was 16 and I was 13. She wanted to know if my mother would take her. Of course, my mother would take her. But then there seemed to be no reason for my going. And I remember this was a subject for a lot of talks at table, as to whether they could afford for me to go. It was pretty much of a luxury for me to go. They finally decided it would be too much of a disappointment, that they'd make out somehow or other and I could go. So the three of us started out on this narrow gauge train. And the first day we got to Hawthorne, Nevada, where we had to stay all night. There were no sleepers. And so the conductor went to bed and the engineer went to bed, and everybody stayed overnight. The engineer and fireman had to get up early and get the engine rolling so they could get started at some reasonable time in the morning on the next part of the trip, which would take us to Reno. We finally got going the next morning and we spent that night in Reno. We could've gotten a sleeper at Reno and gone on down. But that wasn't good for my mother's condition. So we went on the next day and we got to Sacramento. My mother had been educated down there. My mother was an educated woman. She'd been to college. My grandfather had so much troubles and still educated his two daughters. She only knew one hotel in Sacramento, it was known as the Golden West. It was about a block and a half from the station in Sacramento. So we lugged her baggage around there and got there and it was full. Even in those days they had conventions or something. Absolutely full. Well, my mother wasn't to be daunted. She insisted that we were there, she'd been there in the past, she was an old customer. She probably had only been there once, if she ever had. But at any rate, she finally wangled a room out of them with a double bed. Then of course came the real problem. What are they going to do with me? The girls could sleep in the bed. So they finally decided that they'd put a cot in there. And they decided that I'd go to bed first and cover up my head. And then the two girls would go to bed, and we reversed it in the morning. I'd cover up my head and the girls would get up. So that's what we did. You wouldn't believe it, but we did.

We hung around there long enough to get a look at Sacramento, which was the only city we'd seen. We got into Reno too late and got up too early to see much of Reno. Wasn't much of a town anyway. And still isn't. Then I got on the train at Sacramento and went up to Shasta County, where my grandfather's logging camp was. I got up there about nine o'clock at night. And he was down there—the camp itself was about four miles from the railroad, up in the hills, the mountains. Very heavily timbered country. Riding up in his buckboard, my grandfather wanted to know all about the trip and I was telling him. And I told him about this experience of sleeping all night, how I was proud of my mother, the way she worked it out and so forth. And he said,

"Well, you didn't cover up your head, did you?" And I said, "Yes, I did. I certainly did." And he said, "Goddamn it, you're no grandson of mine." I can still remember that.

My earliest memories go way back. You know, there was no lights or anything. They had sort of cellars in the ground. And they had a trapdoor on the top. Well, we had one in the backyard of this house that my father bought. And it had a slanting one. The back part of it was built up. And it slanted enough so you could make a little slide out of it. And I think that I remember more than anything else—it's clearer to me than anything else—sliding down that door. I was about 4 years old. But I also can remember just a wisp of Candaleria, the mining town before we left there. I can remember the buildings across the street, and I can remember the tin shop next door to us, which was run by a man who married my grandmother's cousin. They were also from Arkansas. But come to some real thing that I can put my finger on. I was given a big dog. I'd never seen one like it. There were two of them. One belonged to a butcher and I had the other. And we had a cart, I don't know whether my father made it or not, but it was painted red. And we could hook up that dog and ride around town. Only just a few years ago, I ran into someone who remembered me riding around town. I'd ride my dog around.

I gotta give credit to a woman in Sunday school. My mother was quite religious. It was not a fetish with her, but she insisted that we go to Sunday school. And we had a Sunday school that was right across the street. I had a teacher by the name of Fligger—no, Frager. Her husband was a rancher. And she was a good teacher. And they had cards they gave out every Sunday, and it had a picture, a biblical picture. And it had on the back of it the lesson, and also a quotation. My mother had learned all those quotations. And we had to. We had to recite them by the month of the year. And I remember collecting those after I was in college. I think I had a stack about that high, my first collection, a collection of Sunday school cards. I paid attention to what they said and it stuck. Well, they were good people. Nothing bad ever happened. You don't hear any bad examples. We never locked the doors. I don't remember any stealing ever being done. I think once in a while we had a murder, but I don't remember who was murdered.

I don't know what's happened to the family. It didn't happen in my family. It may be that the parents got something else they want to do and they're not concentrating on their children. I think it's a lot of that. They may not be concentrating on each other, either. Everything about life today baffles me more every day. I found out something the other day. For a week here I've been worrying about the sixty-six thousand abortions we had in Los Angeles last year. Just think of it. Sixty-six thousand girls were aborted here in Los Angeles last year. That's just one hell of a thing, don't you know? The so-called liberation of sex. Well, I think it's terrible. Sure, we have to control population, but I'd much rather see it be like it was back when I was in college. I think of my fraternity house. I only belonged to the local club. I didn't belong to a Greek. But I can't remember around the house, around the clubhouse, anyone talking about women or about their characteristics. I remember the girls' dresses dragged on the ground, you know. We weren't going to see any legs or ankles or anything. When I was a senior, the girls developed a dress they called the Directoire gown. And it had a slit on the left-hand side, and if you had a quick eye you could see an ankle. Now the kids all used to laugh a little bit about that. Did you see an ankle today? Did you see one of those Directoire gowns they talked about? That was the first somebody gave a darn one way or the other. Wasn't giving it much thought, you know. It was a little fun to try to see an ankle. But that would be a game, don't you know?

I never tried to define love. I've been very fortunate in love myself. I happened to get a classmate of mine who I think is the loveliest girl in the world, and I've had her for sixty-three years. And I've never had to worry about it. It's a good feeling. You don't have to do a lot of things—you don't have to worry. You're confident that the house is going to run all right. And it's a smooth way of living, smooth and sweet and gentle. All those qualities you like. Nothing rough about it.

Well, we've had divorce in our own family. My daughter had to get rid of her husband after twenty-seven years. But you know exactly what had caused it. It was liquor. Marriage used to be hard to destroy. Yes, indeed. In fact they weren't destroyed. I don't remember any divorces when I was a boy. I would think that the excesses of liquor has a good deal to do with it. Now, men can't leave women alone. They have to go off with some other one.

I don't ever remember finding it necessary to adjust myself in any way to marriage. Of course, my wife is a very beautiful woman. You can tell that by looking at her now at 87 years old. But she had an inner beauty. It just shone right through. She is gentle. She's kind. She's compassionate. She's always wanting to do something for somebody else. She's that way with me. I mean, we never had any reason to fuss. We just meshed all the time, since we first met. That was in college. Another classmate, a girl whom I had met once or twice, called up my clubhouse one night and asked me if the next Friday night I could come over to her place where she was having a dance, and bring a couple of fellows along with me. She said they needed some more men. So I went over there with the other fellows, and soon after arriving, I met this girl, this tall brown-haired, brown-eyed girl. And she was with another fellow. And she was dancing around with him. But I managed to get a dance with her. And I was fascinated by her. She's a marvelous dancer. She had a way with it. You couldn't help but feel captivated. Well, I was so fascinated by her and by her compassion and by her lively way and her fine dancing and her beauty that after we got home that night, we guys spent a couple of hours discussing the women we met that night, and everybody wanted to see if they couldn't take this girl out. But they admitted I should have the first chance because I brought them over there. Well, of course, I eagerly looked forward to seeing her again. Two days later, on Monday, I was walking up the campus with another classmate, and here she comes down the street, her arms full of books. She comes right past us. And speaks gently and beautifully to this classmate of mine and never even recognized me. Passed me up. And well that was a terrible blow.

Well, I'm studying shorthand and typewriting so I can get a better job. I'd been putting up real-estate signs and digging postholes for billboards and so forth. I still hate billboards. I got a job in the recorder's office where all the records of the students are kept, don't you know? First thing I did was make a dash over to take a look at her record. Well, it was so very much better than mine that that scared me even more. I thought this country boy is in a bad way. She's too beautiful. She's too charming. She's too this and she's too that, and now she's too darn smart. I just better leave her alone. So I did. I didn't get to know her very well for a year or two afterwards.

Then we resumed. With a year of correspondence, that first year I was in Washington, before I came back and claimed her. Finally got her. It really was a long-distance courtship.

There was one part of my life that could've thrown me clear off. Fortunately didn't. One of the lucky things that happened to me. When we were coming down from that summer in Shasta when I went up with my grandfather, my mother took me to San Francisco. I had always been interested in soldiers. Clipped out pictures of them in the paper. Of course, I went through the Spanish-American War. I had lots of pictures of soldiers, but I never saw one. And after I'd been there several days, I said to my mother, "I wish I could see a soldier." A troop ship was going to sail from a certain dock on the following Tuesday, just a couple of days away. So she decided to get lunches and we'd go down and eat them on the dock. And we found the soldiers. They were going to go to the Philippines.

Not very long before the boat sails, two officers came by, went right past us. Both of them about six feet tall and fine-looking men, and they were each dressed in full uniform, shoulder straps, stripes down the legs, maroon color. I remember it very well. Well, that really excited me. That really excited me. The next day their pictures were on the front page of the paper. They were Second Lieutenant Douglas MacArthur and Second Lieutenant U. S. Grant III, just graduated from West Point, and were on their way to the Philippines on their first assignment. And the man who was in command was General Arthur MacArthur, who was the father of Douglas MacArthur. They were going to be serving under him. Well, nothing in the world looked good to me except getting to West Point, where they'd been, don't you see? So I began deviling the congressman when I got home. He lived in Bakersfield. I was 13. All during the years I was 13, 14, 15, and 16, I bedeviled that congressman, until finally, I guess, just to get rid of me, he named me first alternate for the commission in the fall of 1907. I'd have been in the class of 1911 at West Point. So I went down there and took the examinations. But the principal passed. Both of us alternates passed, too, but we couldn't get in on account of him.

There was a man from the mountains up there who knew my father and mother. And he lived over in Oakland. And he insisted that when I got through with the examinations, that I had to come on over there to his place and see his family. And while I was over there—I was a junior in high school—they took me up and showed me the University of

California, and that made the difference. But I would always think back on how it happened that I might just as well have been the one who had gone to West Point in 1907. Everything else would've been different. It would've been World War I, absolutely. Might have been dead.

We should all have just two children, no more. Two. I'm for zero population. I'm a little bit disgusted with two of my grandchildren right now. They're going to have two more and then they've got three for each of them. They're at three. Up to the present time for three generations, both sides we've had zero population. Each two. I had two. My daughter-in-law had one. My son's wife was an only child, and my daughter's husband was an only child.

It's not that I'm sorry I had children, at all. There are so many surprises, so many things happen. Questions that interest them. And some new thing dawns on them. I got a big kick out of my great-grandson. I stayed one night with them in May. They know everything about *Star Wars*. I'd never seen the picture and I didn't know anything about it. They were just so full of telling me all about it. I got a thrill out of them.

I never have gone out of my way to take care of myself. But I've never smoked. I'm not particularly proud that I don't smoke. When I was a boy about 12 years old, 13 years old, everybody was smoking in other places, but not where we lived, however. That particular place, that particular community, if you wanted to be a he-man, you had to chew tobacco. And if you smoked, you had to play with the women, the girls. I wish I had, because I'd never been with them enough. But I tried to chew tobacco and it made me sick every time I put that stuff in my mouth. I stole my mother's chocolate and spit it out on the sidewalk. I bought licorice. I did everyway in the world to be a he-man at that particular stage. Every once in a while I'd go back to the tobacco and it made me sick. I said, Well, tobacco is not for me. So I just quit it and I never went back to it at all.

I think I'm more careful now because I know I'm in a precarious situation. I mean, I could fall down here and harm myself because I can't see very well. I've got arthritis in my left knee and both shoulders. I'm not steady, in that sense. And my eyes are not too good. But I never took any medicine. I was in a hospital when I was in college, for mumps. It went down on me, but not enough to knock me out. And then I was in Alaska, in my work as head of the national parks and I got an appendicitis. And when I was superintendent of Yellowstone Park, I had my tonsils out. That's about the extent of my illness. I never took any aspirin until they prescribed it for my arthritis.

The most beautiful place in America? Of course, that depends upon what you mean by beauty. I suppose I'd have to say Yosemite Valley. You've got this great gorge, three thousand to four thousand feet deep, carved by glaciers, with great domes and spires, individual monoliths standing out. And waterfalls running hundreds of feet up and down. And the great river at the bottom, white water. If you are down on the ground looking at wild flowers, dogwood and other flowering trees, it certainly is an exquisite situation. Now that's one kind of beauty, it's a more living beauty, more exciting. Lots of people say the Grand Canyon. Well, the Grand Canyon is spectacular. It's just there, always. You've got to get your changes with light. There may be some views, when the sun is creeping through and hitting someplace, where you'd say that's the most beautiful. On the other hand, I hate to put Yellowstone down. I love it more than any of them, because I was there ten years. I know every feature of it. I was superintendent of it for ten years before I became director of all the parks. That's the best job I ever had, I think. That was 1919 to 1929. I was the first superintendent after the military. The military had it for thirty years, had cavalry in there protecting it. I was put in charge to reorganize it to a civilian park. I seem to have had a knack for organizing.

I've read so darn many books. I just gave about four or five thousand to the university. I've got a wonderful library, a conservation library. I gave it to UCLA. It's going to be kept intact. I have all the reports going back one hundred years on Yellowstone. But I can't think of one single book that comes to mind. I just read and read. The only thing that bothers me now is I can't read much. I've been trying to read a book on Harry Truman and a book on the Presidents and the Park Service.

I've never been in politics, but I've had an awful lot of dealings with them. I know so much about politics I don't want to be in with them. But I did think that Watergate was a piddling thing. If he'd a been a Democrat, there wouldn't have been anything about it.

I don't think women need the ERA. I think they're already there. I think it's just going too far. I don't know what they have in mind. But I've always been for women. I cast my first vote for women's suffrage in this state in 1911 when I was 21 years old. That's the first vote I ever cast. I hired the first woman ranger when I was superintendent of Yellowstone. I hired her in 1920. I've always been for giving them an even break. On the other hand, I see no sense at all in sending them to West Point and Annapolis. I know that they're there. That's just the trouble. They've got to have complete freedom of everything. They've got to have access to everything, whether they ought to be there or not. Their physical characteristics, their strength, other things about them, the very fact that they're women.

Civil rights? Well, I think that was coming. I think we needed an awful lot of that, although I don't know what it's going to do to efficiency. I was for Bakke in that Bakke case. I think when you get to a thing like medicine, I think you gotta have the very tops. And I don't think you ought to take into consideration race or anything else. They're giving an examination and they've got certain standards, and those are the standards you ought to follow. And if that drops out all the exotics and the aliens, out they go. And the same way with the women.

Right now, I'm scared to death about America. They just don't seem to be able to do anything about inflation. And of course I don't think this is only a wage-inflation situation. I'm just as sore as I can be at these postal people getting fifteen thousand dollars a year and still going on strike. I think that's a damn outrage. I told our postman down here. I'm very fond of him. Wonderful guy. I said, "Now Tom, you aren't going to strike, are you?" He said he hoped not. Well I said, "Don't do it. Defy them. They can't do anything to you." They're getting too much. And that's what's causing the damn inflation. You're never going to lick it if you're going to let eveybody have a 5- or 10-percent increase every year. You take this postal thing. Over 90 percent of the operations of the postal department is personnel. That's a plain case of wage inflation.

I've been in Russia. I've never been able to get too excited about them. Maybe I didn't meet the people that should've scared me. I was only there for three weeks. But I just have a feeling that the leaders have got themselves nicely situated. And they're not going to give it up. And on the other hand, they wouldn't dare precipitate a war. So you've just got to live with this thing for a while. Now sooner or later there something will happen to it.

In our country, I think that the two-party system should be in effect. It's not been in effect for forty years. And I think if it was in effect, we'd have been better off. I think Democrats have been in for too long. I was there when they captured the House of Representatives in 1930. Hoover was halfway through his term. And the Republicans have never gotten it back yet. For only four years in all these nearly fifty years, only four years when the Republicans had the Congress. I do believe that this is the best country. I do believe that, but I don't know how long it can last.

You know, I think Hoover was the best-qualified President. He never had a chance. The Depression hit him before he'd been in a year. He never had a chance to show what he could do. But I saw quite a bit of Hoover before he was President. He was out there with me. He had a fish hatchery out in Yellowstone. He'd come out there and we'd be fishing together. I spent lots of time talking to him. And even while he was President, his summer place was at the dam, and I helped him discover that. He wasn't the fellow you'd want to go out on a spree with or go camping with, particularly. But he was a terribly interesting fellow. My first experience with him I thought I'd never like him. We had a well-developed fish hatchery in Yellowstone. But we didn't have any in Yosemite and we needed one. And the commissioner of fisheries, a man named Henry O'Malley, wanted one in Yosemite. But he couldn't get it. He couldn't get his budget approved. So we finally decided we'd tackle Hoover ourselves. He was Secretary of Commerce. I remember just about the way it went—something like this. We went up there to his office and he was ready for us. He got up, but he didn't shake hands. He spoke to us and then he sat down. We all sat down. Then he got our relative rank right away in the introduction. He just shifted his eyes to the highest ranking one of us. Not me. Well, it was a pretty cool situation. That guy didn't feel like talking. It just chilled him to the bone apparently. And so he stammered a little bit and he said that he thought that someone else could tell him better what we wanted. Well, that guy had never been before a cabinet officer or a congressman or so forth. He stammered a little bit and he said, "Well, as much as we want a hatchery like we have in Yellowstone, perhaps you should talk to Albright from Yellowstone." Of course, I had nobody to shift it to, so I had to do the job of telling him about it. And after we got through, he looked at us for a minute or two and he said, "It ought to be done."

I don't know how you're going to take care of people if you don't have retirement. I mean, the jobs are needed. If my company hadn't merged when I was 66 years old, I would've felt that I should leave anyway. I was past the time at age 66. And I was grooming a fellow to take my place. And I think I should've gone. I don't think I should've stayed on until 70, because that fellow never would've had a chance. I had an awful lot of things I liked to do. I wanted to do some writing. There was a lot of travel that I wanted to do. I had plans. I had things to do. And I think people should do that. Now of course, if they can't afford it, although I never was a wealthy man at all. Everything I seemed to be doing was just starting. I mean, we started this company from scratch. Never did make big pay. But I was one of these fellows that if I liked my work, I didn't care so much about what I got as long as I got enough to get along, get going. You really ought to know what you're doing. But I do think you've got to make room. I think that retirement is an important feature because you've got to make room for others. They've got to come along.

I don't get mad easily. I suppose I have been mad. My wife tells about me being mad one time. When I was superintendent of Yellowstone, she said she came into the office one day and I'd been out all night on an inspection, some other part of the park. The park is bigger than Rhode Island plus Delaware, you know. You started out to inspect, you couldn't do it in a day. And she asked an assistant, "Have you heard from my husband?" And he said, "Yes, we did this morning. Except for the words 'hello' and 'good-bye,' I couldn't tell you what he said. I'll tell you he was mad." And so when I came back in, she wanted to know what I was so mad about. In those days we sprinkled 105 miles of the roads—they were dirt and dust, they didn't have any pavement on them. Couldn't get money to pave them. We hired ranchers down in the valley who kept horses to rent out in the summertime in the park, to draw these sprinklers. Well it had rained all night, and part of the day before. And I was starting on my inspection and here was one of these four-horse sprinklers, sprinkling the road that it had rained cats and dogs on top of, don't you see. And apparently that's what made me mad. I probably was sore.

I haven't had a family crisis for a good long time. We lost our son twenty years ago. I lost my mother about thirty years ago. We haven't lost anybody lately. But I'm losing friends all the time. I've got one right now, John D. Rockefeller III, I've known him since he was 18 years old. I've just been sick about that. But you just have to take it, as far as friends are concerned. And family, you have to make adjustments inside the family, I suppose.

I deal with grief by keeping busy. I would say that's about what it is with me. I think I feel it very keenly. I had two the other week. One was John Rockefeller and the other was a man named George Marler. Now, Marler was undoubtedly the best-posted man on hot springs, geysers, and all that sort of thing in the world. I don't know what he was, a teacher or something, and we picked him up about forty years ago and gave him a summer job in Yellowstone. He never did work except for the summer. I'd been going back every year till last year. I'm not going back now. I just feel like the bottom's dropped out so far as George Marler is concerned. I don't want to go back up there again. I wouldn't know what to do without that fellow going with me.

I was for many years on the board of trustees of Colonial Williamsburg. John Rockefeller was the chairman for fourteen years. So I spent many an hour with him going back and forth to Williamsburg. I was at his wedding and the wedding of his daughter and the wedding of his son. And it's just a crushing blow to have that thing happen. But on the other hand, I'm three thousand miles away. I couldn't go to the funeral, and I just had to go on doing what I've been doing.

I know it's going to happen to me pretty soon because I'm practically 90 years old. I think the idea is we're going to live quietly and safely as long as we can. We're not going to take a lot of chances. That's why we're not going to go East anymore. Stay pretty much here. We got this place where we want it, and I've got some more writing I want to do. I write mainly for our Park Service papers. My daughter is trying to get kind of a biography worked out. Of course, there was a book written about me. Written by Professor Swain at the University of California, an historian. He wrote it ten years ago. Very good book, I think. I feel lucky to have somebody want to write it.

# Dr. Mary Calderone

*Compared with the lives most Am rican women lead, Dr. Mary Calderone's has been extraordinary. Her father was the distinguished photographer Edward Steichen. Carl Sandburg was her uncle. She spent much of her early childhood in France. She went to Vassar, spent a few years discovering that she didn't want to be an actress, and got an M.D. (then a master's in Public Health). But after practicing medicine as a public school physician, she turned to another branch of science, the study of human sexuality, when she was almost 50. She served as medical director of Planned Parenthood–World Population from 1953 to 1964, leaving it to continue her crusade as the head of the Sex Information and Education Council of the United States (SIECUS). She remains the guiding force in that organization's efforts today.*

*Dr. Calderone has been married twice and has three daughters (another died at the age of 8 of pneumonia), two grandsons, and two great-grandsons. She is a fervent Quaker, and her belief in God, together with her belief in the value of sexual counseling, has helped sustain her passion for life.*

*She has been praised for her valiant and successful effort to bring sex out of the closet; and she has been attacked, viciously, by those who believe she encourages promiscuity and licentiousness. She has withstood the criticism and moved forward to persist in her mission.*

*From the SIECUS office in New York—where Dr. Calderone rules with the demanding style of a dedicated zealot—she can look ahead to work to be done, and when she permits herself the luxury, she can reflect on the honors she has won. She has been awarded eight honorary degrees and innumerable awards for public service. She was named Humanist of the Year by the American Humanist Association in 1974. She was given the Woman of Conscience Award by the National Council of Women in 1968. And she was listed among "America's 75 Most Important Women" by the Ladies' Home Journal in 1971.*

*She lives and works in Manhattan and travels extensively to further the SIECUS cause. She writes, when time permits. She is the author of* Release from Sexual Tensions *(New York: Random House, 1960) and the editor of* Manual of Family Planning and Contraceptive Practice *(Baltimore: Williams & Wilkins, 1970), and she has published many magazine articles.*

*Her style is crisp, informed, articulate, passionate. At the age of 75 (she was born in New York on July 1, 1904), she does not show a single sign of weakening. Her smile remains winning; her spirit is contagious. She does not plan to slow down.*

I sometimes get the feeling that the singing has stopped for this country. Well, I have to qualify that. It means to me that people no longer spontaneously experience joy in simple things. They seem to have developed the conviction that you have to buy joy and yet they rarely have it. Simple joy for me as an adolescent growing up was sitting and listening to the grown-ups talking. Simple joy was the fact that when I would visit my aunt, she would broil a steak in the fireplace and I would watch. And then I would watch my sculptor uncle peeling his fruit with his beautiful sculptor hands, handling his knife as though it was the finest little tool. Can't tell you the pleasure I got out of that, and in retrospect I still get it. That sounds awfully silly and corny to a lot of people. I miss the joy of biting into a ripe piece of fruit. I'll wager nine out of ten Americans have never tasted fruit really ripe and off the tree, as I remember it. And when those white peaches, which are very delicate and don't ship, so nobody ever has them in this country—when those white peaches started to get ripe on my Aunt Charlotte's tree, that was a moment for rejoicing for the whole family, and for sharing the joy of that. Now, it wasn't so much the delicious pleasure of eating it as it was the joy of sharing.

We played word games. When I was with Dr. Leopold Stieglitz and Mrs. Stieglitz, with whom I lived for four or five winters while I went to school because my family was scattered and abroad and so forth—that was during my very formative years of 11 to 16—Uncle Lee—Dr. Stieglitz—would play simple mathematical games. He would say, "What's nine times ninety-nine?" And I'd start multiplying in my head. And he'd say, "It's nine times a hundred minus nine." He did this not to buffalo me as a child, but as something that was fun to know. And it was. I learned that way of simplifying a mathematical job. What's nine times forty-five? Well, it's nine times fifty minus forty-five. And so forth. It gives me pleasure also when I use it because I think of my uncle and his thought for me.

I don't think it's technology that's led us astray but I miss the sense of joy that we ought to get out of television, for instance. I was thinking last night as I watched something and as I listened to radio this morning, we are not conditioned to equate noise with pleasure. Our commercials are so noisy. After a while you think, Oh God, if I only lived in Great Britain, where the commercials are quiet. You're hearing the message. And the comedians are quiet. It's all very subtle. You're getting pleasure out of getting what they give. But it's so noisy in this country. So intrusive and so blatant and so meaningless. It comes through technology. I suspect it's because of the kind of people we are. Even today technology hasn't taken over all of the European countries the way it's taken us over.

It parallels the feeling I've had about people's attitudes about sexuality. It's very parallel. We have sort of gotten used to thinking that sexual pleasure can only be had in an atmosphere of excitement and hyped-up false pleasure, false noise. There was, for instance, the kind of sexual pleasure that as a young teen-ager I used to get in the slow waltz, dancing cheek to cheek. We didn't have to go out and have intercourse afterwards and we didn't, as a matter of fact. But there was something very sensuous and very enjoyable sexually in this. And now I look at the kind of dancing in which the kids never look at each other. Even the grown-ups never look at each other. They're twisting their bodies in all sorts of ways, but you don't look at your partner, you never touch your partner, practically speaking. And you never have a moment of intimacy and quiet. It's all rackety-packety and noise. I just think we're alienated from our bodies and from other people's bodies.

I'd like to have carried the good things with us into these days so that the technology would have freed us. What have we done with the time that the technology has freed us to have? More noise. More traffic. More excitement and so forth. More shouting. Instead of deep enjoyment of one other person, in quiet, or five other people in quiet. I miss that. I don't miss the lack of technology. I love the technology today. I take every advantage of it. Love my dishwasher, love my washing machine. I love all the things that get me to places or from places fast so that I can then do something I want to do.

Until I was 9, I lived with my mother and father in a sort of magic, enchanted garden in France, a walled garden which my father has made famous in some paintings and photographs. It was a very free existence. He believed that nude bodies were beautiful for children. Nudity wasn't practiced so much by adults in those days. But I have a lovely photograph of him holding my sister's hand, my hand, one on each side of him, and our little nude bodies are prancing along with him in the garden. It's a lovely photograph.

My mother had a bad influence on me. She was a sad, very unhappy woman. She was compulsive. She was angry. She was hostile. I've analyzed it looking backwards, and from my own knowledge, because she was very jealous of my father, who was a womanizer in a very sensitive and wonderful way. She took it out on me by being destructive and hostile and jealous and cutting me down all the time, with truly destructive phrases which I prefer not to repeat. My sister she did the opposite to. She fastened onto her and lived her life vicariously through her. And manipulated and controlled her. I was fortunate to be separated from my mother by the time I was 10. She went back to live in Europe and I had to go to school in America.

My father had an enormous influence on me. First of all, we were alike in many ways. He was very bright intellectually and so was I. He must have had a very high IQ. And I know I have a high IQ—not genius range, but high. And I was intellectually minded. I loved learning. I read enormously. It's true, my favorite books that I remember are the Andrew Lang fairy books, but I read a lot of others, too. And he encouraged this. He encouraged anything I wanted to do. There was never a word said that might imply, Well, you'll never be able to do this because you're a female. So I actually grew up without any sexist upbringing at all. And this was lucky, because when I said at the age of 14 and 15 I wanted to be a doctor, both he and Dr. Stieglitz and my other mentors said, Fine, great, go ahead. We'll help you. So it was fine. There was no problem, even in 1918.

My earliest memory? I suspect it was when I was 3 and my mother was having morning sickness. That is, she was vomiting every morning. And the reason, of course, I know now, was because she was pregnant with my sister who was 4 years younger than I. And I also remember other things. Somebody must have given me a candy frog. We were living in France. Mother was very suspicious of the food and particularly of anything that was cheap. It had to be expensive candy, then it was good. But this was cheap because it was a present from the maid. So she said, "Don't eat that." And, of course, I did and bit the head off, and it did taste horrible. So I spat it out and I threw it all into the garbage pail in the kitchen. And she came along and she said, "What are you doing in there, Mary?" And I said, "Oh, it was a worm rolling along the ground." That phrase is burned in my memory. She went right into the garbage pail and there she found the headless candy frog. And she said, "You lied to me." And then she took me across her knee and paddled me. What I remember is, "I'll teach you not to lie, a worm rolling on the ground indeed!" She repeated that phrase, "I'll teach you not to lie." And she paddled me, and the maid looked so sad and embarrassed for me.

My next memory about being paddled must have been when I was around 9. I don't remember what for, but I remember crying on purpose so as not to hurt her feelings, so she wouldn't see that she wasn't strong enough to hurt me. Those are some of my earliest memories.

And of course the house in France and the garden, and the people who visited us there from the United States. They were some of my father's wealthy patrons. John W. Simpson, who'd bought some of his paintings and brought their daughter Jean, who was later my very good friend of mine. She was about four years older than I. And we used to play in the garden together. I have a photograph of us in the high swing.

I think I developed a sense of ethics and morality—I was fiercely, fiercely bound and determined to be a good person. To be a worthwhile person. I can't trace it to any one factor. But I remember having that determination, and it had nothing to do with being paddled or with going to church, which we never did. It was there—to be a worthy person, to be a worthwhile person, to do something that was good. And I remember there's a painting of mine that Alfred Stieglitz hung in his 291 gallery in New York along with other children's paintings. I have it still. "The soul of God is like a lily, pure white with golden spots in it." And I drew something vague, the soul of God, and wrote on it, "Good, good, I must do good. And good He always did."

The physical life has been very important to me. Very. Not from the view of exercise. I am very much and always have been in touch with my body. It speaks to me and I speak to it. This has been very useful. First of all, I knew what I enjoyed. Secondly, I knew when something was going wrong very early before symptoms showed. And could speak of this. I have gone to the dentist and said, "Something's going wrong with this tooth." And he'd say, "I can't find anything wrong with it." And three months later came the pain, sure enough. I listen to my body's needs and I fulfill them—but I don't need to overfulfill them. I'm not overweight, I've never wanted to smoke, I love wine with fine food, which I cook and eat for my own pleasure even when I'm alone.

I've had a lot of surgery done. But it was always surgery done early and preventively. So my body spoke to me. It was important to me. And the sensuous part, the pleasure part of my body has been a part of this. Because sexual pleasure I have always known. I don't remember not knowing it.

I don't agree that the family unit is disintegrating. I think we're simply learning to change our definition of the family unit. It's always been a mother and father and two or three children, staying together, obviously. Well, recently, in the last ten years, when I've been on a university campus and I go to teach a class, I start out with, What is your definition of a family? And I've seen the change from mother and father and two or three kids to a kind of fumbling for new meanings which gave me the key to my own definition: "A family can be two or more people, of any age, relationship, or sex, who come together in a committed way to care for and about each other." Well, now we're learning that you can create families of older people, three or four or five, who can help each other—one can cook and one is mobile—you know, that sort of thing. And they will do things for each other and they will look after each other. Or disabled people. This brings me to that book and the film *Tell Me That You Love Me, Junie Moon,* about that very topic. It didn't get enough attention because at that time we weren't into looking at the disabled as people. They were non-people. But that was what gave me the clue to the fact that we needed to resexualize the world of people with disabilities. Sexual rehabilitation is now a big thing in rehabilitation centers.

So there can be many kinds of families besides the ones that we traditionally think of. There will be families by adoption. There already are homosexual families. There will be families that live together nonlegally, but are families, more families than some of the legally married ones—and so forth. I think we're learning that it isn't divorce that breaks up the family, but the *reasons* leading to the divorce. And divorce may actually make it possible for new families to be formed that are more creative and more stable and more nurturing than the old ones.

There are studies showing that sexual behavior has really changed very little since Kinsey, though we are certainly hearing more about it. An older woman who bemoans the rise of "promiscuity" obviously had little chance to know how sexual behavior really was in her day. But we have the studies now that tell us how it was. For instance—this is a fascinating thing—we can truthfully say teen-age pregnancies have increased. But then so have the number of teen-agers. What we need to be careful about is to say the *rates* of teen-age intercourse and pregnancies have increased. They are also occurring at younger ages, which would also increase the rates. One more thing. The sociologists are also saying that the accessibility of birth control services has not really changed sexual behavior. Otherwise, you wouldn't have these teen-age pregnancies, you see. We have made contraception available to make safer sexual behavior, but that was already occurring. And I wish young people *would* use it.

And you have the number of sociological factors that enter into the increased venereal disease rates, which I don't want to go into. They were social factors. You have—all across the world—an enormous number of factors that go into changed sexual behavior. And they have very little to do with contraception. And you have a large number of factors that influence girls to become pregnant. There are a large number of these girls who say, "I did it deliberately." There are studies on this. Why did they do it deliberately? Well, they have a number of social reasons why they did it deliberately. So I think that my efforts, when these things come up, my efforts are dedicated completely to saying, Now look, description is not advocacy. I am not advocating a certain type of behavior. But I am telling you what science has found. If you don't choose to accept research figures, I can't help that. Because it's not the job of a scientist to make value judgments. It's the job of a scientist to hold a mirror up and say here is the situation. We know that sexual repression in early childhood—traumatic sexual repression—can have effects far later on in marriage or in sexual behavior. Bad effects. So parents really should stop worrying about masturbation, which is natural and to be expected. It is the norm. Far more people masturbate than do not. They've done it since time immemorial, and they're not going to stop because somebody—the law or the church or the parents—says stop. My mother tried to stop me and she didn't.

She traumatized me though, and it was that that made the trouble—in such a way that I later on had to go into therapy. It really affected my early marital life quite severely. Now, it's perfectly true, as a very good theologian the other day pointed out to me—and he's also a psychiatrist, a marvelous combination. He said, "After all, we have to remember that masturbation can be used pathologically, compulsively as a way of retreating from the world, of avoiding an involvement with somebody else, a human being. And if this is compulsively permanent, we can't recommend that." And I said, "Yes, that's perfectly true. But then it's a symptom of something wrong, and the person should be in therapy not for the compulsive masturbation, but for the reason for it. Then the masturbation will take care of itself."

When somebody else means the world to you, your world, that's what love means.

An awful lot of people are still choosing marriage and remarriage and—you know, what was marriage before? Let's examine what marriage is now, in the blue-collar class. It's a very painful thing, as Lillian Breslow Rubin has pointed out in her study. She's written a book called *Worlds of Pain: Life in the Working-Class Family.* Well, I would not wish on you what she's found. In the whole marital and sexual field, you'll find that there is very little sexual pleasure in working-class marriages. There is at first, of course, the novelty of rolling in the hay. But very soon, probably with the first pregnancy, the pattern gets set. The husband and wife lead parallel lives which very seldom meet in any kind of communication. Sex for them is very likely a quickie, with his ejaculating almost immediately. She may never have experienced orgasm, or if she did experience orgasm occasionally, she may be left unsatisfied. And because it's a blue-collar background, masturbation is an evil and bad and dangerous thing. So then she has very little sexual satisfaction in life and is really deprived. And sexual deprivation can result in various emotional and family disturbances.

Study Victorian marriages, the middle-class marriages in the early part of the century, and you will find that the upper class and the literati, so to speak, were liberated, didn't live the same lives that the middle-class Victorians led. The upper class of the Edwardian era were all for it. Was that ever free! So that spilled over then into the upper class of the United States in the years following. But not into the middle and the blue-collar classes. Today the middle class is doing what the wealthy and the literati have been doing right along. So this is not such a change. But no, I don't think marriage is on the way out at all. What is happening is that marriage is solemnizing a committed relationship very often. With the young and with the older people. A relationship that may have been going on for maybe one, two, or several years. And suddenly they want to solemnize it, they want to signalize it, to recognize it with a contract that's often religious or semireligious. I think that's a beautiful thing.

At SIECUS we deal with the people who might be dealing with blue-collar children. In terms of preparing them to have more open, less traumatizing, less depriving, less punitive attitudes about the sexuality of children, young children. And to help the parents understand this. Now, of course, we're also trying to reach the pediatricians. I'm a doctor, an M.D. I was trained in public health, not in clinical medicine. But I did have pediatrics at Bellevue. I interned. And one of the questions I would like to see added to the well-child examination at the age of 6 or 9 months is, "How does it make you feel, Mrs. so-and-so, when your child plays with his penis or with her clitoris?" That takes for granted that he or she does. That says it's okay. It happens. It also tells the mother that if it troubles her she can talk to the doctor about it.

You can't separate parents out and say, "Now come in for your sex class." You have to teach the staff—or have a trained consultant—who would meet parents who had really a lot of questions and were really open, and so here education would act as therapy so that when an intern or a resident or a pediatrician or a nurse meets a mother, this question would routinely be a part of the examination. So that eventually the parent would be freed to free the child to enjoy its body, which is built into being human. But parents need also to know how to socialize this self-pleasuring, so that by the age of 3, the child would know to seek privacy for it. Sex should always be a private thing, and this is not hard to teach children.

I ran across a recommendation of a psychiatrist who says that the best age to teach sex education is between the ages of 3 and 5 or 6, when the basic attitudes about sex are laid down. In fact, you can even begin to teach the basics of birth control at this age. It goes something like this: "The reason that mothers and daddies have intercourse is not just for having babies. We have two children, but we didn't just have intercourse twice. We had it many times, and we will do it many times because this is the way we talk to each other, love each other. Why don't we always have a baby? Oh, because doctors know how to plan exactly when to have the babies you want. Don't worry, when you've grown up and need it, the doctors will tell you." It's really so simple even a 3-year-old can understand and be satisfied.

My own children certainly have given me joy. Even more so now. First of all, I loved the experience of carrying a baby. I was an old-fashioned woman—so I didn't have the experience of birthing, the Lamaze method. But I did nurse them and take care of them during their infancy. It's just one of the most rewarding things. Four times I did this, loved every minute of it. And then, growing up, they were also a joy, but then as teen-agers, because of circumstances, they all had to go away to boarding school, so I didn't have as close contact with them as I'd like to have had. And now we're very close, they all say that I did not traumatize them about sex, which I'm very glad about. Don't forget that I was bringing up one batch in the twenties and one batch in the forties. We didn't know then as much about childhood sexuality as we know now, so although I knew enough not to traumatize them, I didn't know enough to free them positively in the way I now know I could and should have.

I think I remember almost everything about them—but not specifically. The goodness of having them. The fulfillment of having them. Right now our relationship has never been so good, never. In fact, my oldest daughter who is now 50 and a grandmother has become, in the last four years, a psychotherapist, a transactional analyst. And in the last year when I've had a great deal of stress and pressure in my personal life, she has filled a double function. I can call her at any time and she will be a professional for me, but she's also my loving daughter. It's very unusual. I have had a therapist here whom I can consult, but I've been able to handle most of the stress alone, because of my daughter.

My youngest almost died three years ago from a ruptured appendix, and that brought the whole family together in an extraordinary way. This includes my 22-year-old grandson. We can talk about anything. It's really wonderful.

I became a Quaker in my fifties when my oldest daughter, who was sixteen to nineteen years older than the two youngest, said, "Mother, I'm going to suggest that you bring these two girls up with a more formal religious background than I had, for I have felt the lack of this very much. When I got to college, I couldn't even discuss religion." And I said, "You have an important point and I'll do it." So I did. However, I was not about to go into any kind of a religious group that would trammel me, that's the word that always comes to my mind. I wanted to be free and untrammeled in my religion because by then I was a mature and liberated woman. And I knew what I wanted *out* of life, because I also knew what I was ready to put *into* it. So I looked in the Yellow Pages and there was a Friends Meeting, a Quaker Meeting, not too far from us. So I started bringing the children there, and I found, in their First Day of School, Sunday school, classes, that there were many non-Quakers, including many Jewish children. And so I would sit out in my car and wait for them and read the Sunday *Times*. This is a classic story. They love to tell it, but a couple of times they were bothered by it. So finally, one of the Friends came out to me and said, "We would love to have thee join the adult class, Mary. Feel free." And finally someone did come and say, "We are very unhappy that thee sits here with thy Sunday paper. We would like to have thee join us." So I thought, Oh dear, I've got to do this. So I did. And then I was pulled into helping with the Christmas festivities and leading the singing. And then all of a sudden, one day, I discovered I really was feeling the Quaker recognition of finding God in every person. And that they were not laying bands on me, iron bands on me. I could take what I wished out of their beliefs. So I asked to become a Quaker, and we were visited by a committee of Elders. My daughters also joined, and it was a very wonderful thing, to join in such a peaceful, loving experience for so many years. I never can get to meetings anymore because in the last ten years my life has been such that Sundays I'm away lecturing or am so exhausted I just have to sit at home. But they know that I'm with them, and I was invited to give the Rufus Jones Lecture, which is a great honor for it is then published and circulated widely among Friends. And I called it "Sexuality and the Quaker Conscience." And then I was honored by Haverford College with an honorary doctorate in recognition of my work as a Quaker. This gave me great joy.

Everything I do, I do in the light of my faith. Absolutely. I fully believe that there is that of God in every man. I fully believe that the people who have attacked and vilified me, who have called me, publicly in print and on television, a moral degenerate and a pervert, are simply people who do not have access to the truth. I won't even say that they're willfully blind to the truth. It's very difficult sometimes when someone deliberately misquotes me from speeches or puts parts of two speeches together so that it makes it seem as if I had said something that I didn't say, it's very difficult for me to stick to that. But I know that the people who were important and who mattered to me knew the truth about me. And I know the truth about myself.

One thing more about Quakerism and the truth. Truth, as a scientist, is obviously an important thing for me. But as a Quaker it's sacred because, once established as truth, then it has to be God's truth.

I feel fear every day. I've always felt pure fear that something that I'm passionately into I may not succeed in keeping alive. I felt fear when my oldest daughter died of pneumonia at the age of 8. It was ten days illness. Before the sulfa drugs even came in. That was ten days of pure fear, when I literally had pains in the heart, physical, physical pain. And I have always had the fear that I may not be able to raise the funds to keep SIECUS going. This organization has a powerful reason for being: It is the only organization in the world that functions in quite this way. The American Association of Sex Educators, Counselors and Therapists is a professional organization of professional people, a training and accrediting organization. And the Society for Sex Research is to report research. But SIECUS exists to bring sexual truth to people, all people, and the majority of professional people in the U.S. have access to it. Now we want to bring it down to the people, where it's so terribly needed. And I'm so afraid every day that I won't raise the money this year. It's a real fear.

Ask me when I was last inside of a moving picture or a theater or a ballet or musical, whatever, all things that I adore. I haven't been for five years, ten years. My profession really occupies my whole life. And doing things alone is lonely. But when I think back, I think it's very curious that the book *Kristin Lavransdatter* by Sigrid Undset was one book that had an enormous impact on me. I read it first in my teens. I read it again in my twenties, and I must have read it again in my forties. And always, in those three times, I lived her life. And always the part that was most poignant to me, and probably I was anticipating what might happen to me and really has—was when she went up into the mountains during her last pregnancy. And what her pregnancy did—

this is in essence what it also did for me—it rejuvenated her. But by then Erland, her husband, was no longer interested in her. And she went up there to the summer place in the mountains and she could see herself becoming young again and vital and full of juices, and if Erland had come, he would have found something quite wonderful there, something the French have known about for years and we are just finding out—an older woman *"d'un certain age"* in the prime of her sexual maturity—but he never came. And for some reason this said something to me when I was in my teens. Almost prophetic.

A *Man and a Woman* is a fine film. Now, there were two people who out of a blasted life on each side were able to reconstitute something beautiful, poignant, strong. I loved it, and at that time it was a very far-out movie. Maybe it was sentimental. You can tell a story straightforwardly and it can be a sentimental story. I'm a very sentimental person. *Romantic* is perhaps a better word for it. Yes, I am a romantic.

I've never been active in politics. No, not at all. I didn't even join NOW. First of all, I feel I am a liberated woman. Secondly, I didn't have the time. Thirdly, I'm not a joiner, not a movement person. But I created a movement. I really did. But being a Quaker, you see, and being a solitary subjective person, the early stridency and combativeness of the women's lib movement put me off. I didn't want to have anything to do with that, and they thought I was an old fuddy-duddy. Well, that was also the period when I was talking at Vassar and at Notre Dame, and then my speeches were published in *Redbook*. I had what they would have called highly moralistic views. It's very interesting that one piece called "How Young Men Influence the Girls Who Love Them" has just been reprinted again in a Roman Catholic textbook on families and sex and marriage. What it said in essence was, "Young man, are you ready to take the responsibility for turning this girl into a woman? Is *she* ready for it?" Well, the NOW people, of course, were ultraliberated. And to me sex out of the context of a relationship is relatively meaningless.

I react to politics, of course. Oh, yes. In fact, I brought it in in a rather neat way, I thought, in a number of speeches and writing. I pointed out that the gift, let's say, or the talent, for developing a conscience is today rather blunted. We don't really know what a conscience is. We don't know how to converse with our consciences. In fact, I think some people have, in a sense, had three consciences which they kept conveniently in a drawer, and when it was necessary, they'd pull out a conscience for sex. Or when it was necessary, they'd pull out a conscience for politics, or a conscience for business. Three different kinds of consciences, which let them do in one sphere things they wouldn't think of doing in another. But in the end, as the Report to the Catholic Theological Society of America study on human sexuality stated very clearly, there is nothing special to sexual morality. And I've been saying this for years. Sexuality itself is morally neutral, it's how we use sex that is subject to moral judgment. But sex should not have a special set of moralities. It should be the same set of moralities for the government or for life. Do no harm to yourself or to anyone else. Or to society. And so forth.

Today there's nothing individual or personal about work at all. Recently I watched a TV documentary on a lung disease that comes from being exposed to cotton. And the mechanization of cotton processing is so incredible that it's Charlie Chaplin's *Modern Times* all over again. It's absolutely deadening. But work can be exciting if it has variety. The trouble is that the very thing in our society that has taught us to look for variety, variety in your sex life, variety in your occupations—we're bringing up a nation that's not going to be able to handle these routine jobs. Who's going to do them?

At 35, I changed everything which I'd failed at and went into medicine. It excited me, impassioned me—I'm passionate about what I'm doing. Now, true, I never went to work until I was 50, and it was luck that got me to be medical director of the Planned Parenthood Federation of America—my first real job. I discovered why it had been offered to me—because no self-respecting male physician would take the job, would touch it with a ten-foot pole. But it turned into something exciting for me, because what happened was that I was able to make the medical profession aware of family planning as a part of responsible medical practice. Actually the AMA came out with that as a policy statement in 1964. Then it was no longer exciting. Everyone was climbing on the bandwagon. So then I left to form SIECUS. Work has to be something that grabs you. Now, writers, or artists like my father, were grabbed by what they did. They never had a dull moment in their lives. I don't have a dull moment in my life, my working life. So in a sense my work is my passion, and it's my vacation as well as my vocation.

I think that the human sexuality movement has been one of tremendous growth of concepts and insights in the last ten years. SIECUS is fifteen years old. I co-founded it fourteen, fifteen years ago. I have a clipping here—from 1963, one year before SIECUS was founded, in which I'm predicting SIECUS and what we wanted to do. I couldn't believe, my hair stood on end, because we've done it! However, the terms in which we've done it are different, for we had no idea how it was going to happen. For instance, I had no idea that some day we would be seeing training films to help the handicapped or disabled learn that they could make love again—in different ways. What a beautiful thing that is. I serve as a consultant on some of those films for the Institute for Rehabilitation Medicine of which Dr. Howard Rusk is founder and director. And I had no idea that we were going to develop groups into the kinds of therapeutic arms they are proving to be. The group movement has helped sexuality and individuals enormously; we couldn't have foreseen how much when we founded SIECUS. I don't know how we thought we were going to do it. We just knew we had to do it. It was a blind faith that the way would be opened for us. That's a very religious thing to say, but I really believe it! The way was opened for us.

Yes, I love this country, because it has absolutely infinite possibilities for being itself and for allowing people to be themselves. It's our fault if there is a gap between dream and reality, that we're placing values on the wrong things. Well, let me say that I'm a catalog sucker. I get fifteen to twenty catalogs all the time. All kinds. And when I go through those catalogs I get nauseated. I say to myself, how can people spend their money for *junk* like this? I admit I'm a catalog fancier because they save me time and energy—I hate shopping but I love certain gadgets that I still have that nobody else has now, because I bought them through a catalog, and everyone says, where'd you get this? You can't buy it anymore. Because you know, we like to drop things and pick up something new. I think that we value and teach our children to value the wrong things. To value quickies. You know, the ads for Kool-Aid just drive me up the wall—empty calories, flavored colored water with some Vitamin C in it. How can mothers fall for this? It's just terrible. It's meretricious. And I don't like fakery. That was one thing my father taught me. That was a very favorite epithet of his: "That man's a fake." Or "His work's a fake." "She's a fake." I remember it very clearly. And very early I found myself engaged in trying to spot fakery. I see a lot of it.

Kennedy was my favorite President. He gave me something to believe in. Well, he gave me a personal feeling that he had integrity in the sense that he was willing to work like mad for this country. He may not always have done it in the right way. He certainly made mistakes. But I think he did them in honesty, not in dishonesty. My father was awarded the Medal of Freedom by Kennedy. But Kennedy didn't have a chance to bestow it, so it was bestowed on him by Lyndon Johnson, and, of course, my father's third wife was the one who went along. I would have loved to have been there. But those things are limited.

I can't imagine retiring. But I *can* imagine not having to carry the kind of load I'm carrying now. In fact, I've been imagining it for a couple of years. But I think people should understand what they should look for—I think we're getting a bit better about this, we're understanding that doing nothing is not the ideal, that very few people can be satisfied doing nothing. Now obviously, some people are perfectly happy doing what I would call nothing. Which means running around playing cards or golf and so forth. But that's fine. To each his own, you know. I have no criticism at all. We should do what gives us pleasure. I think that retirement is the time for pleasure. Since my work *is* my pleasure, I don't see myself retiring for some time.

But I do know women whom I'm itching to tell, "Look, go out and be a Gray Lady twice a week in a hospital. Do something for somebody. Get involved with them because they need you." But when I suggest it, they have all sorts of reasons for not doing it. I have to respect those reasons for not doing it, for their not becoming involved. Apparently they have a block. And maybe they wouldn't have been happy. But I do know that people who literally do nothing tend to disintegrate. And they die earlier.

Our children will do lots of things better and some things not so well. I'm a better housekeeper than two of my three children, and I'm a better cook than my youngest daughter, who hates cooking. But generally they do things better than we do. They'd better run the world better! They must. They must. We have to find a way out of the mess we're in now, in which wars and violence are increasing—particularly personal violence. And here I'm with James Prescott, who is convinced that one of the origins of violence is deprivation of sensory and sensuous pleasure during early childhood. I believe in this because I think all the evidence points to this. We find that abusing parents had abused childhoods. And they suffered great sensory deprivation because they were punished for masturbating, for finding pleasure in their own bodies. Among primitive tribes there are certain ones that are warlike, and those are the ones that are depriving their children of sensory pleasure. The gentle, peaceful tribes are those that stroke and nurture their children, that accept the child's sexual play. We have a lot of learning to do here, a lot of research, too.

At present and probably through most of my life, I have not lost many people. People live longer now. My father was 94 when he died, but he had been, in a sense, not living for two or three years. So that was a gradual thing. My aunt in the same way. The one crucifying death in my experience was the death of my 8-year-old child, my firstborn. She would be 52 now. And the only way I found to deal with that, ultimately, was to realize that I was simply part of a long chain, that I could almost literally—and in my mind I did this—reach out my hands into the future and into the past, and feel other mothers' hands touching mine. This was a fantasy exercise that I did, not forcing myself, but it came to me. And I felt comfort flow in from the past and from the future, in the sense that I was one with those other mothers who had also lost a child.

But I don't want to live to be as old as my father and my aunt did. I don't want to live that long. And hopefully I'll be able to handle it so I won't. The trouble is that by the time you realize you're there, other people are in charge of you. And they won't listen, of course. But I'll be able to handle this, because I don't want to live that way. I don't want to be that kind of burden on my family. It's too bad for them.

I've thought, I lived my good life. When I fly, if the airplane falls, I've had a good life, I'm ready to go.

# *Impressions*

There were others.

At the Source Academy on New York City's Upper West Side, I found Joseph Dunn: headmaster, only teacher, college guidance counselor, secretary, and other roles without title. He founded Source Academy in 1964, when students and their parents at a school Dunn had decided to leave urged him to start his own school. Tucked into the main-floor rear of an inconspicuous brick building, it is one classroom, a bathroom, and Dunn's small, spare office. He teaches approximately fifty students in all. Seventy-five percent are graduated (the graduating classes number about twelve, and the ceremony is held in a neighborhood restaurant), and 95 percent of those go on to four-year colleges. Dunn remembers his childhood in Pittsfield, Massachusetts, as having taught him responsibility. "But not in the way we use the word today. Responsibility that you were an integral part of the family. You were important too. You worked in the family store. You helped make it a success, and you felt just as much satisfaction out of achievement. You learned a sense of responsibility to anyone you associated with. Your wife, your children. These students of mine—I feel like a parent. I feel the same sense of responsibility. Most of the time I'll ignore them, but they must go where they want to go. I've got to get them where they've got to go."

The son of an immigrant Irish woman ("She came over on a boat when she was 11 years old, in steerage, with a tag around her neck, because no one could understand her brogue"), Dunn had a Catholic upbringing. When he was ready for college, he was packed off to Holy Cross, though he fully intended to enter Williams. "I am not anti-Catholic, not by a long shot. But I am afraid I'm a little bit anticlerical. I trust my own mind. You hear much talk of heaven or paradise, whatever religion you're in. I hear of Buddha, and I hear of Muhammed and Allah. And Zeus. It makes no difference. They all take the form of people. One day my mother said to me, and I think this started me thinking, she said, 'Do you think my father's up there waiting for me?' And I should've said, 'Oh, I know he is.' And I didn't. I said, 'What makes you think he wants you?' I didn't mean it to hurt my mother. It did. I apologized. I've been apologizing for saying it ever since. But I didn't mean that. What I really meant was, What is this heaven? What is this hereafter?

"What is there in the world that for me would be perfection? Pure intellect. The knowing of all, omniscient. Know the past, the present, the future all at once. Just intellect, just knowledge. Then God must be the intellect. No features, no color, no creed, race—he just knows all. If always, of course, there is a God. I don't know that any more than you. But if there is, and I want there to be one, I don't want to feel that I was just an unfortunate incident on a Saturday night, and I fought my way through this life and gave up the ghost happily and they buried me happily and forgot me happily. I don't think that's why I'm doing all this. So I've got to improve myself. Just me, not you. You do your thing. I've got enough trouble with my own. To the point that I can be assimilated as part of that intelligence. Now, right now, you see, I'm starting to swing off into Hinduism and Buddhism."

I found Ola Mae Page in a small house in a black neighborhood in Los Angeles. She lives alone, having liberated her children by spending her life working hard as a domestic. Born in the rural South, she has spent most of her life in the North and, in recent years, in California. It hasn't been an easy life for her, but she has survived. When I asked her to talk about love, she said, "Love is what I haven't had too much of in my life. In my life it's just been hard, heartbreaking, backbreaking work. You didn't have time to sit down and say, 'I love you.' My work, my keeping soul and body together—I didn't have to do it, but I did it more conscientious than most mothers. Lots of mothers just say, 'Away with it.' I just feel it's my duty. And my duty makes me feel that I haven't lived my life in vain.

"When my time come, I say, well, I did the best I could and I've had a good long life. I can't look back and say, about any one thing, I wish I had done it different. Doing the best you can is all right. But you have to use your ability and your understanding to know that it's the best you can. Not something quick or flashy. Now how would I struggle along and raise these kids the best that I could if I had been like that? I know a lot of mothers didn't even keep the kids. They didn't care if they had shoes. I used to go with paper bottoms in my rubber shoes so they could have their boots and corduroy pants and snowsuits. I never made enough to get around to me. I'd keep them warm and comfortable. Well, a lot of mothers didn't care. I've known children, my children's age, who would go to school in little shirtsleeves in the cold wintertime. Nose running and everything. There's a lot of people didn't try like I tried. And I wasn't doing it because I thought I was better than them. I was doing it because I knew that was the thing to do. You supposed to do that."

Marie Kalish, a career social worker in her seventies, sat in her neatly furnished apartment in Manhattan and thought about then and now. "You stayed put more then," she said. "You stayed put socially, economically. If you were born in one neighborhood, you stayed there. And your children would marry and kind of stay there, too. And there wasn't this shoving and pushing. And I think that is—taking it one step farther—why I'm enjoying my old age so much. Although I'm very active in a number of different things, I find that the people with whom I associate, people my own age, have a certain sense of serenity. I'm very comfortable with people my own age. I'm not one of those who has to be with younger people to feel alive. We've made it one way or another or we have not made it and we have accepted that, and there's no longer this competitive business that there was for many years."

Ilya Bolotowsky is an abstract painter who has also written plays, short stories, films—and taught. He came to America from Russia in 1923, when he was 16—and it has been his home ever since. He is fascinated by cultural patterns, here and abroad, and that fascination inspires his beliefs. "Our sexual revolution exists within our cultural patterns," he said. "What may be good in one cultural pattern may not be in ours. Among the Eskimos, a very excellent people, certain customs might be shocking to us, and they work fine for them. I lived in Alaska, and a very good Eskimo wife before she wants to have an affair must go to the husband and ask his permission. And he, of course, if he is an honorable man, must grant permission. If he refuses, then he loses the respect of his neighbors. And he is dishonored. If he grants permission, he is honored. Now, the wife who has an affair without permission is dishonorable. Which to us seems ridiculous. But for them it's very important. On the other hand, let's say an Eskimo likes you and he offers you his wife and you refuse, you are a dishonorable man.

All these rules may be, to us, preposterous. Now, if you give up our cultural patterns and don't develop any other structures, you go to pot. You merely disintegrate. Whether we're developing new cultural patterns or merely going to pieces, that's the problem. In other words, I'm not saying that promiscuity is necessarily bad if it develops some serious structures."

Brother J. H. Vaughan is a Christian Brother, a teacher in a Roman Catholic high school in New Jersey. He has spent most of his life in the teaching order (it is not, Brother Vaughan likes to point out, the order that makes wine). He has dealt with students and their parents and feels he knows something about family life: "Good parents keep a good home. Have devotion to the children, and to each other. They set good examples. I think of my own mother. She was strict, but not stern or severe. I can never remember either of my parents ever going off the handle with one another or with us at any point. The very atmosphere of the home just wouldn't allow that. I didn't see any rage. My father was very placid. He died in 1918, when I was only 11, but my mother held the family together. There were three of us in grade school when my father died. She went out and worked in a dentist's office, put my brother through high school, my sister through high school, and I came to the Brothers. So she was kind of the evident strong influence I needed."

Al Schwartz is a Chicagoan who has run a summer camp for boys in Wisconsin for fifty years. One of ten children in an immigrant family, he couldn't finish high school; he had to go to work, and he's worked ever since. His wife and his children have been very important to him. "My wife is a great dancer, a good singer, and she still is very pretty," he said. "We fight. That's how we stay married. When I say we fight, we don't really, but we have our arguments. But anyway, that's part of love. I love the way she does things. I love her perfectionist ideals. It has to be done right or don't do it. You know, we couldn't have been very happy in an empty house without children. Children cause things to happen—good, bad, or indifferent. And these things that are caused to happen keep you involved and keep you on your toes and keep you interested and keep you running. A house without children is rather dull. You have to spend your time reading, or listening, or going out."

Woody Herman, the bandleader, has been working most of his life and has no plan to stop. "I'm in a business where you don't have to retire," he told me. "It's terrific." But he hasn't forgotten his father's retirement. "One of the hardest things that I had to do in my entire life was make a telephone call to the president of the company that employed my father. He had been with this shoe-manufacturing company for close to fifty years and now they had let him go, now this was it. He had to leave. And he pleaded with me to call his boss. I was completely at a loss because I didn't know if I was doing the right thing or the wrong thing at that moment. I was now asking a man to let my father continue to work. And yet my father's desire came first and that's the reason I did make the call. Well, I got a simple, typical response, that due to insurance problems and that, they just couldn't keep him on.

"Retirement affected my father as it does most humans. His judgment became a little faulty. For instance, he decided he would go across the street to get something at the grocery store and the ice and snow was up to his can. He had very poor eyesight and one leg was a little bad and he had a cane and he never made it across. And that was the beginning of his demise, because once the great bones go . . . he was 84. That's why I'm absolutely opposed to forced retirement for anybody."

Charles Okerbloom, a retired art professor in Fayetteville, Arkansas, doesn't mind living alone, in retirement. "I used to see my doctor quite often," he told me. "When you're earning a living, you tense up, you know. And then you have problems. But when you're free, they dissipate. My father had similar problems. He had terrible headaches, migraine headaches. Then, after retirement, when my parents were just living in their summer home, all that disappeared. So I think most of these ills are brought on by that. One can't avoid them—the drives and tensions of just earning a living. Anxieties and problems. So if you throw away all your newspapers and destroy your TV and get rid of these communications and live like turtles, you'll be healthy."

Hallie Huntington's grandfather came to Oregon in 1847 and she has been there since 1898. A widow who is active in various community activities, she feels that her life has taken on a sort of calm. "I think as you grow older, you meditate much more," she said. "And you think of things that you wouldn't as a young person who's aggressive and who's getting on in the world. I think you mellow a bit with age and before you know it, you're a little kinder and your viewpoint changes somewhat. I think you learn from everyone. I'm learning every day I live. And unless you're learning, you're stagnant. You're getting no place fast.

"My husband died with cancer and it was a very trying time. And when he died, as much as I regretted it, I didn't shed a tear. I felt that there must be something better. I myself have leukemia. And I live with it. I have for several years. I hope I continue to live with it a few years longer. But when I don't, that's part of living. I take my medicine and say, 'Lord, just let's take care of this.'"

For some, there is the loneliness. Yvonne Rudié, who was born in Paris in 1892 and came to New York to stay when she was 16, is a part-time actress, a widow who keeps busy. She is happy to be alive, but she knows what is missing from her life.

"I've got wonderful children, wonderful friends. As far as money is concerned, well, I'll tell you something about money. I haven't got much money at all. And I don't care. What more do I need? I've got a nice little home. I have nice children. I have nice friends. I have an interesting life. What more do I want? Money—I don't care. You know what I really want? That I must say I miss? To have a friend, a man friend, who is not looking for what he's going to get out of me. What I mean by that is sex. Forget about that. I'm not looking for that. I'm looking for somebody who will understand me, who I will understand, and somebody that I will be able to admire. I'm not looking for someone who's going to admire me. I want somebody that I'll have respect for, love as a friend. I'm not looking to be married. I don't want to."

Pat Schulman was a schoolteacher for thirty-five years; she still substitutes. She lives in a compact Manhattan apartment in a neighborhood in transition; she has lived in it for years and refuses to move. Like others I talked to, she understands the nature of grief, and death.

"I've had a few friends with cancer. It wasn't too much of a shock because, you know, it's inevitable. It isn't like somebody getting run over and killed, immediately. But I've missed them. I used to see a lot of them. I miss them. But in everyday living there's so much to do and places to go that it goes far back in your mind after a while. I'm not worried about dying, no. I felt I've done everything and seen everything I wanted to. I've made a will and I've tried to put my house in order so the family won't have a lot of difficulty after I'm gone. I have names in back of all the pictures on my walls, for people who have come in and said, 'Oh, I love that.' Once upon a time I would have been fearful about doing anything like that. In my young years I wouldn't even think about dying. But now I think that my house should be in order, so I just take it as a phase of life that's to come."

For Emma Bongartz, it is something different. She was born in Sweden more than 90 years ago, now lives in the Midwest with her daughter. She has spent much of her life in America, much of that as a nurse. She looks both backward and forward. In anticipating what is to come, she depends upon her religious faith. "I have a feeling that death isn't the end," she said. "I think that we are going to meet again. And most often death is preceded by pain and unhappiness and that is gone. I feel that we're happier then. You probably wouldn't believe this at all. One of my very close friends was ill. She was very religious and she had cancer. She was a teacher. And she would tell her class that she wasn't going to be with them very much longer. She talked about it openly. Well, I was a friend of hers and then the time came and she had to go to the hospital. I would visit her. And one day when I came, I knew she was sinking. I knew it was coming. She hadn't said anything for quite some time but she was still breathing. I don't know if when I put my hand on the bed, if somehow she knew I was there, but she opened her eyes and I've never seen such glory in my life. It was the most beautiful thing. And I thought that she'd been over there and come back. And I said, 'It's Emma.' She said, 'I know.' It was as if she came back with the message to me, that it was meant for me, because she was glad I was there. And there wasn't anything phony about any of it. It was so beautiful that I was just speechless. And I thank God for it, because it seemed a gift to me, a gift."

Genevieve Elden is an affluent widow who lives in a lavish apartment on Chicago's lakefront; she is a busy volunteer, in her mid-seventies. When the subject of death came up, she said, "They're gone. I'm sorry.

I believe in cremation. I don't believe in funerals and all that monkey business. I had two husbands who both died suddenly. At nine P.M. Sam was in the hospital, having some fluid taken out of him. He wasn't sick. He hadn't had a heart attack or anything like that. I came home and I was just getting undressed. It was eleven P.M. And my son called me. I said, 'What happened?' He said, 'Dad passed away.' Just like that.

"Then with Abe, I went to his bathroom. We each had our own bathroom. I wanted to tell him to come out, that I'd fix breakfast. And he was on the floor. I grabbed his wrist. This was as much as I knew about what to do. And I listened. I couldn't feel any pulse. So I ran to the phone and called downstairs and got them to send somebody up quick. And before I knew what happened, they were all there. And a policeman came in. I said that I wanted an autopsy. So they took him to the hospital and they found that he had a ruptured aorta. It was a shock.

"I've had such shocks, but I got over them. I just decided to start going out. After all, life is for the living. I don't worry about death. I just don't think about it. It's going to happen."

These people, the ones who speak out in this book, have become a part of my life, my consciousness. I did not know any of them before I began my travels. Now, I know them all. I am grateful for that. In looking back on the sequence of interviews, on the eventful meetings I had with these strangers, some thoughts surface.

I had loved my grandmother, admired her, respected her. It was her memory that moved me to find others like her. Yet I knew, all along, about the mythology of the aging. I knew that old people were supposed to be undesirable as companions, unproductive as citizens. I had been taught that they could not accept new ideas, that they clung to the past, tenaciously and ignorantly. I had been led to believe that senility was inevitable, that sex in old age was an absurdity. Old people simply waited, immobile and silent, to die. How rare the TV commercial in which old persons were portrayed as vigorous, alert, knowing; they were there, of course, but usually as comic presences, as eccentrics, to make us laugh in order to make us buy. The young ruled the world, and they didn't have the time or the will to deal with the aging.

And yet not one person I interviewed substantiated that mythology. Individually and as a group, they contradicted it. They are people of undiminished resources. Are they exceptional? Perhaps certain of them may seem extraordinary in their virtues or their skills, but to meet and be with them, one gains no sense of special powers, certainly not to alter the state of the world. They do not astonish.

Despite the advances in gerontology, and the countless studies being done by scientists involved with the aging process, we do not know enough, and we do not appreciate the little we do know. Too many Americans use the aged as their scapegoats.

Before going out to interview people for this book, I read a variety of material about aging—from almost impenetrable government surveys and studies to reports of various investigative bodies. In laboring through it all, I discovered Dr. Robert N. Butler, whose book, *Why Survive?*, subtitled *Being Old in America,* offered the most powerful case for revising our views of old age. In an interview Dr. Butler gave after the book was published, he said, "If you're asking for the secret of life, I'm afraid we don't have it yet. But we do have data that suggests that having a partner is very crucial to survival. It may be because two people have an emotional involvement that keeps them alive. Or it could be the advantage of having someone who can care for you if you're sick."

And he went on to cite other factors: involvement in activities, having specific goals and tasks, physical fitness, the ability to keep learning. He also noted, "Long-lived parents are a good sign, but you can undo that by poor self-care."

After I had completed all of my interviewing, I began to go through the notes I had taken. I found a small slip of paper on which I had written a series of brief generalizations. They were: Take care of yourself, get preventive medical care, be active and involved, see other people, don't worry about dying, and avoid poverty. It is difficult, for many of us, to live a life that makes those objectives possible, especially the last one. But we must know that our old age is, to a large degree, an extension of the life we have led along the way. Dante wrote: "The happiest man is he who can connect the evening of his life with the beginning."

At one point in my journey, while driving along a dusty country road in Missouri, I got lost. I pulled into a farm and asked for directions. A teen-ager came up, listened to me, and said blankly, "Don't know." I drove on. A few miles down the road, I stopped again at a farmhouse. The farmer was a very old man. He gave me flawless directions, graciously. Perhaps that, symbolically, is what I had been looking for when my memory of my grandmother sent me out into the world.

—Don Gold

# Acknowledgments

Dozens of people nominated candidates for me to interview. In a lifetime I could not have gotten to all of them. But in gratitude for leading me to those I did interview, I want to thank the following people: Al Barkow, Roy Bongartz, Roberta Burrows, Christopher Davis, Pamela Fiori, Michael Frome, Ethel Gofen, Paula Gordon, Peter Greenberg, William Harrison, Daphne Hellman, Nina Herman, Emilie Jacobson, Arno Karlen, Carole Kessie, Ed Keyes, Burt Korall, Ben Kremen, Peter Levinson, Barry Lopez, Anne McGrath, James T. Maher, Glenn Mason, James Michener, Gerald Orange, William Russo, Al Silverman, John Lewis Stage, Richard Story, Dawn Tyson-Hare, Danise Weiss, John Williams.

Others were invaluable as well. Catherine Travis transcribed tapes and typed my edited transcripts; the high quality of her work made my life easier. So did the intelligent, gentle, kind guidance of my editor, Don Hutter, whose loyalty to the project kept me going in the heat of Oklahoma in midsummer and the blizzards of New York in midwinter. And to Hedy Weiss, friend and supporter, who encouraged me whenever I needed encouragement, whose presence helped me to do my best.

Finally, my thanks go out to all those strangers who welcomed me into their lives, who sat patiently while I asked all my questions, who answered them with frankness and enthusiasm, and who, invariably, sent me away feeling better than I had when I arrived. A book is not enough to honor their presence in our midst.

# About the Author

Don Gold has been a magazine editor—with *Down Beat, Playboy, The Saturday Evening Post, The Ladies' Home Journal, Holiday,* and *Travel & Leisure*—and has written many magazine articles. His books include *The Human Commitment* (an anthology of fiction), *Letters to Tracy, Bellevue,* and a novel, *The Park.* He spent many months traveling throughout the United States collecting material for *Until the Singing Stops.* It is, in his words, "a continuation of my passionate interest in people, how they survive, how they deal with the stresses of life, how they sustain a sense of ethics despite all obstacles to their well-being."